A Mosaic of Victims

A MOSAIC OF VICTIMS

Non-Jews Persecuted and
Murdered by the Nazis

EDITED BY
Michael Berenbaum

NEW YORK UNIVERSITY PRESS
NEW YORK AND LONDON

c 10 9 8 7 6 5 4 3 2
p 10 9 8 7 6 5 4 3 2 1

Library of Congress Cataloging-in-Publication Data
A mosaic of victims : non-Jews persecuted and murdered by the Nazis /
    edited by Michael Berenbaum.
        p.   cm.
    Includes bibliographical references.
    ISBN 0-8147-1131-6 (alk. paper)
    ISBN 0-8147-1175-8 (pbk.)
    1. World War, 1939–1945—Atrocities. 2. World War, 1939–1945–
    –Prisoners and prisons, German. I. Berenbaum, Michael, 1945–
    D804.G4M63   1990
    940.54'05—dc20   89-13784
                            CIP

New York University Press books are printed on acid-free paper,
and their binding materials are chosen for strength and durability.

Book design by Ken Venezio

To my aunt and uncle,
Lottie and Henry Neiblum, of Tucson, Arizona,
who taught me the values of courage and quiet dignity
and the importance of stoicism.

Contents

Foreword:
The Triumph of Memory

Carol Rittner, R.S.M.

The Holocaust was the systematic, bureaucratic extermination of six million Jews by the Nazis and their collaborators as a central act of state during the Second World War; as night descended, millions of other peoples were swept into this net of death.—*Report to the President,* President's Commission on the Holocaust

The Holocaust was the planned, systematic attempt by Hitler and the Nazis to annihilate the Jews of Europe and to eradicate every vestige of Jewish life and culture from the European continent. Others, before and after the German Third Reich, have left their bloody fingerprints on history, but the Holocaust was something more than just another brutal chapter, something more than just the central event of the twentieth century. The Holocaust was the hinge of modern history, the definitive refutation of the grand illusion that human beings become better as they become more educated.

For centuries civilized society has targeted certain people, Jews in particular but also Gypsies, as "outsiders," people who "did not belong," people beyond the moral universe of concern for their well-being. Cruelty to Jews and other vulnerable people is nothing new, but the Nazi assault constituted an unprecedented mobilization of the resources of the state to single out a people for extinction. As the Ukrainian-American scholar Bohdan Wytwycky writes,

Jews were slated for total annihilation as a people, and Hitler in fact managed to kill an estimated 65 to 70% of all European Jewry, including virtually all of the German and East European Jews. The circle neighboring that of the Jews was reserved for the Gypsies, who also were designated for complete extinction. However, the German mania for exterminating the Gypsies did not quite achieve the same pitch of madness as that directed toward the Jews.[1]

The historical record during the Third Reich demonstrates all too clearly that not all victims of the Nazis were Jews. Millions of other people were swept into the Nazi net of death. If one calculates all the civilian casualties—not including those killed as part of the systematic mass murder, or those who died as accidental victims of battles, air raids, and military operations, but *only* those categorized as *Untermenschen* (subhumans) and killed as a result of conscious persecution—the number is staggering. The Nazi reign of terror brought suffering and death to Jews, Gypsies, Jehovah's Witnesses, the mentally and physically disabled, homosexuals, Communists, Slavs, Poles, Russians, Ukrainians, political opponents, and others. In short, anyone who opposed or did not fit into the Nazi worldview was vulnerable.

Like many others, both Jewish and non-Jewish, Elie Wiesel, a survivor of the Holocaust and the first chairman of the United States Holocaust Memorial Council (1979–1986), believes there is "a moral imperative" for giving special emphasis to the six million Jews—more than a million of them children—murdered by the Nazis: "While not all victims [of the Nazis] were Jews, *all* Jews were victims, destined for annihilation solely because they were born Jewish. They were doomed not because of something they had done or proclaimed or acquired but because of who they were: sons and daughters of the Jewish people."[2]

Memory is at the heart of Elie Wiesel's work. He has devoted his life to writing and speaking, with extraordinary power and eloquence, about the Holocaust. The starting point for his work has always been what happened to his people, the Jewish people, during the Holocaust, but he has not neglected other victims who suffered and died at the hands of the Nazis and their collaborators. In 1979, as chairman of President Jimmy Carter's commission on the Holocaust, he wrote:

Our Commission believes that because they were the principal target of Hitler's Final Solution, we must remember the six million Jews and, through them and beyond them, but never without them, rescue from oblivion all the men, women and children, Jewish and non-Jewish, who perished in those years in the forests and camps of the kingdom of night.[3]

I believe it was that spirit, as well as the recognition that many non-Jewish victims of the Nazis feel their particular suffering has been overlooked, that prompted Elie Wiesel in late 1986, as chairman of the United States Holocaust Memorial Council, the successor organization to the president's commission, to courageously convene an international conference on "The Other Victims: Non-Jews Persecuted and Murdered by the Nazis."

As a Jew, a survivor of Auschwitz, and as a scholar, he knew there were risks that such a conference might blur the unique aspect of the Jewish tragedy during the Holocaust, that it might simplistically but conveniently group the various victims together, dump them all into the same file: Jews and Resistance fighters, Jews and anti-Nazis, Jews and political prisoners, Jews and homosexuals, Jews and Gypsies, Jews and Jehovah's Witnesses, Jews and Soviet prisoners of war, Jews and social deviants, Jews and . . . Nevertheless, once he was committed to the conference, he moved ahead.

It took almost a year to organize the meeting. The herculean task of identifying topics and contacting scholars, in addition to developing a conference process that allowed for both presentation and discussion, fell to me as the conference director. Elie Wiesel offered his support, gave his advice, suggested ideas and people. He led a small delegation of council members to the Soviet Union to meet with scholars and survivors of Nazi concentration camps in order to invite Soviet participation in the conference. Regrettably, Wiesel resigned as chairman of the U.S. Holocaust Memorial Council three months before the February 23–25, 1987, meeting, but without his initial support and encouragement, the conference would never have taken place. Harvey Meyerhoff, who succeeded Elie Wiesel as the chairman of the council, also gave his invaluable support to the project. Without it, at the last moment, the conference might have been postponed indefinitely.

When the conference opened on February 23, 1987, Secretary of State George Shultz set the tone for the deliberations:

. . . while the attention of civilized humanity has been focused, and rightly so, on the unprecedented Nazi murder of six million European Jews . . . the acts of unspeakable evil committed by Nazi Germany against non-Jewish people also deserve to be studied, to be condemned, and above all to be remembered.[4]

For two days more than 250 scholars, survivors of Nazi concentration camps, and other participants from the United States, Canada, France, West Germany, Norway, Austria, Poland, the USSR, Hungary, and Israel met at the State Department in Washington, D.C., to explore, discuss, and learn more about the "other victims" swept into the Nazi net of death. Who were the people categorized by the Nazis as "undesirable," "useless mouths," "enemies of the state," "Untermenschen"? How did their fate parallel or differ from what happened to the Jews? What role did the medical and legal professions play in this organized barbarism? How did industry profit from slave labor? These are a few of the questions and issues participants confronted, discussed, and explored during the conference.

Of course, there were moments of tension during the conference; of course there were misunderstandings; of course there were people who only wanted to talk about their own suffering. But there also were moments of insight and sensitivity, moments when the reality of shared suffering transcended ideology. Jews and non-Jews, scholars and nonscholars tried to listen to one another with compassion and understanding, and for that reason the conference never degenerated into a kind of "suffering one-upmanship." The conference was an effort on the part of Jews and non-Jews to find common ground for shared remembrance.

From my perspective, the fear expressed by some Jewish survivors of the Holocaust—that the uniqueness of the Jewish tragedy would be ignored, distorted, or denied by giving attention to non-Jewish victims of nazism—never materialized. As Dr. Michael Berenbaum, a scholar whose sensitive and astute advice proved invaluable during the months I organized the conference, said at the closing session:

Years from now, as we look back at this conference, at the communities that were represented and the issues that were raised, we may see that it pointed the way for solving the problem of uniqueness and universality. It showed us how to include the other victims of Nazism without distorting history or backing away from the Judeo-centric nature of the Holocaust itself. . . . Only by understanding the fate of others who suffered, where it paralleled the Jewish experience and more importantly where it differed, can the distinctive character of the Jewish fate as a matter of historical fact be demonstrated.[5]

"The Other Victims" conference was important not just because of the scholarly attention and research it stimulated, but because of its effect on those of us who participated in it. Only when we see what happened to the Jews as compared with the Gypsies, the Ukrainians, the Poles, the Slavs, the gays, the Communists, the Jehovah's Witnesses, the physically and mentally disabled, and so many other victims of the Nazis can we come to recognize more clearly, even if we never understand it, the unique evil that was the Holocaust.

All of us, Jewish and non-Jewish, need to stretch our thinking and expand our hearts, perhaps to the breaking point, to include the suffering of "others" in our consciousness. And we must do it even as we struggle to bear with our own particular suffering. Otherwise, how shall we come to recognize that our moral claim to life is not only individual, but also social and common? In the moral community of human beings, each of us is related to every other, and we must expand our universe of human concern to include not just those who are "our own," but also those who are *"not our own,"* yet one with us in our common humanity.

These are issues not just for the past, but for the present and the future. Serious people who wish to learn from history have much at stake in understanding the profound importance of remembering what happened to the Jews during the Holocaust and to millions of other peoples swept into the Nazi net of death. As the Baal Shem Tov teaches us, "Forgetfulness is the root of exile. Remembrance is the seed of redemption."

NOTES

1. Bohdan Wytwycky, *The Other Holocaust: The Many Circles of Hell* (Washington, D.C., 1980), p. 17.
2. Elie Wiesel's letter to President Jimmy Carter, which serves as the preface of the *Report to the President,* President's Commission on the Holocaust (Washington, D.C., 1979), p. iii.
3. Ibid.
4. George Shultz, "Remarks" (Delivered at the conference, "The Other Victims: Non-Jews Persecuted and Murdered by the Nazis," U.S. Department of State, Washington, D.C., 1979, mimeographed), no. 45.
5. See chap. 2 of this work.

Acknowledgments

This work is the result of the joint effort of many people. First of all, it is a tribute to the United States Holocaust Memorial Council, which sponsored the conference "The Other Victims: Non-Jews Who Were Persecuted and Murdered by the Nazis." The conference was planned when the council was under the chairmanship of Elie Wiesel. It was held two and a half months after his resignation as chairman and within a fortnight of Harvey M. Meyerhoff's appointment as Wiesel's successor. Were caution rather than truth his major concern, the incoming chairman could have canceled or delayed the conference. Instead, Meyerhoff chose to go forward, which is a credit to his leadership.

Sister Carol Rittner, R.S.M., organized the conference. Her work was not merely competent but inspired. She was ably assisted by the council staff and most especially by Marian Craig.

It was my good fortune to be invited by Dr. Rittner to edit this manuscript. I could not have undertaken this project without the able assistance of my summer 1988 intern, Beth Cohen, who reviewed all submissions and suggested the general format for the work. Margery Grossman, assistant in the oral history department of the United States Holocaust Memorial Museum, has been diligent, disciplined, organized, and cooperative in succeeding Beth and handling the major preparation of this book. All of the scholars who had the pleasure of dealing with her have benefited from a gentility of spirit and intellectual mastery. Her supervisor, Dr. Linda Gordon Kuzmack, who directs the museum's oral history program, has been most generous in permitting Margery to handle this additional assignment. Margery has been ably assisted by the support staff of the museum including Susan Perrault, Jennifer Gold, Steven Koppel, Michelle Leopold, and Susan Greenhouse.

I would like to thank Lydia Perry who handled this extra burden on her already difficult assignments with dignity and grace and, as always, without complaint.

I could not have completed this work or the other major undertakings of this year without the understanding and the love of my children, Ilana and Lev, whose presence and being add immeasurably to the quality of my life. This is the only major work that I have undertaken in the past decade that has not benefited from the unique creativity and criticism of my wife, Linda Bayer. Her special touch has been missed, but this year rightfully belongs to her work, *The Blessing and the Curse*.

Kitty Moore, senior editor of New York University Press, has been both a critic and a conscience. She has believed in this work from the beginning. Barbara White has been of invaluable assistance.

Though I have been aided and assisted by many, the responsibilities of omission and of commission are mine and mine alone.

Introduction

For three days in February 1987, scholars from ten different countries met at the Department of State in Washington, D.C. Many of the professors had themselves been victimized by the Nazis. Others were the descendants of ethnic and religious groups persecuted by the Germans and their allies during World War II. They represented many separate ethnic groups who had been historically at odds with one another.

These scholars had come to ponder controversial questions: Who were the victims of the Holocaust? What distinctions, if any, can be made between the Final Solution to the Jewish question and Nazi policies toward other ethnic and religious groups?

Seemingly, these questions may be of scholarly interest alone. Yet lurking behind the disciplines of history and theology, medicine and ethics, were the concerns of diverse ethnic and religious groups, and the content of the United States Holocaust Memorial Museum—the American national memorial to the Holocaust. The museum is committed to including all the victims of nazism while remaining faithful to the uniqueness of the Jewish experience. And for the ethnic leaders, the recollection of a historic past is shaped by current and future communal interests.

Led by the indomitable Elie Wiesel, Jewish survivors were concerned that the Holocaust not be de-Judaized and that the uniqueness of the fate of Jews not be overshadowed by a concern for the universality of victims. Wiesel has proposed a poetic solution: "While not all victims were Jews, all Jews were victims destined for annihilation solely because they were born Jewish."[1] Jewish survivors also harbored historic resentments toward other victims of nazism who they felt might have collaborated with the enemy in the Final Solution. Anger of betrayal is not assuaged even by the passage of time.

Other ethnic leaders harbored their own resentments. Historians of Poland spoke of the forgotten Holocaust. Ukrainian scholars refuted charges of collaboration and argued for a rewriting of Jewish-centered history. All

I

of the ingredients were present for confrontation rather than conversation, for monologues or diatribes rather than dialogue.

Yet civility prevailed and the result is a collection of essays, written from a variety of perspectives, that explores the scholarly issues that the conference raised and the ethnic politics associated with remembrance of the victims—all the victims—of nazism. For the first time, in A Mosaic of Victims all major groups victimized by the Nazis are represented in one work.

A Mosaic of Victims begins with a general essay on the history of genocide by Richard Rubenstein and with a sustained treatment of the uniqueness and universality of the Holocaust that I wrote.

The second section explores the problems associated with German slave labor policies. Two essays explore the Nazi forced-labor program and the tension between ideology and economics in Nazi labor policies. Much to our regret a third essay on the cause and effect of forced and foreign labor could not be presented. Professor Gyorgy Ranki died before he could finish the essay.

The third section explores Nazi policies in the occupied territory. This part of the book is divided by countries—Serbia, Croatia, Belgium and France, Poland, the Ukraine, and the USSR.

The fourth section of the book looks at the Nazi policy toward children. Additional sections of the book focus on Nazi policies toward the churches, Jehovah's Witnesses, and Pacifists; their treatment of homosexuals and Gypsies; and Nazi medical experiments.

While not all of the papers presented at the conference "The Other Victims" could be published in this work, all of the essays included were first presented to the extraordinary gathering of scholars who met in Washington.

Discussions were intense as they should be. They were painful as could be expected. They also pointed the way to solving the dilemma the conference was convened to consider; that is, how to memorialize all of the Nazis' victims while remaining faithful to history and mindful of the unique state-sponsored policy of annihilation directed with particular fury against the Jews.

NOTES

1. Elie Wiesel, preface to *Report to the President,* President's Commission on the Holocaust (Washington, D.C., 1979), p. iii.

CHAPTER I

Modernization and the Politics of Extermination

Richard L. Rubenstein

Although thousands of books have been written about the destruction of the European Jews, until recently few have been devoted to the problem of genocide per se.[1] At the 1983 convention of the American Political Science Association a session on genocide, which featured papers by a number of leading authorities, drew an audience of no more than ten. It is my thesis that the relative silence on the subject of genocide stems from the unwillingness of both the scholars and their audiences to confront the fact that, far from being a relapse into barbarism, genocide is an intrinsic expression of modern civilization as we know it.

Put differently, the genocidal destructiveness of our era is an expression of some of its most significant political, moral, religious, and demographic tendencies.[2] If indeed genocide expresses some, though obviously not all, of the dominant trends in contemporary civilization, it would hardly be surprising that few researchers would want to spend much time on the night side of the world we have made for ourselves.

In a recent essay, Tony Barta of La Trobe University, Melbourne, Australia, raised the issue of the connection between civilization and genocide most directly.[3] According to Barta, the basic fact of his nation's history has been the conquest of the country by one people and the dispossession "with ruthless destructiveness" of another people, the Aborigines, those who were there *ab origine,* "from the beginning." Barta argues that, although it was by no means the initial intention of the British government to destroy the Aborigines, Australia is nevertheless a "nation founded on genocide," for genocide was the inevitable, though unintended, consequence of the European colonization of the Australian continent.

Barta's thesis puts him somewhat at odds with those scholars who insist that genocide is the *intentional* extermination of the target group. To comprehend genocide, we need a conception that embraces relations of destruction and de-emphasizes the elements of policy and intention with which the term is normally associated. Barta argues that Australian history amply demonstrates that genocidal outcomes can arise without deliberate state planning. Far from being a consequence of the actions of isolated men acting out their aggressions on a lawless frontier far from metropolitan centers of civilization, the destruction of Australia's aboriginal population was very largely the projected outcome of modernizing transformations in the mother country, the first European nation fully to enter the economically rationalized world of the modern era.

If we wish to comprehend the roots of genocide as a modern phenomenon, the beginnings of the modernization process in Great Britain provide an excellent point of departure.[4] These beginnings are to be found in the acts of enclosure that transformed the subsistence economy of premodern English agriculture into the money economy of our era. In the process, the customary rights to land usage of the economically unproductive English peasant class were abrogated and that class was largely transformed into a congeries of individuals whose survival was entirely dependent upon their ability to find wage labor. Absent gainful employment, the dispossessed peasants could only turn to a harsh and punitively administered system of poor relief, vagabondage, or outright crime. A crucial social by-product of England's economic rationalization was the creation of a large class of people who were superfluous to England's new economic system.

A class of more or less permanently superfluous people is a potential source of acute social instability. Having no hope of receiving society's normal rewards, it has little incentive, save fear of punitive retaliation, to abide by society's customary behavioral constraints. Even if such a group is tied to the rest of the population by common ethnicity and religion, it is likely to be perceived and to perceive itself as having been cast outside of society's *universe of moral obligation* (I am indebted to Helen Fein, *Accounting for Genocide: National Responses and Jewish Victimization,* for this concept). A measure of self-sacrificing altruism rather than self-regarding egoism will normally characterize the behavior of members of such a universe toward one another. At a minimum, members will not normally regard other members as potential sources of injury or even of personal destruction. To the extent that trust is possible between human beings, the actors within a shared universe of moral obligation are more likely to trust one another than those they regard as alien. Such attitudes have less to do with the moral virtuosity of individuals than with the way social relations are usually structured. The enclosure laws had the effect of expelling England's displaced peasants from the only universe of obligation they had ever known, that of the manor and the parish. This was clearly understood by English decision makers as early as the enactment of the Elizabethan poor laws, which were as much police measures aimed at controlling England's first redundant population, as they were philanthropic efforts to supply that population's irreducible needs for survival.

As is well known, in the economic rationalization of English agriculture, arable land taken from the displaced peasants was devoted to sheep raising, a cash crop, and large-scale cash farming. Out of the vast social dislocation engendered by the process, England was able to finance its first modern industry, textiles. However, the transformation of arable land to pasture seriously diminished England's ability to produce its own food supply. In addition, by the beginning of the nineteenth century, that country was no longer able to produce all of the raw materials necessary for its burgeoning industry.

Australia was an ideal land for sheep raising. It was also a convenient outlet for the elimination of a significant portion of England's redundant population. As Barta points out, the convict population exported by England to Australia was not unrelated to the dispossession of England's peasantry by the acts of enclosure. England also had large numbers of undercapitalized smallholders and artisans who were faced with the prospect of downward economic mobility in an increasingly capital-intensive domestic economy. Many of the more enterprising smallholders took their meager assets to Australia in the knowledge that an ever-increasing demand for both sheep's wool and sheep's flesh in the mother country presented the undercapitalized free colonizers, who were willing to work and capable of prudent management, with opportunities for prosperity that could not be duplicated at home. Like North America, Australia served as a demographic safety valve for those segments of England's population made redundant by the progressive rationalization of her economy and society.

Unfortunately, neither North America nor Australia was an unsettled territory when white settlers arrived. In Australia the aboriginal people had developed a viable human ecology that was altogether incomprehensible to the settlers, as indeed the ways of the settlers were incomprehensible to them. Moreover, sheep raising and the settlers' rationalized and desacralized agrarian economy were incompatible with Aborigine land use. Since both sides were unconditionally dependent upon the land, albeit in radically different ways, loss of the land necessarily entailed the complete destruction of the defeated way of life. As Barta writes, coexistence was impossible.

The issue was decided, as it almost always is, by superior power and technology. Since their survival was at stake, the Aborigines had no choice but to resist. As in North America, the predictable response of the settlers was to root out the aboriginal menace to their way of life. There were a number of bloody massacres. There were also government-sponsored attempts to diminish settler violence, but even without direct violence, the Aborigines were destined to perish. Having lost their way of life and having been deprived of a meaningful future, most of the Aborigines who were not killed by the whites "faded away." Barta writes that between 1839 and 1849 there were only twenty births recorded among the seven aboriginal tribes around Melbourne. He concludes that, whatever the official British intent, the encounter between the white settlers and the blacks was one of living out a relationship of genocide that was structured into the very nature of the encounter.

Barta distinguishes between a genocidal society and a genocidal state. National Socialist Germany was a genocidal state. Its genocidal project was deliberate and intended. Australia was a genocidal society. It had no genocidal project. Nevertheless, its very existence had genocidal consequences for the original population. The basic pattern of the colonization of Australia was everywhere the same. It consisted of white pastoral invasion, black resistance, violent victory of the whites, and finally the mysterious disappearance of the blacks.

Although Barta confines his description to Australia, the process he describes was repeated in other European colonial settlements. In his biography of Oliver Cromwell, the English historian Christopher Hill comments:

A great many civilized Englishmen of the propertied class in the seventeenth century spoke of Irishmen in tones not far removed from those which the Nazis used about the Slavs, or white South Africans use about the original inhabitants of their country. In each case the contempt rationalized a desire to exploit.[5]

Hill could have added that Cromwell was fully prepared to exterminate those Irish Catholics who resisted exploitation and refused to turn their lands over to Protestant colonizers. The towns of Drogheda and Wexford refused to surrender to Cromwell. They were sacked and those inhabitants unable to flee were massacred. In Wexford, after all the inhabitants had been killed, Cromwell reported that the town was available for colonization by English settlers. An English clergyman commended the place for settlement: "It is a fine spot for some godly congregation where house and land wait for inhabitants and occupiers."[6] Even in the seventeenth century, England's leaders recognized that the more Ireland was cleared of its original Catholic inhabitants, the more available it would be for Protestant English settlement.

The extremes to which England was prepared to go to empty Ireland of its original inhabitants became clear during the famine years of 1846–48. Estimates suggest that within that period the population of Ireland was reduced by about 2,500,000 out of an estimated 1845 population of 9,000,000. Approximately 1,250,000 perished in the famine. About the same number were compelled to emigrate in order to survive.[7]

Elsewhere I have attempted to show that the relief given by the English government to the Irish, who were technically speaking British subjects at the time, was deliberately kept at levels guaranteed to produce the resultant demographic changes and that those changes were welcomed by leading members of England's society and government. The deaths by famine and the removal by emigration did for Ireland what the enclosures had done for England, namely to clear the land of uneconomic subsistence producers and to make it available for rationalized agricultural enterprise.[8] The candor of an 1853 editorial in the *Economist* on the benefits of Irish and Scottish emigration is instructive:

It is consequent on the breaking down of the system of society founded on small holding and potato cultivation. . . . *The departure of the redundant part of the population of Ireland and Scotland is an indispensable preliminary to every kind of improvement.*[9] (italics added)

Unfortunately, the "departure" welcomed by the *Economist* entailed mass death by famine and disease for a very significant proportion of Ireland's peasant class. In the eyes of the British decision-making class of the period, Catholic Ireland was an inferior civilization.[10] A class indifferent to the fate of its own peasants was hardly likely to be concerned with that of the Irish.

The basic colonizing pattern described by Barta, namely white settlement, native resistance, violent settler victory, and, finally, the disappearance of most if not all of the natives, was played out in North and South America as well.[11] If Australian society was built upon a genocidal relationship with that of the indigenous cultures, so too was American society. Not so long ago it was taken for granted that "the only good Indian is a dead Indian."

The link between genocidal settler societies of the eighteenth and nineteenth centuries and twentieth-century genocide can be discerned in Adolf Hitler's *Lebensraum* program. As a young man, Hitler saw the settlement of the New World and the concomitant elimination of North America's Indian population by white European settlers as a model to be followed by Germany on the European continent. Hitler was keenly aware of Germany's population problems. He was determined that there would be no surplus German population even if a significant portion of Germany's Slavic neighbors were exterminated to provide "living space" for German settlers adjacent to the homeland. Hitler proposed to repeat in Europe, albeit with infinitely intensified viciousness, the exploitative colonialism practiced by other Europeans overseas. In Hitler's eyes the Slavs were destined to become Europe's Indians. They were to be displaced, uprooted, enslaved, and, if necessary, annihilated to make way for Germany's surplus population. Unlike the earlier European colonizers, Hitler had no illusions concerning the genocidal nature of such an undertaking. He had the historical precedents of earlier European efforts at colonization and imperial domination. He regarded the defeat of native cultures by white settlers and colonists as evidence for his version of social Darwinism, the belief that history is the theater in which the races enact their life-and-death struggle for survival and the superior races destroy their racial inferiors. As is well known, this same social Darwinism became an important component in the legitimating ideology for the Holocaust. In Hitler's eyes, the Jews were the most contemptible of the inferior races destined by fate and German strength for destruction.

Hitler differed fundamentally from the older European colonizing powers in that his policies were intentional and deliberately formulated. If the destruction of the aboriginal cultures of Australia was an unintended consequence of state policy, the destruction and eventual extermination of Germany's neighbors were fully intended by Hitler and National Socialist Germany. Nevertheless, that difference should not obscure the fact that (a) both colonizing policies were intended to solve the same fundamental problem, namely the relatively humane elimination by the mother country of a redundant or potentially redundant sector of its domestic population; and that (b) both could be successfully implemented only by the merciless elimination of the indigenous population of the colonized lands. Moreover, the very success of the earlier projects invited their repetition by political leaders, such as Hitler, who believed their nation to be faced with the problem that had led to the original colonization. Such leaders could no longer pretend ignorance of the consequences of their policies.

One of the differences between Hitler and his predecessors was his lack of hypocrisy and illusion concerning the extent to which his project entailed mass murder. Nevertheless, the history of the English in Ireland and Australia as well as the Europeans in the New World clearly indicates that the destruction of the indigenous population never constituted a reason for calling colonization to a halt. There is thus a historical continuum between the unintended genocides of the period of Europe's demographic projection beyond its original territorial limits and that of the period of Europe's deliberate autocannibalization.

If the above argument has merit, it will be possible to define genocide as *the most radical means of implementing a state- or communally sponsored program of population elimination.* Note, however, that (a) the issue of intention is not raised in this definition, and (b) genocide is grasped conceptually within the wider context of programs of population elimination. This definition allows for comprehension of the larger historical conditions under which a population is likely to be identified as redundant and targeted for one or another form of elimination. This definition also helps to suggest the connections between population redundancy, emigration, expulsion, colonization, modernization, and genocide.

A fundamental issue in the decision to initiate a program of genocide can be discerned in the question, Who is to have a voice in the political order? The issue of a voice in the political order is in turn related to the question of the universe of moral obligation. In ancient Greece, members of the polis belonged to a common universe of obligation. This was especially evident in war. Only those who shared common origins, belonged by *inherited right* to the same community, and saw themselves as partaking of a common fate, could be trusted in a life-and-death struggle. Neither the slave nor the stranger could be so trusted. Hence, they were regarded as outside the shared universe of obligation.

A very grave problem arises when, for any reason, a community regards itself as having within its midst a subcommunity or a group of strangers who cannot be trusted. The problem is especially urgent in time of war, and even more urgent when a community has experienced what it perceives to be humiliating national defeat. The perception of disloyalty may be mistaken, as was initially the case of the Armenians in Turkey during World War I and Japanese-Americans during World War II. The fundamental reason for the mass incarceration of the Japanese-Americans was the belief of most Americans that the majority of Japanese-Americans were loyal to the emperor rather than to their adopted country.

Sometimes the question of a voice in the political community takes on a class rather than an ethic dimension. When Kampuchea fell to the Pol Pot regime in 1975, the victors had a very clear idea of the kind of agrarian communist society they proposed to establish. Rightly or wrongly, they regarded Kampuchea's entire population as *objectively hostile* to the creation of the new political order. This perception was consistent with the Marxist idea that the bourgeois class is destined to disappear with the coming of socialism. Not content to let this process take its course nonviolently, the regime determined upon the immediate elimination through genocidal measures of all those who were regarded as either incapable of fitting into the new system or of being objectively committed to its destruction.[12] In the aftermath of the Russian revolution, a very similar logic compelled the departure from the Soviet Union of millions of "objective enemies" of the new system. Similarly, the Cuban revolution resulted in the enforced emigration of over a million Cubans who could not fit into Castro's system, primarily to the United States.

A related development is currently taking place in South Africa. Because of the overwhelming number of blacks and their indispensability to the functioning of the economic order, it is impossible for the Afrikaners to eliminate them. Indeed, except for some ultrarightist groups, there is no evidence of any Afrikaner interest in doing so. Nevertheless, the Afrikaners have answered the question, Who shall have a voice in the political community? by excluding all nonwhites. Of crucial importance is the consistent refusal of the Afrikaners to admit the blacks to any meaningful kind of suffrage. Apartheid and the denial of electoral rights are attempts to limit membership in the political community without resorting to outright mass murder. Nevertheless, it is important to recognize that all of the policies cited above—segregation, concentration camp incarceration, expulsion, and genocide—are attempts to cope with a common problem.

The question, Who is to have a voice in the political community? was absolutely decisive for National Socialism. The political emancipation of the Jews in Europe in the late eighteenth and nineteenth centuries bestowed upon the Jews a voice in the political communities in which they were domiciled. With the dour wisdom of historical hindsight, the extermination of the Jews can be seen as an unintended consequence of their emancipation. Emancipation made membership of the Jews in Europe's political communities a political issue for the first time. Emancipation was opposed by all who believed such membership should be restricted to Christians. It was, as we know, also opposed by those who sought to restrict membership to those who regarded themselves as bound together by ties of blood. An important reason why so little was done to assist the Jews during World War II, both in Germany and throughout occupied Europe, was the almost universal European acceptance of the National Socialist objective of excluding the Jews from membership in the political communities in which they were domiciled. This certainly was true of the mainstream Protestant and Catholic churches, which everywhere saw the denial of political rights to the Jews as a beneficial step toward the creation of a Europe that was culturally, intellectually, socially, and politically Christian. The fundamental difference between Hitler and the churches was that Hitler had no illusions concerning the extreme measures necessary to implement such a program. The churches never faced frankly the question of implementation. Nevertheless, one must ask whether the silence of the overwhelming majority of Europe's church leaders during World War II concerning the Holocaust may have been at least partly due to the fact that church leaders fully understood that extermination was the only viable means of eliminating the Jews. Having no direct responsibility for carrying out the process of elimination, they preferred to leave the question of implementation to the German government. In any event, it is now clear that the insistent call for the elimination of the Jews from membership in the body politic of the European nations was in fact a demand for their extermination.

The question of uniqueness looms large in the discussions of the place of the Holocaust in the larger subject of genocide. Surprisingly few discussions of the question deal with one aspect of the Holocaust that was absolutely unique: In no other instance of genocide in the twentieth century was the fate of the victims so profoundly linked to the religiomythic inheritance of the perpetrators. In Christianity, the Jews are not simply one of the many peoples of the world. They are the people in whose midst God himself deigned to be incarnated. According to the classic Christian account, instead of being the first to recognize this supreme act of divine graciousness, the Jews both rejected God-in-the-flesh and were responsible for his viciously painful removal from the human scene. Alone among the victims of genocide, the Jews are depicted as the God-bearing and God-murdering people par excellence. No other religion is as horribly defamed in the classic literature of a rival tradition as is Judaism. Moreover, starting with the fall of Jerusalem in 70 C.E., Christianity has taken the disasters of the Jewish people to be the principal historical confirmation of its own truth. They have been interpreted in the classic sources to be God's punishment of a sinful Israel for having rejected Christ.

The practical consequences of the ascription of a demonic identity to Jews and the interpretation of their misfortunes as the just chastisement of a righteous Lord was to cast them out of any common universe of moral obligation with the Christians among whom they were domiciled. In times of acute social stress, the demonic characterization of Jews had the practical effect of decriminalizing any assault visited upon them, as Hitler and the leading National Socialists fully understood. The implementation of the Holocaust was greatly facilitated by the deicidal and demonic interpretation of the Jewish people in the Christian religious imagination. If the Holocaust was to some extent a unique event, its religiomythic dimension constituted a significant component of that uniqueness.

In addition to the religious aspect of the Holocaust, there was a highly significant economic element. To a large extent the European Jews constituted a middleman minority. The question of the proneness of middleman minorities to genocidal assault has been raised by Walter P. Zenner and a number of other scholars.[13] Zenner points out that the Armenians were also a middleman minority targeted for extermination, as were the Hoa or ethnic Chinese of Vietnam, who were the object of a large-scale, state-sponsored program of population elimination.[14] Zenner argues that there is no necessary link between middleman-minority status and genocide. He does, however, concede that such a status can be a precondition for genocide if other factors are present.

According to Zenner, middleman-minority theory has yet to face the question of why "economically integrated non-wage labor groups" are more likely to be victimized than wage laborers, the marginalized, and the poor, who are not usually targets. In actuality, middleman minorities are usually permitted domicile in a community to do work that for some reason is not being done by the indigenous population. Their presence as strangers is tolerated because they constitute an economically or vocationally complementary population. They are most likely to be targeted for elimination when their roles can be filled either by the state or by members of the indigenous population. When this development takes place, the minority members compete with members of the majority. They usually compete against one of the most dangerous and potentially unstable groups within the larger population, the majority middle class. In the case of indigenous wage workers, the marginalized, or the poor, the same bitter rivalry with a dangerous class does not arise. When political leaders perceive vocationally redundant members of the majority to be a source of social or political instability, they encourage emigration, as was the case in western and central Europe during much of the nineteenth century. Nevertheless, there is usually some residual sense that the marginalized or superfluous people remain to some extent part of the shared universe of moral obligation. This is not the case with middleman minorities, especially when they are outside the majority religious consensus. They are often tolerated only as long as they are needed.

In premodern societies it was not socially or economically functional for middleman minorities to share a common religion with the majority. The impersonal, objective attitudes necessary for successful commerce were less likely to develop between people who considered themselves to be kin worshiping the same gods. The flow of commerce often depended upon an in-group, out-group double standard. It was only with the rise of Protestantism that the personalized ethics of tribal brotherhood gave way to universal otherhood and a universal money economy could come into being.[15]

As an economy modernizes, the situation of middleman minorities is likely to become increasingly precarious. The condition of Europe's Jews became progressively more hopeless as the economies of western and eastern Europe were modernized.[16] As the agriculture of eastern Europe was progressively rationalized during the second half of the nineteenth century, large numbers of Polish and Russian peasants were dispossessed of their holdings and forced to seek scarce wage labor in the villages and cities. The peasants' predicament was further aggravated by yet another aspect of modernization: improved medicine and hygiene, which yielded unprecedented population increase. Desperate for any kind of work under conditions of massive unemployment and underemployment, members of the former peasant class began to compete with the Jews for wage labor and those middle-class slots that had previously been predominantly Jewish. In seeking to displace the Jews, the dispossessed peasants and their urbanized offspring had the support of the tsarist government. Their policy toward the Jews differed little from that of the National Socialist regime in Germany. Both sought the elimination of Jews as a demographic presence. Most American Jews are alive today because the two regimes did not share a common method of implementation.

In addition to serving as a method of radically redefining and restructuring society, genocide has been since ancient times the most unremitting kind of warfare. Elimination of a potential future threat became a powerful reason for wars of genocide. The human cost to the perpetrator undoubtedly played an important role in determining when a war was carried to such an extreme. After total defeat, the cost to the victor of eliminating a future threat was minimal. Since the enemy was outside the victor's universe of moral obligation, defeat removed the only practical impediment to genocide. As long as an enemy retained the power to injure, a would-be perpetrator had to weigh the relative costs of a precarious peace against those involved in genocide. If neither side had the power to achieve a decisive victory, there was no possibility of a Final Solution. In the case of the Holocaust, the Jews were perceived as a defenseless enemy with no significant capacity to retaliate. The problems involved in their extermination were reduced to the bureaucratic management, transport, and elimination of the target population. A principal motive for the establishment of the state of Israel was to escalate the cost of killing at least those Jews who are Israeli citizens. There is little doubt that the cost now includes nuclear retaliation.

Programs of genocide frequently are initiated in the aftermath of military defeat, especially under the devastating conditions of modern warfare.[17] An important element in the decision of the Young Turk regime to initiate the program of extermination against its Armenian Christian minority was Turkey's defeat by Bulgaria in 1912. Similarly, Germany's defeat in World War I created the conditions in which a radically anti-Semitic, revolutionary, revisionist National Socialist movement could come to dominate German politics. As a consequence of defeat, the fringe became the center. In addition to the role of a defenseless minority as a surrogate object of revenge for the victorious enemy, military defeat can intensify the urgency with which the question of membership in the community is posed. As noted above, a fundamental issue in genocide is the question of who can be trusted in a life-and-death struggle. All minorities suffer some discrimination and experience some degree or resentment and incomplete identification with the majority, a situation that is as obvious to the majority as to the minority. In normal times, such tensions can be held in check. In the aftermath of catastrophic military defeat, they can get out of hand. Aggressive energies can achieve cheap victories over a defenseless minority. The reality of defeat itself can be denied and responsibility for the misfortunes of war ascribed to the minority's hidden "stab in the back." The accusation of secret treachery can legitimate genocide against the minority. If such a group is perceived as bringing about national catastrophe, *while appearing to be loyal,* it can become a matter of the greatest public urgency to eliminate them from the body politic.

Almost from the moment Germany lost World War I, the Jews were accused of bringing about her defeat through treachery, an accusation that appeared ludicrous in view of the extremely high proportion of German Jews who had served as frontline soldiers and who had made the ultimate sacrifice for what they regarded as their fatherland. Elsewhere I have argued that the tradition of Judas betraying Jesus with a token of love, a kiss, provided an enormously powerful religiomythic identification of the Jew with betrayal in the minds of German Christians.[18] Since the identification of the Jew with Judas takes place in earliest childhood and is constantly reinforced by religious tradition, it is more deeply rooted and less subject to rational criticism than beliefs acquired at a later stage in the life cycle. When Hitler and the German right ascribed Germany's defeat to the Jews, they had working for them this immensely powerful pretheoretical archetype. Here, too, we discern a unique religiomythic element of enormous power that sets the Holocaust apart from other instances of genocide in our times.

Given the presence of religiomythic elements in the Holocaust, it is not surprising that many scholars have argued that the Holocaust was irrational in its objective if not in its methods. I have not agreed with such arguments in my major writings on the Holocaust. In contrast to spontaneous outbursts of intergroup hatred and violence, modern, systematic, bureaucratically administered genocide can be understood as a form of instrumentally rational *(zweckrational)* action in contrast to value-rational *(wertrational)* action. Max Weber, to whom we are indebted for this distinction, has observed that instrumental rationality refers to the choice of means whereas value rationality is a matter of ends.[19] Above all, one must not confuse humane action and instrumentally rational action. The experience of our era should leave no doubt concerning the enormous potential for inhumanity present in morally autonomous instrumental rationality. The perfection of this mode of political and social action is indeed one of the most problematic aspects of the modern era.

The idea that genocide could in any sense be regarded as rational has been rejected by Ronald Aronson. In *The Dialectics of Disaster*, Aronson argues that the Holocaust systematically outraged the norms of the "normal world."[20] He insists that the Holocaust was a product of madness, which he defines as a systematic derangement of perception, a seeing what is not there. The National Socialists saw the Jews as the source of Germany's problems and regarded their riddance as a major element in the solution. Aronson argues that when rulers organize a society against false enemies and falsely propagate the view that society is mortally threatened by them, we may speak of madness as much as when a paranoid individual behaves in a similar delusionary manner. Aronson insists that the Nazi attempt wholly to eliminate the Jews as a demographic presence first in Germany and then in all of Europe was insane because the Jews in no way constituted the threat the National Socialists alleged them to be.

Aronson's analogy of the individual and the group is questionable. He fails to deal with the underlying reason why the question, Who shall have a voice in the community? is raised in the first place. As noted, genocide is a violent means of determining who is to have a voice in a community whose members may have to sacrifice their lives in a life-and-death struggle with external enemies in a crisis. When a group regards itself as secure, it can afford to take a relatively benign view of the presence of a limited number of strangers in its midst. However, in times of acute national stress, such as economic dislocation, modern warfare, or military defeat, insiders are likely to view outsiders with intensified suspicion and hostility. When middleman minorities specialize in commerce, insiders may suspect that the outsiders' love of gain will outweigh their loyalty to the homeland. In an extreme situation, the insiders may decide upon the total elimination of the outsiders.

Contrary to Aronson, the issue of the patent untruth of National Socialist defamations is irrelevant to the critical fact that the overwhelming majority of Germans regarded even the most assimilated Jews as aliens whose elimination would be a positive benefit to the nation. The Germans were not duped by mendacious Nazi propaganda. They wanted the *volkisch* homogeneity Hitler promised them. When it was all over, some of them regretted the method of implementation employed by their government, but not that Europe was largely empty of Jews.

Unfortunately, one cannot even say that it is irrational to want an ethnically or religiously homogenous community consisting of those with whom one shares a sense of common faith, kinship, and trust. At least in the urbanized sections of much of the modern world, pluralism is a given. Nevertheless, there is nothing irrational about the desire for a community of moral trust and mutual obligation. Recent historical scholarship has demonstrated that a singularly important political purpose of the biblical religions of covenant was to unite under a common God in a shared community of moral and religious obligation those whose diverse tribal membership precluded them from creating a community based on kinship.[21] This was as true of biblical Judaism as it was of early Christianity. Moreover, one of the reasons for the astounding success of contemporary Japan has been its ethnic homogeneity. The irrationality of nonpluralistic communities is not the problem, but rather the extreme cruelty and inhumanity that must be practiced by the modern state in order to transform a pluralistic religioethnic or multireligious political entity into a homogenous community. Neither Hitler's ends nor his methods were irrational. They were, however, obscenely cruel and they graphically demonstrate what citizens of one of the world's most advanced civilizations were willing to do to other human beings for the sake of national homogeneity.

Finally, there is the issue of genocide and national sovereignty, an issue that has become ever more important with the end of political imperialism and the attainment of national sovereignty by so many of the nations of the world. It is a well-known fact that the United Nations never detected a single instance of genocide by a member nation. Elsewhere I have argued that as a sovereign community National Socialist Germany probably committed no crime at Auschwitz.[22] Under no circumstances was it my intention to mitigate the inhumanity and the obscenity of what the Germans did, but instead to point to one of the most urgent moral dilemmas involved in the notion of political sovereignty in our era. Crime is a violation of behavioral norms defined by political authority. Homicide, for example, is only a crime when the victim is protected by the state's laws. Even in National Socialist Germany, there were actually a very small number of SS officers who were punished for the *unauthorized* murder of Jews during World War II. The state determined when homicide was an offense against its law and when it constituted the implementation of those same laws.

If it be argued that the National Socialist state was by its very nature a criminal state because it violated God's laws or the laws of nature, one must ask what practical difference such violations made to the perpetrators. As long as the leaders of National Socialist Germany were free to exercise sovereignty, no superordinate system of norms constituted any kind of restraint on their behavior. As is well known, neither the German churches nor the Vatican ever asserted that the genocidal program of the National Socialist state was a violation of God's law although the program was well known. In reality, there are no human rights; there are only political rights. That is why the question, Who is to have a voice in the political community? is the fundamental human question. Membership in a political community is no absolute guarantee of safety. Nevertheless, to the extent that men and women have any rights whatsoever, it is as members of a political community with the power to guarantee those rights. This was clearly evident in the fate of the Armenians in Turkey during World War I. Genocide is the ultimate expression of absolute rightlessness.

While highlighting the extreme moral limitations of contemporary civilization, genocide is nevertheless an intrinsic expression of that civilization. Genocide is most likely to occur when men and women refuse to extend the benefits and protection of their societies to strangers whom they cannot or will not trust. Obviously, that perception is highly subjective and may very well be in error. One of the privileges of power, however, is the ability to define social reality. The objective facts are of far less practical consequence than the subjective perceptions of the majority.

NOTES

1. For an important new work on the subject, see Isidor Wallimann and Michael N. Dobkowski, eds., *Genocide and the Modern Age: Etiology and Case Study of Mass Death* (Westport, Conn., 1987). See also Leo Kuper, *Genocide: Its Political Use in the Twentieth Century* (New Haven, 1987), and Irving Louis Horowitz *State Power and Mass Murder* (New Brunswick, N.J., 1980).
2. This is a generalization of my fundamental thesis concerning the Holocaust as expressed in Richard L. Rubenstein, *The Cunning of History* (New York, 1975), p. 6.
3. Tony Barta, "Relations of Genocide: Land and Lives in the Colonization of Australia," in Wallimann and Dobkowski, *Genocide*, pp. 237–52.
4. This thesis is spelled out by the author in Richard L. Rubenstein, *The Age of Triage: Fear and Hope in an Overcrowded World* (Boston, 1983), pp. 34–59.

5. Christopher Hill, *God's Englishman: Oliver Cromwell and the English Revolution* (New York, 1972), p. 113.

6. R. P. Stearns, *Hugh Peter: The Strenuous Puritan, 1598–1660* (Champagne and Urbana, Ill., 1954), p. 356, as cited by Hill, *God's Englishman*, p. 117.

7. Cecil Woodham-Smith, *The Great Hunger: Ireland, 1845–1849* (New York, 1980), pp. 411–12.

8. Rubenstein, *The Age of Triage*, pp. 120-27.

9. "Effects of Emigration on Production and Consumption," *The Economist*, February 12, 1853, pp. 168-69.

10. See "The Irish Priesthood and the Irish Laity," *The Economist*, June 19, 1852, pp. 67–73.

11. For a study of the fate of the Indians of North America, see Bernard W. Sheehan, *Seeds of Extinction: Jeffersonian Philanthropy and the American Indian* (Chapel Hill, N.C., 1973).

12. See Rubenstein, *The Age of Triage*, pp. 165–94.

13. See Walter P. Zenner, "Middleman Minorities and Genocide," in Wallimann and Dobkowski, *Genocide*, pp. 253–81; Zenner, *Middleman Minority Theories and the Jews: A Historical Assessment*, YIVO Working Papers in Yiddish and East European Jewish Studies Series, no. 31 (New York, 1978); Edna Bonacich and J. Modell, *The Economic Basis of Ethnic Solidarity: The Case of Japanese-Americans* (Berkeley and Los Angeles, 1981).

14. For a discussion of the elimination of the ethnic Chinese from Vietnam, see Rubenstein, *The Age of Triage*, pp. 165–94.

15. See Benjamin Nelson, *The Idea of Usury: From Tribal Brotherhood to Universal Otherhood*, 2d ed. (Chicago, 1969).

16. Rubenstein, *The Age of Triage*, pp. 128–64.

17. See Irving Louis Horowitz, "Genocide and the Reconstruction of Social Theory: Observations on the Exclusivity of Social Death," in Wallimann and Dobkowski, *Genocide*, pp. 61–80.

18. Richard L. Rubenstein, *After Auschwitz: Radical Theology and Contemporary Judaism* (Indianapolis, 1966), pp. 30ff.

19. Max Weber, *Economy and Society: An Outline of Interpretive Sociology*, ed. Guenther Roth and Claus Wittich (New York, 1968), 1:24–26.

20. Ronald Aronson, *The Dialectics of Disaster* (London, 1983).

21. See George E. Mendenhall, *The Tenth Generation: The Origins of the Biblical Tradition* (Baltimore, 1973), pp. 19ff. and Rubenstein, *The Age of Traige,* pp. 229–40.

22. Rubenstein, *The Cunning of History*, p. 90.

CHAPTER 2

The Uniqueness and Universality
of the Holocaust

Michael Berenbaum

The question of the uniqueness and universality of the Holocaust is being considered with increasing frequency not only in scholarly quarters with a focus on historiography but also in communities throughout the United States where Holocaust memorials and commemorative services raise a consciousness of the Holocaust that then enters the mainstream of American culture. The debate over the place of the Holocaust in history is being conducted within the academy, in the streets among ethnic politicians and community leaders, in schools by educators developing curricula, among a cultural elite in literature and the arts, and in religious and philosophical circles. In the process the word *holocaust,* shorn of its particular reference along with its article, threatens to become a symbolic word connoting mass murder and destruction whatever the magnitude.

Perhaps the force of personality, as much as circumstance, has brought the definition of the Holocaust to the fore. The chief protagonists for alternate conceptions, Elie Wiesel and Simon Wiesenthal, are both survivors, both European Jews, both men of towering stature who have brought the Holocaust to the world's attention. Yet these two men differ markedly in their personal history, their legacy and destiny. Simon Wiesenthal defines *Holocaust* as the systematic murder of eleven million people, six million of whom were Jews killed because of their Jewishness, and five million of whom were non-Jews — Gypsies, Jehovah's Witnesses, homosexuals, political prisoners, Poles, Ukrainians, the handicapped, and the mentally ill — killed for a variety of reasons in an apparatus of destruction designed for mass extermination. The machinery of destruction included the *Einsatzgruppen,* the concentration camps, and the extermination camps with their gas chambers and ovens. Wiesenthal maintains that although all

Jews were victims, the Holocaust transcended the confines of the Jewish community. Other people shared the tragic fate of victimhood.

Wiesenthal personifies two traditional self-characterizations of the Jewish people, *din* (justice) and *am ke'she oref* (a stiff-necked people). Wiesenthal has been tenacious in his pursuit of law, demanding that the European nations bring their Nazi war criminals to trial. He has stubbornly refused to abandon the quest for justice after some forty-five years, even when its meaning may have been tarnished by international lack of interest and by the absence of appropriately severe sentences. (One war criminal was recently sentenced to the equivalent of 1.5 minutes in jail for every person he killed.) Wiesenthal has resisted the temptation to resort to revenge—a swifter, more primitive form of punishment. He hounds both the criminal and the state to reaffirm the value of justice.

Wiesenthal's inclusion of non-Jewish victims enhances his basic post-Holocaust commitment, the prosecution of Nazi war criminals. When apathetic governments are reminded that their non-Jewish citizens were also killed, a greater measure of cooperation can be enlisted. By more broadly defining the Holocaust, Wiesenthal can intensify the political pressure he exerts. Wiesenthal's more universal predilection may also reflect his present status as a European Jew; he belongs to a demoralized community that may be psychologically incapable of taking a Judeo-centric perspective in the public domain, preferring instead the aphorism of Judah Leib Gordon: "Be a Jew in your own home and a man in the street" ("Awake My People," *Ha-Karmel*, vol. 7, no. 1 [1866]). Wiesenthal's statements regarding Kurt Waldheim's Nazi past similarly indicate the limits of his situation as an Austrian Jew. Wiesenthal feared the resurgence of Austrian anti-Semitism and was reluctant to press the Waldheim matter. He also failed to take the lead in challenging President Reagan's visit to Bitburg. (The Los Angeles Center for Holocaust Studies that bears Wiesenthal's name is led by more secure American-born Orthodox Jews who were less inhibited in exposing Waldheim's past and decrying Bitburg.)

Wiesenthal's insistence that the non-Jew was also a victim of the Holocaust mirrors his experience in Mauthausen where Jews constituted only a minority of those incarcerated. Unlike Wiesel, who was deported and incarcerated almost exclusively with Jews, Wiesenthal spent the war years in an integrated environment.

Nevertheless, it should be noted that among two hundred panels on display in the Simon Wiesenthal Center (as of 1988), less than 7 percent deal with non-Jews, and half of these displays concern righteous individuals who lived and fought with Jews or helped rescue Jews. Critics who would contend that the Wiesenthal Center dilutes the Jewish meaning of the Holocaust had better look elsewhere for the substantiation of their accusations.

Wiesenthal is not the only person who has included non-Jews among Holocaust victims nor has he become an active participant in the debate over definition. Rather, his general position in the past has led others to perceive his stance in universalist terms that some interpret as an affront to the unique experience of the Jews in the Holocaust.

By contrast, Elie Wiesel is regarded as the poet laureate of the Holocaust, a man who has become, in the words of Steven Schwarzschild, "the de facto high priest of our generation, the one who speaks most tellingly in our time of our hopes and fears, our tragedy and our protest."[1] For Wiesel the Holocaust is a sacred mystery that can be approached but never understood; the Holocaust is the modern *Pardes,* a world that can only be apprehended at great peril and that should not be studied without preparation and caution. Elsewhere I have written at length of Wiesel's significance as a thinker and his impact on contemporary Jewish consciousness.[2] He is invaluable as a storyteller who has passionately conveyed the memory of the Holocaust.

Wiesel fears that Wiesenthal's definition of the Holocaust may trigger an irreversible process that will erase the memory of six million Jews. He contends that people will speak first of eleven million people, six million of whom were Jews; then of eleven million people, some of whom were Jews; and finally of eleven million people, deleting any reference to Jews.[3]

Wiesel is the only major American Jewish novelist who writes solely from a Jewish perspective and for whom the process of Americanization was peripheral to his personal story and literary contribution. Even though Wiesel has been an American citizen for three decades and was twice honored with medals by his country, he continues to write in French and sets most of his novels in Europe and Israel; few American characters ever appear. (*Day,*[4] a rare exception, is set in New York but deals with the psychological scars left by the Holocaust on a survivor, thus rendering the American setting irrelevant. *The Fifth Son*[5] begins in America but quickly moves to Europe.) Nevertheless, it was as an American figure that Wiesel was appointed chairman of the President's Commission on the Holocaust and its successor body, the United States Holocaust Memorial Council. These public bodies were created to transmit the legacy of Jewish suffering to a general American audience.

The task of the U.S. Holocaust Memorial Council involved the Americanization of the Holocaust; the story had to be told in such a way that it would resonate not only with the survivor in New York and his children in Houston or San Francisco, but with a black leader from Atlanta, a midwestern farmer, or a northeastern industrialist. Millions of Americans make pilgrimages to Washington; the Holocaust museum must take them back in time, transport them to another continent, and inform their current reality. The Americanization of the Holocaust is an honorable task provided that the story told is faithful to the historical event. Each culture inevitably leaves its stamp on the past it remembers. The intersection of historical event and social need, what happened and what can be understood, leaves neither history nor society unchanged. This process is integral to what sociologists term the civil religion of a given society.

Designing a Holocaust museum in America will be far more difficult than planning Yad Vashem in Israel because the United States Holocaust Memorial Museum must address an audience that finds the tale itself alien. The American museum also runs the risk of creating a magnet for anti-Semitism if others who perceive themselves, rightly or wrongly, as victims of the Holocaust feel excluded from the memorial and/or sense that their suffering has been trivialized or denied. The museum must grapple with the problem of complicity with the Nazis in the destruction of the Jews by people who were themselves the victims of nazism. The American museum must also explore the dilemma of the bystander in a way that makes sense of the few successes and many failures of American policy regarding the Holocaust during and following the war. Because the American museum is a government project (appointments to the council are made by the president), the council cannot be fully insulated from the political context in which it operates.

Yehuda Bauer, the prominent historian and head of the Institute of Contemporary Jewry at the Hebrew University in Jerusalem, voiced the fear that historical truths would be sacrificed for political expediency in the American council's work. Bauer noted two definitions of the Holocaust offered in speeches by President Jimmy Carter. Carter spoke of a memorial to "six million Jews and millions of other victims of Nazism during World War II." On another occasion he decried the "systematic and state-sponsored extermination of six million Jews and five million non-Jews." Bauer interpreted Carter's comments as follows:

The memorial as seen by the President [not the commission] should commemorate all the victims of Nazism, Jews and non-Jews *alike* and should *submerge* the specific Jewish tragedy in the general sea of atrocities committed by the Nazi regime.[6] (italics added)

Bauer attributed the "submersion" of the specific Jewish tragedy to pressure from American ethnic groups and warned that an Americanized, non-Jewish memorial would misrepresent the Holocaust.

Bauer marshaled three highly emotional arguments to foster his claim. He invoked the Russian attempt to deny the Jewishness of the Holocaust, which resulted in the abominable memorial at Babi Yar where no mention of Jews is made in either the content of the sculpture or the inscription on the memorial. Second, Bauer referred to the Western denial of the "War Against the Jews," which led to the failure to rescue Jews. Third, he alluded to international anti-Semitism, which seeks to deny the Holocaust altogether.

We must separate the emotional elements of these arguments from their substantive components. Ironically, Bauer focused on Carter when the responsibility for designing and implementing the museum had been delegated to the U.S. Holocaust Memorial Council, which consistently emphasized the uniqueness of the Jewish experience.

Bauer gave undue importance to a president's words on a ceremonial occasion while neglecting the deliberations of the presidential commission and its *Report to the President,* as well as the actual work of the council. Furthermore, Bauer mistook the intention to "include" others (non-Jews) in the museum for a total "submergence" of Jewish suffering in a "sea of atrocities." In fact, the uniqueness of the Jewish experience can best be documented by comparing it with the Nazi treatment of other persecuted populations. Only by understanding the fate of other groups, detailing where it paralleled Jewish treatment and more important where it differed, can the distinctive nature of Jewish fate be historically demonstrated.

With respect to Bauer's fear of Americanization, the question of audience should not be confused with content. The Holocaust is only "Americanized" insofar as it is explained to Americans and related to their history with ramifications for future policy. The study of the Holocaust can provide insights that have universal import for the destiny of all humanity. A national council funded at taxpayers' expense to design a *national* memorial does not have the liberty of creating an exclusively Jewish one in the restricted sense of the term, and most specifically with regard to audience. A purely Jewish museum is the task of the American Jewish community operating with private funding and without government subvention, as is the case with the New York Holocaust Memorial (appropriately titled "The Museum of the Jewish Heritage"). In the final analysis, private Jewish memorials and the national Holocaust museum (along with scholarship, art, and media productions) will define the Holocaust for the American public, not the words of an ineloquent president.

Bauer does provide his readers with a valuable definition of the uniqueness of the Holocaust: the planned, total annihilation of an entire community and a quasi-apocalyptic, religious component whereby the death of the victim became an integral ingredient in the drama of salvation. Bauer presents two necessary but not exhaustive conditions for the uniqueness of the Holocaust.

Survivors (and some other Jews as well) have been fundamentally ambivalent about bequeathing the story of the Holocaust. For the Holocaust to have any sustained impact, it must enter the mainstream of international consciousness as a symbolic word denoting a particular, extraordinary event with moral, political, and social implications. Yet the moment it enters the mainstream, the Holocaust becomes fair game for writers, novelists, historians, theologians, and philosophers with different backgrounds and unequal skills. Some lesser minds or insensitive thinkers are bound to disappoint, dilute, and misrepresent.

Transmitting the Holocaust entails a degree of uncontrolled dissemination. Jews cannot simultaneously maintain the Holocaust as a horribly sanctified and inviolate topic while complaining that the world is ignorant of its occurrence. Even for Wiesel, the decision to run the risks of exposure began when he published *Night* in French.[7]

Uniqueness of Intent or of Methodology   Bauer displayed no discomfort with the word *holocaust* even though the term itself is not without its problems. In origin *Holocaust* is a theological term rather than a historical one. It is an English word derived from the Greek translation of the Hebrew word *olah*, meaning "a sacrificial offering burnt whole before the Lord." The word itself softens and falsifies the Holocaust by imparting religious meaning.[8] The Yiddish word *hurban*, meaning "destruction," is more stark and refers to the results of the event itself. The Hebrew word *shoah* shares much in common with its Yiddish antecedent. Bauer locates the uniqueness of the Holocaust in the intentionality of the perpetrators. This view is essentially supported by Lucy Dawidowicz, Uriel Tal, George Mosse, and Steven Katz. These scholars emphasize intent and ideology.

By contrast, Raul Hilberg and other historians have focused on results rather than intentions. Hilberg concentrates not on the philosophy that underscored the destruction but on the processes of execution. Emil Fackenheim, Lawrence Langer, Hannah Arendt, Richard Rubenstein, Joseph Borkin, and I concur with this functionalist approach. *How* the terrible crime was committed, as much as its theoretical conception, distinguishes the Holocaust from previous manifestations of evil.

Joseph Borkin has argued that Auschwitz represented the perverse perfection of slavery. In all previous manifestations of human slavery, including the particularly cruel form practiced in North America, slaves were considered a capital investment to be protected, fed, and sheltered by the master. Slaves were permitted to reproduce and hence to increase the master's wealth. By contrast, the Nazis reduced human beings to consumable raw materials expended in the process of manufacture. All mineral life was systematically drained from the bodies, which were recycled into the Nazi war economy—gold teeth went to the treasury, hair was used for mattresses, ashes became fertilizer. At I. G. Auschwitz the average slave lived for ninety days; at Buna, he lived thirty days. One survivor explained: "They oiled the machines, but they didn't feed the people." These corporate decisions were made in Frankfurt, and *not* in the field, for "sound" economic reasons and not under the exigencies of battlefield conditions.[9]

Beyond the "perfection" of slavery, the elimination of surplus population was also carried to its logical conclusion. Bureaucracy was employed to solve complex problems in implementing mass destruction. The coexistence of demonic evil with banality pervaded the bureaucratic structure.[10] The camps themselves were a society of total domination.

A *Lachrymose Theory of Jewish History* Ismar Schorsch, the prominent Jewish historian and now chancellor of the Conservative Jewish Theological Seminary, advocated a limited role for the Holocaust in the civil religion of American Jews. Schorsch feared the development of a lachrymose theory of Jewish history.[11] The history of Jew as victim threatens to dominate Jewish consciousness, to diminish the totality of Jewish history in which Jews were the authors of their own destiny and to overwhelm the vital celebration of life or the hope for redemption. In addition, Schorsch argued, the consequence of an overemphasis on the Holocaust has been an "obsession with the uniqueness of the event as if to forgo the claim would be to diminish the horror of the crime."[12]

The truth, Schorsch maintained, is that Jews were the only victims of genocide in World War II. "To insist on more is to imply or overindulge in invidious comparisons." When used indiscriminately, the argument for the uniqueness of the Holocaust is a "throwback to an age of religious polemics, a secular version of chosenness."[13] This misuse of the uniqueness argument to reinforce chosenness is seen most clearly in the writings of the Orthodox Jewish theologian Eliezer Berkovits:

The metaphysical quality of the Nazi-German hatred of the Jews as well as the truly diabolical, superhuman quality of the Nazi-German criminality against the Jews are themselves testimonies to the dark knowledge with which a nazified Germany sensed the presence in history of the hiding God.[14]

For Schorsch, the claim of uniqueness may be true, but it is politically counterproductive because it "impedes dialogue and introduces issues that alienate potential allies from among other victims of organized depravity," such as other victims of nazism, Armenians, Gypsies, blacks, and so forth. Schorsch recommends that Jews translate their experience into existential and political symbols meaningful to non-Jews without "submerging our credibility."

What for Schorsch is the process of translation appears to Bauer as Americanization and de-Judaization. Bauer's characterization of the Holocaust's uniqueness is inadequate (since it is limited to intentionality), and Schorsch's resistance to history is inappropriate. Both Bauer's assertions and Schorsch's reticence could be informed by a more comparative approach. The fruits of such consideration are amply apparent in such important works as Irving Horowitz's study of the Holocaust and the Armenian genocide, *Taking Lives;* Helen Fein's *Accounting for Genocide,* and the literary analysis of Terrence Des Pres.[15] A recognition of uniqueness need not alienate potential allies for it can sharpen insight and encourage research. Nevertheless, Schorsch's inhibiting cautions, like Bauer's misplaced fears, should be taken as warning signals of what must be avoided in order to secure serious scholarship and its responsible application.

Conferring Status John Cuddihy of Hunter College is a brilliant yet eccentric critic of contemporary American Jewry. His insights sometimes glisten even if they do not long endure; yet his information is wide ranging and his understanding of modernity and the Jewish condition is comprehensive and original. Cuddihy probes not the history of the Holocaust but its historiography.[16]

Cuddihy cited numerous scholars, all of whom are making similar points regarding the Holocaust's uniqueness in character and organization, in its systematic and noninstrumental preoccupation with murder, in its totality and its focus on death. Henry Feingold, an important historian of the Roosevelt administration,[17] fears that the Holocaust may be robbed of its "horrendous particularity." People may generalize history and modulate nazism by treating it not as a uniquely demonic force but as the dark side of the human spirit that lurks in all of us. A. Roy Eckhardt, a Christian theologian of the Holocaust, terms the event "uniquely unique," a category apart from all other historical events. In his critical work *The Cunning of History,* Rubenstein projects the precedent of the Holocaust toward its present and future ramifications, as noted by William Styron both in his introduction to Rubenstein's work and in his novel *Sophie's Choice.*[18] For both Rubenstein and Styron, the Holocaust looms as the ultimate technological nightmare, the manifestation extraordinaire of the potentialities of Western civilization. Emil Fackenheim, by contrast, believes that the uniqueness of the Holocaust is found in the uniqueness of its victims. The Holocaust was directed against Jews who were "not the *waste products* of Nazi society but its *end products*" (emphasis added).[19]

In reviewing these claims of uniqueness, Cuddihy has noticed that the distinction between Jews and non-Jews is the key element that unites Fackenheim and Feingold, Bauer and Wiesel. The "residual category" of non-Jews that continues to divide the world serves three critical functions for Jews. It preserves a sense of sacred particularity, freezing the presence of anti-Semitism in Jewish consciousness, and thus preempting Sartre's question, "Why remain a Jew?" It continues to separate Jew from Gentile not as a free choice by Jews but as a decision imposed by Hitler, who radically divided Jews from non-Jews. Finally, according to Cuddihy, uniqueness functions not so much for preventing historical fraud or de-Judaization but as a device for conferring status.

In fairness to Cuddihy, we must stress that his concern is not history but sociology, and he is writing something of a crypto-sociology of historiography. Often one can dissent from his views with ease, especially when his statements are flip or inaccurate. Yet one must examine his claim that inherent in the desire to affirm the uniqueness of the Holocaust—apart from the issue of its factual validity—may be a secular translation of Jewish chosenness wherein a people's specialness, once derived spiritually from the divine revelation at Sinai, is now recast as the inheritance of those wronged by the demonic anti-God (so to speak) who acted at Auschwitz.

In response to Cuddihy's critique, we must consider the factual basis for the Holocaust's uniqueness and the resistance to its centrality in contemporary Jewish consciousness.

The Holocaust in Jewish History The discussion of the uniqueness and universality of the Holocaust in world history is accompanied by queries regarding the place of the Holocaust in Jewish history. The current discussion centers on two major questions: (1) Does the Holocaust occupy an excessively prominent position in contemporary Jewish consciousness, threatening to obscure the promise of Sinai, the triumph of Israel, and the totality of previous Jewish history? and (2) Does the Holocaust have normative implications for Jewish history and theology? The parameters of the dialogue have been set by Jacob Neusner, Irving Greenberg, Paula Hyman, Michael Wyschograd, Robert Alter, Arnold Wolf, and me.[20] Essential to the general argument for the uniqueness of the Holocaust is the conclusion that the Holocaust is not only quantitatively but also qualitatively different from other episodes of persecution in Jewish history, a point not universally accepted by scholars in the field whose objections are often motivated by the politics and aesthetics of Holocaust commemoration rather than by specific historical data.

Another set of objections to the Holocaust's uniqueness comes from religious Jews who seek to minimize the Holocaust's importance and thereby limit the damage done to religious faith. These pietists view the Holocaust as another event in the long line of Jewish tales of suffering and woe—less significant, perhaps, than the destruction of the first and second Temples though surely more important than the 1492 expulsion of Jews from Spain or the 1648 Chmielnitski massacres in the Ukraine. After all, these thinkers argue, martyrdom and misery have often been the lot of Jews throughout their long and painful history. After each catastrophe Jewish faith has confronted the suffering, and Jews have remained faithful to the covenant.

Most Jews who share this view are believers for whom too much is at stake to permit a fundamental reexamination of faith.

The most serious Jewish critique of the uniqueness of the Holocaust in Jewish history comes from those thinkers who fear that the recollection of destruction is inadequate to sustain the Jewish future. Michael Wyschograd, a philosopher at the City University of New York who fled from Germany shortly before the war, has repeatedly challenged Emil Fackenheim's views:

Israel's faith has always centered on the saving acts of God: the election, the Exodus, the Temple and the Messiah. However more prevalent destruction was in the history of Israel, the acts of destruction were enshrined in minor fast days while those of redemption became the joyous proclamation of Passover and Tabernacles. . . . The God of Israel is a redeeming God; this is the only message we are authorized to proclaim.[21]

Yet Wyschograd refuses to ask the fundamental question: how is it possible to speak of a redeeming God in a world of Auschwitz? When truth is sacrificed to expediency, the result is propaganda (however useful psychologically or theologically). It may be traditional to emphasize good over evil, but in the face of overwhelming destruction, this perspective may cease to be credible.

Similarly, Jacob Neusner, who recently retired as Brown University's Ungeleider Distinguished Scholar of Judaica and university professor, objects to the vacuous quality of Jewish consciousness that is rooted in the Holocaust. He regards the entire enterprise as theologically doomed to failure. Neusner writes that "the Judiac system of Holocaust and Redemption [the restoration of the Jews in the State of Israel] leaves unaffected the larger dimensions of human existence of Jewish Americans—and that is part of that system's power."[22] As people look for answers to the various dimensions of their lives, the vicariousness of American Jewry's new theology will not serve them well.

Neusner also bemoans the demise of the intellect in American Jewish life. An American Judaism of Holocaust and Redemption works only with "the raw materials made available by contemporary experience—emotions on the one side, and politics on the other. Access to realms beyond require learning in literature, the only resource beyond the immediate."[23] Neusner insists that a Judaism of Holocaust and Redemption is not the product of intellectuals but bureaucrats—fundraisers, administrators, and public relations managers:

The correlation between mass murder and a culture of organizations proves exact: the war against the Jews called forth from the Jews people capable of building institutions to protect the collectivity of Israel, so far as anyone could be saved. Consequently much was saved. But much was lost."[24]

In the end, however, even the most distinguished historian and empiricist is forced to become a theologian:

The first century found its enduring memory in one man on a hill, on a cross; the twentieth, in six million men, women, and children making up a Golgotha, a hill of skulls of their own. No wonder that the Judaism of the age struggled heroically to frame a Judaic system appropriate to the issue of the age. No wonder they failed. Who would want to succeed in framing a world view congruent to such an age, a way of life to be lived in an age of death?[25]

In response, we must ask whether any theology can be authentic in the age of Auschwitz and in the nuclear age that followed, if it does not confront the overwhelming legacy and proximity of death.

The Holocaust is unprecedented in Jewish history; it was not simply a continuation of traditional anti-Semitism, for four fundamental reasons. The Holocaust differs from previous manifestations of anti-Semitism in that the earlier expressions were episodic, unsustained, illegal (they took place outside the law), and religiously rather than biologically based. That is, Jews were killed for what they believed or practiced: conversion or emigration were possible alternatives. By contrast, the Nazis were unrelenting; for twelve years the destruction of the Jewish people was a German priority. Trains that could have been used to bring soldiers to the front or transport injured personnel to the rear were diverted to bring Jews to their death. The persecution of Jews was geographically widespread throughout Europe from central Russia to the Spanish border. Furthermore, it was legally conducted, the legal system serving as an instrument of oppression. The persecution of Jews and their annihilation was a policy of state, utilizing all facets of the government. Most important, Jews were killed not for *what* they were or for what they practiced or believed, but for the *fact* that they were—all Jews were to be exterminated, not merely the Jewish soul. Jews were no longer considered, as they were in Christian theology, the symbol of evil; rather, they were regarded as subhuman and were thus eliminated.

Even the traditional category of Jewish martyrdom was denied to many victims of the Holocaust because they lacked the essential element of choice in their deaths. Since they did not die because of their beliefs but because of the accident of their birth as Jews (or as children or grandchildren of Jews), a new category of martyrdom, a new language, had to be invented.

Toward a Solution   There is no conflict between describing the uniqueness of the Jewish experience during the Holocaust and the *inclusion* of other victims of nazism. In fact, the examination of all victims is not only politically desirable but pedagogically mandatory if we are to demonstrate the claim of uniqueness. History should guide the portrayal of all victims of nazism—Jews and non-Jews. There are three historical dimensions to the question of uniqueness.

First, the goal of the Holocaust was unprecedented. Never before did a state sponsor a systematic, bureaucratic extermination of an entire people in a quasi-apocalyptic act promising national salvation. Nazi Germany prioritized the murder of Jews over the war effort.

Second, the Holocaust was without parallel in its methodology. Raul Hilberg traces the process of extermination from definition to expropriation to concentration to deportation and to extermination. Each step was part of a disciplined program borrowing on past policies but breaking new ground, shattering previous boundaries—moral, political, psychological, and religious—and overcoming the inertia of an entrenched bureaucracy, civilian as well as military. The result was the creation of new instruments of destruction; the Nazis created *l'universe concentrainaire,* which Arendt called a "society of total domination," where Fackenheim's *musselman* (the walking dead) inhabit Wiesel's "kingdom of night." Langer speaks of the "death of choice," and Primo Levi writes about a "new language of atrocity."

Finally, the results of the Holocaust were six million dead, one million of them children—an entire world destroyed, a culture uprooted, and mankind left with new thresholds of inhumanity.

To demonstrate each dimension of the uniqueness, the plight of all Nazi victims must be understood. How does one explain systematic genocide of an entire people without contrasting the Jewish experience with the horrendous plight of the Polish people?

Unlike the Jews, Poles were consigned by the Nazis to subservience, not destruction. The Polish intelligentsia was annihilated so that Polish culture could be dominated. Gifted Polish children were Aryanized, kidnapped, and brought to Germany for adoption by "pure Aryan" families. Thus, the Polish future was mortgaged.

Unlike the Poles, all Jews were condemned to death, not just a political, social, or intellectual elite. From Albert Einstein to Mottle the tailor, the Jew was considered the enemy. All Jewish blood was to be eliminated. Thus even blond, blue-eyed, brilliant Jewish children were sent off to be destroyed.

Gypsies shared much but not all of the horrors assigned to Jews. Romani were killed in some countries but not in others. The fate of the rural Romani often differed from that of their urban counterparts. By contrast, the murder of the Jews was a priority in every country; the Nazis pressed the bureaucracy to process Jews for the Final Solution. Even though the Romani were subject to gassing and other forms of extermination, the number of Gypsies was not as vast, and individual death by gassing was far less certain than it was for the Jews. This is not to diminish or minimize Gypsy suffering, which was intense, sustained, and harsh, but to focus on those dimensions of the Holocaust that were unique.

Like the Romani, homosexuals were arrested and incarcerated; similarly, many Ukrainians were sent to concentration camps where they were jailed as prisoners of war. Yet a Ukrainian or a gay could hope to outlive the Nazis merely by surviving. In contrast, all Jews lived under an imminent death sentence of death. The ovens and gas chambers were primarily restricted to Jews. An apparatus originally designed for the mentally retarded and the emotionally disturbed consumed the Jews, although in all likelihood this destruction would not have ceased when the last Jew was killed had the Nazis won both the World War and the War Against the Jews.

Contra Bauer, the inclusion of non-Jews is neither a convenience nor a bow to the realities of pluralistic American life but an intellectual, historical, and pedagogical prerequisite to conveying the truth of what occurred in the Holocaust. Historical accuracy should unite ethnic communities who wish their dead to be remembered with Jewish survivors who appropriately want the Judeo-centric nature of the experience to be told. Particularity need not be sacrificed to false universalism.

Bohdan Wytwycky, a young philosopher of Ukrainian ancestry from Columbia University, has offered a compelling image for describing the Holocaust in *The Other Holocaust: The Many Circles of Hell* (Washington, D.C., 1980). He refers to the many circles of hell in Dante's *Inferno*. The Jews occupied the center of hell with the concentric rings extending outward to incorporate many other victims much as waves spread outward with diminishing intensity from a stone tossed into a lake. To comprehend the

Jewish center, we must fully probe the ripple effects as well as the indisputable core.

In arming themselves to protect the uniqueness of the Holocaust, many defenders of the faith (rather than the fact) have shied away from comparisons with other instances of subjugation or mass murder. Such comparisons do not innately obscure the uniqueness of the Holocaust; they clarify it. For example, inclusion of the Armenian experience in discussing the Holocaust does not detract from the Holocaust's uniqueness but deepens our moral sensitivity while sharpening our perception. Such inclusion also displays generosity of spirit and ethical integrity. We should let our sufferings, however incommensurate, unite us in condemnation of inhumanity rather than divide us in a calculus of calamity.

The analogies between the Armenian genocide and the Holocaust teach a number of moral lessons. For example, Hitler used the world's indifference to Armenian suffering to silence cabinet opposition to his plans for the Poles. The Armenian genocide assured Hitler that negative consequences would not greet his actions. Likewise, the memory of the Armenian genocide prompted Henry Morgenthau, Jr., to confront President Roosevelt with evidence of American inaction during the Holocaust. Henry Morgenthau, Sr., was the American ambassador to Turkey during the Armenian massacres, and his namesake, the secretary of the treasury, remembered his father's example and acted responsibly. In the same manner, the Jewish resistance fighters at Bialystok invoked the memory of Musa Dag, the Armenian uprising, in fighting for freedom and honor. The Holocaust can become a symbolic orienting event in human history that can prevent recurrence.

Common to all these examples are two principles for dealing with events analogous but not equivalent to the Holocaust. The analogies must be historically authentic, and they must illuminate other dimensions of the Holocaust and/or the analogous event. If these principles are followed, then we need not fear engaging in analogies that illumine scholarship and memory. Comparison will neither trivialize nor de-Judaize the Holocaust.

NOTES

1. Steven Schwarzschild, "Jewish Values in the Post-Holocaust Future," *Judaism*, vol. 16, no. 3 (Summer 1967), p. 157.

2. Michael Berenbaum, *The Vision of the Void: Theological Reflections on the Works of Elie Wiesel* (Middletown, 1979).

3. Wiesel's experience with the United States Holocaust Memorial Council reinforced his caution. Romani (Gypsy) representatives first pressed for representation on the council as one of the Nazis' victims. Once included, the Romani representative challenged the uniqueness of the Jewish experience, arguing that the Romani losses were equivalent to Jewish losses, if not numerically, then proportionally. (In my work as a consultant and later a project director of the U.S. Holocaust Memorial Museum, I also encountered a tendency among the professional staff to move from inclusion of non-Jewish victims to a nondifferentiation among the victims.

4. Elie Wiesel, *The Accident* (New York, 1962). In 1985 Wiesel published his trilogy and changed the title of *The Accident* to *Day,* which conforms with the original French title *(Le Jour).* Elie Wiesel, *Night/Dawn/Day* (New York, 1985).

5. Elie Wiesel, *The Fifth Son* (New York, 1984).

6. Yehuda Bauer, "Whose Holocaust?" *Midstream,* vol. 26, no. 9 (November 1980), p. 42.

7. Elie Wiesel, *La Nuit* (Paris, 1960). The Yiddish original was *Un Di Velt Hot Geshvign* (Buenos Aires, 1956).

8. Walter Laqueur, *The Terrible Secret* (Boston, 1980), p. 7.

9. Joseph Borkin, *The Crime and Punishment of I. G. Farben* (New York, 1978).

10. Richard L. Rubenstein, *The Cunning of History* (New York, 1975), pp. 1–56.

11. Ismar Schorsch, "The Holocaust and Jewish Survival," *Midstream,* vol. 27, no. 1 (January 1981), pp. 38–42.

12. Ibid.

13. Ibid.

14. Eliezer Berkovits, *Faith after the Holocaust* (New York, 1973), p. 118.

15. Irving Horowitz, *Taking Lives: Genocide and State Power* (New York, 1981); Helen Fein, *Accounting for Genocide: National Response and Jewish Victimization* (New York, 1979); and Terrence Des Pres, *The Survivor: Anatomy of Life in the Death Camps* (New York, 1976).

16. John Cuddihy, "The Holocaust: The Latent Issue in the Uniqueness Debate" (Presented at Zachor, the Holocaust Resource Center's faculty seminar, January 1980). The Brown Judaica series will soon publish a collection of Cuddihy's essays on the Holocaust, including this one.

17. Henry Feingold, *The Politics of Rescue: The Roosevelt Administration and the Holocaust, 1938–1945* (New Brunswick, N.J., 1970).

18. William Styron, *Sophie's Choice* (New York, 1980).

19. Emil Fackenheim, *The Jewish Return into History: Reflections in the Age of Auschwitz and a New Jerusalem* (New York, 1978), p. 93.

20. Robert Alter, "Deformations of the Holocaust," *Commentary,* vol. 61, no. 2 (February 1981). Arnold Jacob Wolf and Michael Berenbaum, "The Centrality of the Holocaust: An Overemphasis?" *The National Jewish Monthly,* vol. 95, no. 2 (October 1980). Jacob Neusner, *Stranger At Home* (Chicago, 1985); *The Death and Birth of Judaism: The Impact of Christianity, Secularism, and the Holocaust on*

Jewish Faith (New York, 1987); and *The Jewish War against the Jews: Reflections on Shoah, Golah, and Torah* (New York, 1984).

21. Michael Wyschograd, "Faith and the Holocaust," in *Judaism*, vol. 20, no. 3 (Summer 1971), pp. 293–94.
22. Neusner, *Death and Birth of Judaism*, p. 335.
23. Ibid., p. 340.
24. Ibid., p. 345.
25. Ibid., pp. 348–49.

CHAPTER 3

Nazi Germany's Forced Labor Program

Edward Homze

When the Flick concern recently changed ownership, the call for financial compensation for Jewish and foreign workers employed by the firm during World War II was raised anew. The German public was painfully reminded again about another "forgotten tragedy" from their Nazi past. Well over eight million foreigners were employed in the German war economy and most of them were forced—although with varying degrees of pressure—to labor on the farms and in the factories of the Third Reich. The term *forced labor (Zwangsarbeit)*, or *slave labor* as the Nuremberg Tribunal called it, is not very precise. It included prisoners of war, voluntary workers from Germany's allies and the neutral states, workers recruited from northern and western occupied areas, and the brutally recruited workers from eastern Europe. It is fairly clear from the evidence that these foreign workers, who represented about one-fourth of the total labor force in 1944, were instrumental not only in maintaining the German war economy but, ironically, in prolonging their own unwanted stay inside the Third Reich.

In this essay the overall magnitude of the Nazi foreign labor program will be described with special emphasis on the economic and human aspects of the exploitation. In recent years the program has received considerable attention from Western and Eastern European scholars.[1] Western scholars have been intrigued by the ideological, economic, and political aspects of the program while Eastern European scholars have pressed their case linking the program to capitalism and its role within the Third Reich. Whereas Western scholars have treated the program as a peripheral aspect of nazism the Eastern Europeans, especially the East German historians, have always regarded the program as one of the central issues of the Nazi economy. Their underlying assumption has been that German "finance-

37

capitalism" was an integral part of nazism that was opposed by the progressive force in Germany and Europe, naturally led by the Communists. They further assume that an alliance developed between the foreigners in the Reich and progressive forces that sought to oppose Nazi oppression. Newer studies that stress the almost unqualified approval the foreign labor program had among all elements of German society, including the working class, and the relatively high degree of success the Nazis had in integrating German workers into their system, have modified these Eastern views.[2]

Curiously, the sheer magnitude of the program has not been the subject of much investigation. German wartime records indicate that foreign employment peaked about August 1944 with 7.6 million foreigners working within the Reich. Of that figure, 5.7 million were civilians, of whom 1.9 million were women (about one-third) and 1.9 million were POWs. The total number of foreigners employed throughout the war has never been ascertained.[3] Fritz Sauckel, the head of the program, estimated that he had recruited 5.3 million foreigners and that another 5 million were recruited before his appointment, indicating that at least 10.3 million foreigners were recruited. But this figure must be considered a conservative estimate. German records were always based on the number of foreign workers employed at a particular time and never took into account the actual number recruited. The fluctuation caused by expiring contracts (in the case of true volunteer workers mostly from the west and neutral countries), deaths, injuries, arrests, and escapes was tremendous. Sauckel estimated the fluctuation for 1944 alone at close to 2 million. In his pretrial interrogation, Sauckel hinted at the possibility that nearly 12 million foreign workers were recruited throughout the war.[4] Furthermore, these figures are only for workers in the Reich. No one has figured out how many millions of foreigners were employed by German agencies in the occupied areas. The German Army, the railroad, Organization Todt, and the various German ministries were known to be large-scale employers. In this essay, we are only concerned with those employed within the Reich.

As table 3.1 indicates, most of the foreigners came from the East. Of the 5.7 million foreign civilian workers roughly one-third or 1,924,912 were women. The overwhelming number of women (87 percent) came from the East, compared with 62 percent of the men. In other words, more eastern women were employed in 1944 than the combined total of men and women from Belgium, France, and Holland.[5]

The type and nature of the recruitment of the foreign workers varied

TABLE 3.1
Origins of Foreign Civilian Workers and POWs Employed in the Reich
in August 1944

Country	Civilian Workers	POWs	Total
Belgium	203,262	50,386	253,648
France	654,782	599,967	1,254,749
Italy	158,099	427,238	585,337
Holland	270,304		270,304
Poland	1,659,764	28,316	1,688,080
Bohemia-Moravia	280,273		280,273
Soviet Union	2,126,753	631,559	2,758,312
Total	5,721,883	1,930,087	7,615,970

Source: Der Arbeitseinsatz im Grossdeutschen Reich, vol. 31.10.1944, no. 10, Files of the United States Strategic Bombing Survey, National Archives, Washington, D.C.

widely from east to west. In the East, first in Poland and then later in the Soviet Union, recruitment was characterized by violence, racism, and its massive scale. By contrast, in the West recruitment was at first voluntary, devoid of stringent racial overtones, small-scale, and sporadic. Germany capitalized on the widespread unemployment and the vast numbers of POWs to fulfill its labor needs. Gradually, however, they imposed more coercive legal, financial, and political measures to force westerners into working in the Reich.

In Poland, the Nazis drew the major outlines of the labor program. Within the first year of occupation, they subjected Poles to an increasing array of racial, legal, wage, and working discriminations that were then applied to peoples of the Soviet Union. Among these discriminations was the first instance of marking the Poles with a patch on their outer garments, which occurred even before the Jews were marked. In the Reich foreigners quickly came under the control of the SS and the police as they encroached on the jurisdictional rights heretofore exercised by the normal legal authorities.[6] The Nazis moved rather gingerly at first, testing the water to determine the reaction of the German public and especially the German working class to these discriminations. Finding little resistance, they proceeded to implement their racial discriminations with haste. By mid-1940 most of the racially inspired discriminations and the general outlines of the programs were in place.

The method of recruiting eastern workers varied greatly according to where it took place, who was in charge of recruiting, and the time and conditions when the recruitment occurred. In general, it involved establishing compulsory labor laws, drafting workers by age classes, and using force. Force in the East was much more prevalent than in the west. In the east everything was in a constant state of flux; recruitment areas became military operations sectors time and time again, and the proximity of the battle lines stimulated partisan guerrilla activity, which caused the Germans to become more severe in their methods. There was also a ready supply of troops to enforce police measures against the native population. Another reason was the German attitude toward the easterners. Consciously or unconsciously, the Germans believed that they were dealing with racially inferior peoples—*Untermenschen*. Recruitment in the East quickly degenerated into manhunts where the healthy, the ill, the young, and the old were rounded up and deported to the Reich. The results were predictable —increased resistance, the application of more force, and a further breakdown of German occupation rule.[7]

If recruitment methods were cruel and inhumane, the working and living conditions of the foreigners in the Reich were not much better. Whereas western workers were at first generally treated like German workers, the eastern workers were subjected to vast discrimination. They were forced to work longer, harder, and for lower wages than the westerners, and their living conditions were deplorable. Usually they were confined to barbed-wire barracks and fed at the lowest ration rate, regardless of their type of employment. For example, it was not until April 9, 1942, that Reinhardt Heydrich, head of the Security Police, issued a circular removing barbed wire from the Russian barracks and allowing limited, supervised leaving of quarters.[8] A year later labor inspectors were still complaining about camps that were enclosed by barbed wire.[9]

The Nazi attitude toward feeding foreign workers went through three phases: during the first period, from the beginning of the war until the spring of 1942, racial considerations were important; in the second period, from 1942 until the summer of 1944, many of the inequalities were removed; and in the third period, from the summer of 1944 to the end of the war, the Nazis tried selective feeding based on the workers' productivity. The disastrous physical condition of many eastern workers recruited in 1941–42 prompted the German authorities to establish a standard diet in March 1942 for all foreign civilian workers fed in camps. But again eastern workers were exempted.[10] It was a near universal complaint from factory managers, labor officials, and foreign workers that the food problem was the biggest one in the entire labor program. Although the food policy toward easterners changed as the war dragged on, these gains came at the expense of their fellow foreign workers. The amount of suffering the Nazi food policy caused can never be estimated.[11]

Wage discrimination was the most obvious form of exploitation of foreign labor. Although western workers were to receive the same wages as Germans, it was never expected that eastern workers would be paid the same. When the first Polish workers came into the Reich, the German authorities imposed a special 15 percent tax on the Poles called the *Sozialausgleichsabgabe*, or "social equalization fee."[12] Its purpose was to keep Polish wages lower than German wages. The tax was later extended to all eastern workers; it was deducted by the employer and paid directly to the Reich treasury. This tax, along with the other deductions for taxes, room, and board, meant that no eastern worker could receive more than 6.50 Reichsmark (RM) per week after deductions regardless of time worked. The average pay was only 4.60 RM. In June 1942, Sauckel succeeded in slightly raising the earnings of easterners when a ceiling on earnings was lifted. Even then the average weekly earnings after deductions for an eastern worker were only 9.10 RM.[13] The arithmetic of this exploitation was not lost on Hitler who, in his usual exaggerated manner, commented that

integration of twenty million foreign workers at cheap rates into the German industrial system represents a saving which, again, is greatly in excess of the debts contracted by the State.[14]

If eastern workers were badly underpaid, Soviet POWs fared even worse. A Speer Ministry report from September 1944 indicates that Soviet POWs received one-half the payment of non-Soviet POWs. In practical terms this meant that if a Soviet POW was working in a job where the German wage scale was 40 to 45 RM weekly, the Soviet POW received 5 RM compared to the non-Soviet POW's 10 RM.[15]

Western workers faced subtler discrimination. In theory, all foreigners except Poles, easterners, and Jews, were under the normal German social insurance system. They were eligible for unemployment, sickness, accident, social security, and wartime benefits. They paid the same compulsory contributions of 9 percent of their wages as did German workers, and they were to receive equal treatment. In reality, the Nazis rigged the system so the foreigners received far less or had difficulty obtaining services. Insurance benefits were usually systematically directed to foreign occupied funds instead of to German ones. Hospitalization while in the Reich was possible only in "quite extraordinary cases."[16] Normally the foreigners were shipped back to their own countries. These and many other legal bureaucratic procedures were used to sharply reduce the chances of foreigners receiving their legitimate benefits under the German social insurance system. Eastern workers were gradually given benefits similar to western workers. By April 1, 1944, they were included in most facets of the social insurance system.[17] Needless to say, racial considerations blocked full participation. For example, maternity benefits were never paid to eastern women.[18]

The Nazis developed an elaborate policy of discriminations for the eastern foreigners. In 1940 Poles were ordered to wear badges, segregated in their housing, and prohibited from all German cultural life. They had a curfew, could use public transportation only for work, and could not use public baths, attend movies, or eat in restaurants. They had separate barbershops, brothels, and pubs. If they died, they were even buried in segregated plots.[19] Punishment for violating these restrictions were severe, ranging from fines of 150 RM or six weeks in jail for failure to wear a badge, to death for having sexual relations with a German.[20]

The authorities also encouraged, without much success, employers and camp directors to set up separate facilities for western workers to minimize their contact with Germans. Just as in Germany today, every town had certain cafes known as "foreign workers' cafes." Despite continual warnings and threats, German nationals of both sexes frequented these cafes, much to the displeasure of the authorities. By 1944 the Gestapo was even allowing cafes for eastern workers.[21] It was virtually impossible to segregate foreigners from Germans under the existing wartime conditions.

Foreign workers were punished more frequently and more severely than German workers. Fragmentary reports from the Gestapo for the first nine months of 1943 indicate that 388,000 people were arrested for political offenses in the Greater Reich and of these, 260,000 were foreigners. Almost all of the offenses were work related. From July to September of the same year, the Gestapo reported that the arrest rate ranged from a high of 95 per 10,000 for eastern workers to a low of 18 for Italians and only 1 arrest for German workers.[22]

Punishment meted out for labor offenses was also much more severe for foreigners. German workers were normally punished by the labor officials or courts, but the police handled foreigners. Whereas Germans usually received fines or warnings, foreigners were placed under protective arrest or sent to labor reeducation camps or concentration camps. For example, in the Westfalen-Nord Gau during February and March 1944, 80.1 percent of the foreigners punished for labor infractions were sent to camps or placed in protective custody, compared with only 5.8 percent of the Germans.[23] Partial statistics from other parts of the country bear out the same contention that the probability of arrest and detention was much higher for foreigners than for Germans.[24]

During the last months of the war, with the military situation deteriorating, plundering increasing, and an attempt being made on Hitler's life, the authorities panicked. In early November 1944 the Reich Central Office for Security allowed local Gestapo offices to summarily execute foreign workers, starting first with easterners and then including westerners.[25] A bloodbath ensued. Driven by their irrational fears of a Soviet-inspired partisan campaign among the foreigners, German authorities savagely murdered thousands of workers at the slightest provocation. Foreign workers, whom Nazi propaganda had made the scapegoats for plundering, black marketing, and terrorism, now became sacrificial lambs. When the war mercifully came to an end, foreign workers showed remarkable restraint. There was no general revenge, only widespread random looting and some individual murders.[26] After years of oppression, the foreign workers were primarily interested in returning home as quickly as possible.

The millions of foreign workers forced to work in the Reich represent one of the largest groups of victims of the Nazi regime. Although it can readily be surmised that the stereotype of slave labor applied at the Nuremberg war trials to the foreign labor program was too inclusive, it is clear that all foreigners were exploited in some way, ranging from minor legal restrictions to the robbing of their labor, health, and lives. That their plight has been largely forgotten and their grievances never redressed only adds to their sorrow. The foreign workers were indeed the "unknown victims" of the Third Reich.

NOTES

1. The best review of the literature is in Ulrich Herbert, *Fremdarbeiter: Politik und Praxis des "Auslaender-Einstazes" in der Kriegswirtschaft des Dritten Reiches* (Bonn,

1985). A quick review of the East German literature is Lothar Elsner and Joachim Lehmann, *DDR-Literatur ueber Fremdarbeiterpolitik des Imperialismus. Bemerkungen zum Forschungsstand und Bibliographie. Fremdarbeiterpolitik des Imperialismus* (Rostock, 1979), vol. 5.

2. For a thoughtful analysis of new trends see Herbert, *Fremdarbeiter*, pp. 14–20.

3. Pretrial interrogation of Fritz Sauckel, October 5, 1945, Files of the Nuremberg Trials Collection, National Archives, Washington, D.C. Unfortunately, when the Russian prosecuting attorney at the Nuremberg trials attempted to establish the exact number of foreigners recruited during the war, his inquiries were judged irrelevant. At the trial Sauckel admitted to ten million foreigners recruited; see *Trials of the Major War Criminals Before the International Military Tribunal*, 42 vols. (Nuremberg, 1947–49), 15:134–36 (henceforth cited as *IMT*).

4. Sauckel's pretrial interview of October 5, 1945.

5. *Der Arbeitseinsatz im Grossdeutschen Reich*, vol. 31.10.1944, no. 10, p. 271, Files of the United States Strategic Bombing Survey, National Archives.

6. Herbert, *Fremdarbeiter*, pp. 115–22. This is a major theme in his book. He argues that it started with the Poles and was extended to eastern and then western workers.

7. Edward L. Homze, *Foreign Labor in Nazi Germany* (Princeton, 1967), pp. 154–68.

8. *IMT* 14:627; and *Trials of War Criminals Before the Nuremberg Military Tribunals under Control Council Law N. 10*, 15 vols. (Washington, D.C., 1951–53), 9:879–80 (henceforth cited as *Minor Trials*).

9. *Minor Trials* 6:743.

10. Carl Birkenholz, ed., *Der auslaendische Arbeiter in Deutschland, Sammlung and Erlaeuterung der arbeits- und sozialrechtlichen Vorschriften ueber das Arbeitsverhaeltnis nichtvolksdeutscher Beschaeftigter* (Berlin, 1942), p. 222, and *IMT* 41:218–22.

11. Herbert, *Fremdarbeiter*, pp. 288–94; and Homze, *Foreign Labor*, pp. 271–77.

12. *Reichsgesetzblatt*, 1942, pt. 1, p. 42.

13. *IMT* 15:45–46.

14. Norman Cameron and R. H. Stevens, trans., *Hitler's Secret Conversations* (New York, 1953), p. 372.

15. Letter from Speer Ministry, September 29, 1944, National Archives, Microfilm, T-73, roll 97, frames 3251043–46.

16. Birkenholz, *Der auslaendische Arbeiter*, p. 96.

17. *Reichsgesetzblatt*, 1944, pt. 1, p. 68.

18. See "Gesetz sum Schutze der erwerstaetigen Mutter," May 17, 1942, in *Reichsgesetzblatt*, 1942, pt. 1, p. 321. See also amendments in *Reichsarbeitsblatt*, 1943, pt. 5, p. 58; 1943, pt. 3, p. 141; and 1944, pt. 2, p. 60.

19. *Reichsarbeitsblatt*, 1940, pt. 1, p. 528, and 1941, pt. 1, pp. 326, 399. Late in 1944 the special regulations dealing with the burial of eastern workers were amended.

20. *Nazi Conspiracy and Aggression*, 10 vols. (Nuremberg, 1947–49), 3:251–53.

21. Letter from Regensburg *Kreisobmann,* January 12, 1944, National Archives, microfilm, T-81, roll 68, frames 77835–36.
22. Wolfgang Schumann and Gerhart Hass, eds., *Deutschland im zweiten Weltkrieg* (Cologne, 1974–84), 4:407.
23. Herbert, *Fremdarbeiter,* p. 303.
24. Ibid., pp. 302–5.
25. Ibid., p. 329.
26. United States Strategic Bombing Survey, *The Effects of Strategic Bombing on German Morale* (Washington, D.C., 1946), 2:60–61.

CHAPTER 4

Forced Labor in the
Concentration Camps, 1942–1944

Peter Black

The Concentration Camp System and Forced Labor in the Prewar Years Until 1939, concentration camps in Nazi Germany served to physically and psychologically break real and perceived opponents of the National Socialist regime. The goal was to "reeducate" fellow "Aryans" to become loyal members of the *Volksgemeinschaft,* and to encourage Jews and members of other unwanted races to leave the new Germany, preferably without their property. On January 29, 1939, Reichsführer-SS Heinrich Himmler, whose SS administered and guarded the camps, still publicly stressed this "educative" function:

There is only one road to freedom. Its milestones are: obedience, industriousness, honesty, orderliness, cleanliness, sobriety, veracity, sense of sacrifice, and love for the fatherland.[1]

While the Secret State Police, or Gestapo, under Himmler and Security Police Chief Reinhard Heydrich, arrogated to itself authority to incarcerate people in the camps, SS-Obergruppenführer Theodor Eicke, whom Himmler had appointed inspector of the concentration camps on December 10, 1934, consolidated the independent camps that had formed spontaneously during the early months of Nazi rule into a uniform structure dedicated to the application of systematic terror against its victims. A flow of decrees issued by central and regional Gestapo offices revealed that during the prewar years terror in the camps was directed not only against German Jews, but also against political and religious opponents of Hitler and nazism, Gypsies, the mentally ill, professional criminals, and errant members of the Nazi movement itself.

In penal regulations formulated in 1933, Eicke urged concentration camp personnel to treat the prisoners with unmitigated hostility, contempt, and brutality. This attitude, adopted by the personnel of the SS Death's Head Units (*Totenkopfverbaende*), which guarded the camps, was reflected in the postwar comments of Rudolf Hoss, who recalled Eicke lecturing new recruits at Dachau that

> . . . any pity whatsoever for "enemies of the state" was unworthy of an SS man. Weaklings had no place in his [Eicke's] ranks and would do well to withdraw to a convent as quickly as possible. He [Eicke] could only use hard, determined men who ruthlessly obeyed any order. . . . *They were the only soldiers who even in peacetime faced the enemy day and night, the enemy behind the wire.*[2]

Since its fruit was always subordinated to its effect on the human dignity of the prisoners, concentration camp labor in the 1930s was rarely linked to rational economic criteria and served the camps' original purpose: the suppression of political and ideological enemies.

Factors Affecting the Utilization of Forced Labor from the Outbreak of the War until the End of 1941   Nazi leadership took advantage of World War II to draw the ultimate consequence of the struggle against "uneducable" enemies. Concurrent with the German invasion of Poland in 1939, Himmler established under Heydrich a Reich Central Office for Security (*Reichssicherheitshauptamt* [RSHA]), which became the driving executive and administrative force behind the physical elimination of undesirable persons and races within the Nazi sphere of influence. Nor was it mere coincidence that Hitler initiated the first Final Solution against the incurably ill and severely handicapped in the early autumn of 1939. Coincident with the attack on the Soviet Union in June 1941, the Nazis began to implement both the extermination of European Jewry and the mass murder of Soviet prisoners of war. The opportunity to eliminate enemies, so conveniently excused as a national emergency within the context of the war, could not be overlooked. Thus, the camps served increasingly as sites of mass murder after September 1, 1939.

Such wholesale killing, whether by direct methods or through starvation, exposure, and untreated disease, hampered efforts to harness forced labor in the camps to production for the German war economy. Though not always adhered to in practice, Heydrich's decree of January 2, 1941, which classified the camps into three grades of severity based on the potential for reeducation of prisoners, suggests that the SS leadership still viewed reeducation, intimidation, or liquidation of the inmates as the primary function of prisoner labor.[3]

Conversely, the arrival of thousands of Polish and Soviet citizens, most of whom were brought to Germany by force between 1939 and 1942, impelled the SS leadership toward a more rational deployment of inmate labor. Security Police and Nazi party officials, who viewed these Slavic laborers as racially inferior, established regulations strictly segregating them from the German population and threatened them with incarceration in concentration camps for minor violations of the restrictions, which ranged from bans on riding streetcars and having sexual intercourse with Germans to lack of zeal at the workplace.[4] Inadequately housed and fed, and treated by German officials like the subhumans they were perceived to be, thousands of Polish and Soviet workers not surprisingly either failed to show sufficient working zeal, whether through design or simple physical exhaustion, or sought solace in some form of fraternization with Germans, and were sent to concentration camps.[5]

The development of underground resistance in the occupied countries, particularly in Poland, led to a further increase in the prisoner population. Throughout 1940, thousands of Polish clerics, government officials, schoolteachers, lawyers, and other professionals were shipped to the camps.[6] In the winter of 1941, western European political prisoners began to arrive in large numbers as well.[7] Himmler's August 1941 decree requiring that "all strife inciting shavelings, [all] anti-German Czechs and Poles as well as communists and similar low-life be transferred to the concentration camps for a prolonged period as a matter of principle"[8] guaranteed a plentiful supply of labor in a time of severe shortages and was likely to stimulate enterprising minds both within and outside the SS.

Another precondition for the evolution of the camp system into a forced-labor reservoir was the involvement of the camps in projects developed for the peacetime economy. Even before the war, the SS leadership discovered that it need not renounce the by-product of a productive labor output in achieving its aim of "education" and annihilation. On April 29, 1938, the chief of the administrative office of the SS, SS-Brigadeführer Oswald Pohl, and Albert Speer, then general construction inspector for the Reich capital, agreed to establish the SS-owned Deutsche Erd- und Steinwerke (DEST), which, supported by concentration camp labor, was to provide cheap building materials (bricks, stone products, etc.) for Hitler's peacetime construction projects. Between 1938 and 1941 several concentration camps were established near stone quarries: Flossenbürg (May 1938), Mauthausen (August 1938), Gross-Rosen (May 1939), Gusen (December 1939), and Natzweiler (December 1941). Brickwork projects were established in 1938 in the vicinity of Sachsenhausen and Buchenwald and were the impetus for the establishment of Neuengamme as an independent camp in June 1940. Through such projects Himmler and Pohl "intended . . . in good time and through circumspect utilization of the opportunities offered to the SS by the war, to secure a significant sector of the national economy for the future tasks of the National Socialist state."[9] The failure of the Blitzkrieg in December 1941 and the prospect of a long war encouraged the more imaginative in the SS leadership to dream of an expanded war economy fueled by slave labor. As a result, the deployment of prisoner labor in the war economy was a major factor in the development of the camp system from 1942 to 1944.

Forced Labor in the Concentration Camps: 1942–1944   With the incorporation of the Inspectorate of Concentration Camps as office group *(Amtsgruppe)* D into the newly created SS Economic and Administrative Main Office (SS *Wirtschafts- und Verwaltungshauptamt* [WVHA]) under SS-Gruppenführer Oswald Pohl on March 16, 1942, prisoner labor was organizationally linked for the first time to the SS economic enterprises. Matters concerning prisoner labor were centralized in WVHA office D II under SS-Standartenführer Gerhard Maurer, who installed in each concentration camp a labor deployment officer *(Arbeitseinsatzführer)* as the liaison between the camp staff and SS or non-SS industries employing prisoner labor.

On the day that the WVHA took over the camps, Amtsgruppe D chief Richard Glücks met with Wehrmacht and Armaments Ministry officials in the office of Karl Otto Saur, chief of the Technical Office of the Ministry of Armaments and War Production. Glücks stated that Hitler had approved of a greater integration of concentration camp prisoners into the armaments production process and reported that Buchenwald, Sachsenhausen, Neuengamme, Auschwitz, Ravensbrück, and Lublin (Majdanek) had some 25,000 prisoners capable of work. Since Himmler had ordered that the prisoners remain in the camps, Glücks urged that participating firms transfer their plants to the camp grounds and provide engineers and foremen to train the prisoners on the appropriate machinery. Buchenwald and Neuengamme were selected to provide labor for the armaments industry on an experimental basis.[10] In spring of 1942, Himmler authorized the establishment in Neuengamme of a pistol factory managed by the Walther Works from Zella-Mehlis. Toward the end of 1942, the Deutsche Messapparate GmbH Langehorn set up a factory at Neuengamme to manufacture detonators for antiaircraft artillery shells.[11]

At Buchenwald, Dr. Werner Schieber, one of Saur's subordinates, ordered the Thuringia-based Wilhelm Gustloff Works to transfer monthly production of fifteen thousand carbines and two thousand sporting rifles to the camp within four months.[12] On April 2, 1942, Glücks reported to Himmler that Hermann Pister, the commandant, had agreed with the Gustloff Works to deploy three hundred prisoners for rifle production and further five hundred prisoners for pistol production within three and eight weeks, respectively. Himmler gave his blessing to both projects in July 1942 and ordered Pohl to prepare for the utilization of female prisoner labor from Ravensbrück in the manufacture of communications equipment for the Wehrmacht.[13]

In a secret letter of April 30, 1942, Pohl revealed to Himmler his long-term plans for SS entry into the German war economy. He explained that the war had brought "a tangible, structural change in the concentration camps and their function in regard to the allocation of prisoner labor." The incarceration of prisoners for reasons of security, education, or prevention of crime was growing less important, while the "mobilization of the entire prisoner labor supply—first and foremost for war tasks [increased armaments production] and later for tasks of reconstruction—is moving more and more into the foreground." Pohl attached guidelines to his letter that implied "a general transformation of the concentration camps from their previously one-sided political form into an organization responding to economic endeavors." The commandants were now responsible not only for the security of the camp and the discipline of the prisoners, but also for the economic output of industrial plants located therein. Plant managers, though civilians, would serve the commandants as technical advisers. The commandants were also responsible for the deployment of prisoner labor and determined the hours that the prisoners should work each day. To increase work capacity, Pohl suggested limiting both the number and the length of mealtimes, roll calls, and other time-consuming but not directly labor-related activities. Anticipating that prisoner labor would be utilized more frequently at sites outside the camps, Pohl ordered guard detachments to increase mobility through the use of mounted sentries, guard dogs, and portable guard towers.[14]

In general, Himmler had no quarrel with Pohl's intentions, but he remained concerned that the educational function of incarceration not be lost in the enthusiasm for economic integration. Otherwise, "the thought could arise that we arrest people—or, having arrested them, keep them incarcerated—in order to have workers." While Pohl's ideal camp commandant was an industrial manager with "a clear, technical knowledge of things military and economic combined with a clever and intelligent leadership of groups of people which he should fuse into a high production potential," Himmler's man still had to "see to the education of those capable of education,"[15] and presumably to the extermination of those considered uneducable. The conflict between ideological concerns and economic necessities was never resolved; it confronted all personnel in the camp machinery from Himmler to each perimeter guard.

Requirements of the German war effort accelerated the development of the camps as Pohl had foreseen. On September 15, 1942, WVHA and Armaments Ministry officials agreed at a meeting that "the labor force available in the concentration camps must be deployed for armaments production on a grand scale." On the following day, Pohl explained to Himmler that the policy of confining prisoners in the camps during work hours was not efficient, since the bulk of production could not be transferred there. He suggested the firms lacking sufficient labor to meet production quotas be taken over by the SS, which would deploy prisoner labor, thus freeing civilians to meet other labor needs.[16] Although he failed to usurp control of war industry production,[17] Pohl weakened Himmler's resolve not to deploy prisoner labor outside the camps and elicited his permission to establish subcamps in or near armaments plants. From 1942 to 1944, hundreds of subcamps were opened throughout Germany and occupied Europe. Mauthausen developed a chain of satellite camps throughout Austria, Bavaria, and the Sudentenland. For example, the subcamp Wiener Neudorf was established in August 1943 in a Vienna suburb to engage approximately 2,000–3,000 prisoners in the production of airplane motor parts for the firm Flugmotorenwerke Ostmark.[18] Drutte, a subcamp of Neuengamme, was established in October 1942 near Braunschweig-Salzgitter to produce 88-mm and 105-mm artillery shells for the Reichswerke AG, a subsidiary of the Hermann-Goering-Werke.[19] During 1944 no less than forty-three Neuengamme subcamps were established, nearly half in connection with armaments production or related construction. From 1943 to 1945, thirty-four subcamps of Ravensbrück were established; twenty-three pertained to the armaments industry. Subcamps of Flossenburg increased from six in 1942 to seventy-five in 1944.[20]

To meet the demand for labor, the WVHA and the Gestapo combed the Reich and occupied Europe for prisoners capable of work. In December 1942, Himmler ordered Gestapo chief Heinrich Müller to increase the working population of the camps by at least thirty-five thousand before February 1, 1943. To achieve this quota, Muller instructed local Gestapo offices to ship all foreign laborers who were not citizens of a nation allied to Germany and who had either fled their place of work or in some other way breached their work contract to the nearest camp. He also urged local Security Police commanders to comb Gestapo prisons and labor camps for prisoners, sparing only those needed by the police for interrogation.[21] On December 31, 1942, the RSHA informed Pohl that in addition to the required thirty-five thousand prisoners to be provided by Müller, twelve thousand "asocial" prisoners languishing in Justice Ministry prisons and all Polish prisoners in Gestapo prisons in the General Government would be transferred to the camps in the next months.[22]

A February 26, 1943, RSHA decree forbidding the release of Soviet civilian laborers (Ostarbeiter) from the camps reflected the impingement of economic considerations on the policy of "reeducation." The measure was justified in the following terms: "in order to secure the ongoing armaments programs in the concentration camps, we will dispense with the previous ruling that Ostarbeiter be released from the concentration camps after a specific time and be returned to their previous positions, which had been issued originally for its educational effect."[23]

The adaptation of the camps to the war economy brought several changes in labor conditions for the inmates, who generally had to work longer and harder, often under more dangerous conditions. On November 22, 1943, Pohl insisted that the daily work schedule of eleven hours could not be relaxed even in wintertime. Only for security reasons could detachments working outside cease work early in the winter.[24] Prisoners were also engaged in new types of work created by conditions of war, often without proper equipment or protective clothing. From 1940 on prisoner volunteers had been solicited to defuse and remove unexploded bombs from urban areas and industrial plants.[25] In September 1942, after his meeting with

Speer and other Reich Armaments Ministry personnel Pohl authorized the formation of three "construction brigades" (Bau-Brigade) of one thousand prisoners each at Neuengamme, Sachsenhausen, and Buchenwald. The brigades were deployed in the difficult and often dangerous work of clearing rubble in the cities after Allied air raids. Their equipment consisted of picks and shovels.[26]

Visions of a vast SS economic empire induced Pohl, with Himmler's support, to issue instructions that contradicted the killing function of the concentration camps, even for groups singled out for extermination. The first "beneficiaries" of the new wind were the Soviet prisoners of war. Initially slated for immediate liquidation, the Soviets were given a temporary reprieve under Himmler's order of November 15, 1941, which permitted camp commandants to work prisoners to death on stone-breaking details rather than liquidating them outright.[27] Likewise, the WVHA sought to limit the indiscriminate murder of sick and physically incapacitated prisoners that had been initiated in autumn 1941 under the code name "Action 14f13" by instructing the camp commandants to select for liquidation only those persons who had no prospects of ever becoming capable of work. In 1943, the commandants had to limit these selections to mentally ill prisoners; victims of disease and physically handicapped prisoners could work from their beds.[28]

Since the prisoners had been transformed at one stroke from unwanted life to a marketable commodity, the WVHA attempted to reduce the appalling death rate, to reward especially industrious prisoners, and to limit gratuitous torture of prisoners by SS guards. On January 20, 1943, Glucks urged camp commandants to "attempt by all means to hold down the mortality rate in the camps" and held them "personally responsible" for "exhausting every possibility to maintain the physical strength of the prisoners."[29] Developing a sudden interest in the prisoners' diet, Himmler authorized German and non-German prisoners to receive food packages from relatives; he further suggested that for the year 1943 raw vegetables be stored in the camps to improve the prisoners' diet in the winter of 1943–1944.[30] In September 1943, Pohl reported that the death rate in the camps had been dropping steadily from a peak of 10 percent in December 1942 to a low of 2.09 percent in August 1943. To achieve this decrease, the WVHA had increased food rations, introduced basic hygienic measures, shortened the length of roll calls, and permitted prisoners to wear coats in the winter, "insofar as they were not encumbered in their work." Though he assumed that the coming winter would bring an increase in the death rate, Pohl confidently expected that it would not rise above 6 percent.[31]

Himmler and Pohl also initiated what they believed would be positive incentives for the prisoners. On May 15, 1943, Pohl established categories of rewards for prisoners who "distinguished themselves by industriousness, prudence, good deportment, and exceptional performance."[32] At the Neuengamme subcamp Drutte, several prisoners received bonuses of 0.50 RM to 4.00 RM on a weekly basis for what the factory managers determined to be exceptional work.[33] In March 1943, Himmler had ordered the establishment of a bordello for the prisoners in Buchenwald.[34] The Reichsführer considered the option of establishing training programs in the construction industry for especially industrious prisoners to work in SS-owned factories as civilians.[35] Through such incentives, Himmler expected to demonstrate that Germans could "summon up the same cleverness as the Russian, who by means of his wage and nourishment system, impels the Russian people, which in theory is inert, to the most incredible achievements."[36]

So great were the economic needs of the Reich in 1942–43, and so captivated by the economic potential of the prisoners was the WVHA, that it encouraged a reprieve, albeit temporary, for the Jews. Himmler appears to have entertained the idea of utilizing rather than destroying Jewish labor as early as January 1942; but in light of the initial implementation of the "final solution" during the following spring, this notion can scarcely have been more than a passing fancy. Indeed, on July 19, 1942, Himmler ordered that the entire Jewish population of the General Government be liquidated by December 31, 1942. In September, however, with the gas chambers operating at full capacity, Pohl cynically suggested that "those Jews capable of work but earmarked for migration to the east [*Ostwanderung*, i.e., extermination] will have to interrupt their journey and work in armaments production."[37] Nevertheless, the slaughter of nearly eighteen thousand Jews rounded up from various labor camps in District Lublin at Majdanek on the orders of SS and police leader Odilo Globocnik revealed what little significance economic considerations ultimately had in the face of the ideological goal of annihilating the Jews.[38] Elsewhere, however, Jews in the General Government were able to survive as long as they could work; local labor camps at Plaszow (District Krakow), Radom, and Blizyn (District Radom) were transferred from control of the SS and police leaders to the WVHA in January 1944. Their Jewish inmates survived the transition because of their value to economic endeavors managed by the SS firm Deutsche Ausrustungswerke G.m.b.H. (German Equipment Works, Ltd.).[39]

In many ways Auschwitz was symbolic of SS efforts to take advantage of the supply of slave labor. Cooperation between the SS and I. G. Farben in utilizing Auschwitz prisoners for the development of synthetic fuels and rubber at Auschwitz III epitomized the new relationship between the concentration camps and the German war industry. Orders issued in February 1944 by the camp commandant, SS-Obersturmbannführer Artur Liebehenschel, reflected Pohl's ideas for the economic development of the camps. Liebehenschel instructed his staff that their evaluations would henceforth depend on their ability to increase production through rational deployment of prisoner labor. To this purpose, Liebehenschel limited roll calls to one fifteen-minute call per day; threatened severe punishment of SS personnel who unnecessarily tormented prisoners during nonworking hours; ordered that prisoners receive adequate food, clothing, and footgear to perform their duties; ordered that ill prisoners receive medical treatment; and directed that industrious prisoners receive every possible reward, including the promise of freedom, while "lazy prisoners" undergo "all possible punishments in accordance with the camp regulations."[40] Thus Liebehenschel sought to realize Pohl's ideal of a commandant who could fuse the resources at his disposal into a high production potential for the German economy.

Nevertheless, life was not pleasant for the camp inmates during this two-year era of SS entrepreneurship. The 8,491 recorded deaths in the Mauthausen system in 1943 among an average prisoner population of 21,100[41] hardly reflected a commitment to prisoner survival. Moreover, prisoners continued to lack sufficient food, clothing, and equipment to do their jobs properly. For example, during the initial stages of underground tunnel construction at Dora, prisoner mortality was extremely high due to lack of ventilation and severe cold. In the first six months of the camp's existence, 2,882 prisoners died out of an average total of around 10,000.[42]

Concentration camp guards also continued to mistreat the prisoners, as reflected in Himmler's complaint that whipping was used too frequently as a punishment to have any meaningful deterrent effect.[43] Prisoners likewise suffered constantly under the anxiety of being cited for sabotage. Whether actually involved in sabotage or simply too exhausted, hungry, or stressed to work properly or fast enough, prisoners so accused faced certain death. On April 11, 1944, execution by hanging was ordered for any prisoner who had engaged in sabotage; a report from factory management was sufficient for conviction and execution.[44]

The continued implementation of "extermination through labor" despite the efforts of the SS leadership to keep the best workers alive reflected the unchanged attitude of the SS toward the prisoners. Echoing Eicke's characterizations of the prisoners the general inspector of the SS Death's Head Units issued a circular on January 22, 1940, depicting them as "enemies of the state of the worst sort."[45] Guard training material issued in July 1943 taught that the concentration camp was a place for criminals, sexual deviates, and enemies of the state whose release would seriously injure the German war effort. The guards were equated both in the nature of their duties and in their courage in performing them to the soldiers serving at the front.[46] This attitude hampered the rational utilization of prisoner labor and ensured a maximum degree of suffering and death.

With the exception of Auschwitz and other Jewish labor camps in Poland and the Soviet Union, the overwhelming majority of the camp population, approximately 224,000 in August 1943,[47] was non-Jewish between the end of 1942 and the arrival of the Hungarian Jews during the summer of 1944. The majority of prisoners in the Reich camps in 1942–44 were Slavs, primarily Poles and Russians; after these came the resistance fighters and forced laborers from western Europe; Italian laborers, who arrived in the camps after the Italian surrender on September 8, 1943; and finally German political and criminal prisoners. Breakdowns of nationality figures are not readily available, but the best estimates for the period from 1938 to 1945 indicate that out of approximately 191,838 prisoners to pass through Mauthausen, the largest five groups were Poles, 44,000 (22.92 percent); Hungarian Jews, 32,000 (16.67 percent, but only after May 1944); Soviet civilians, 22,000 (16.46 percent); Soviet prisoners of war, 15,500 (8.08 percent); and Frenchmen, 13,000 (6.77 percent). Slavic prisoners numbered approximately 90,470, or nearly half the total prisoner population (47.14 percent).[48]

A breakdown by nationality of prisoner arrivals at Dachau between December 1, 1942, and August 31, 1943, reveals a similar pattern. Of 9,949 prisoners who entered Dachau during this period, Soviet civilians were most numerous, totaling 3,920, or 39.40 percent. If Poles (the second largest group) and Yugoslavs are added, Slavic prisoners arriving at Dachau during this time numbered 5,449, or 54.77 percent of all arrivals.[49] In its seven-year existence, Neuengamme contained approximately 106,000 prisoners, of whom 55,578, or more than 52 percent, were Slavs (33 percent Soviet civilians, 16 percent Poles, 3.5 percent other Slavs and Soviet prisoners of war). The remainder came from western and northern Europe.[50] Figures from Ravensbrück, which had 107,753 prisoners in 1945, indicate that 46.3 percent of the camp population was Slavic.[51] Finally, of the 2,882 prisoners who died during the first six months at Dora, 839 were Russians, 708 Frenchmen, 407 Poles, 373 Germans, 264 Italians, and 291 others.[52] In terms of figures, then, Slavs of all types, but especially Poles and Russians, comprised the largest group of victims in those camps not dedicated to the extermination of Jews. Frenchmen and German political prisoners followed close behind.

By March 1944, the SS leadership had largely succeeded in linking concentration camp labor to the production needs of the German war economy. Himmler boasted to Reich Armaments Minister Speer in June 1943 that 63 percent of the available prisoners had been deployed in armaments production and other war-related industries.[53] When Pohl reported the existence of 20 concentration camps and 165 labor camps throughout Europe in April 1944, Himmler remarked that "one can see precisely with such examples how our affairs have grown, not least owing to your [Pohl's] service."[54] On March 9, 1944, Himmler reported to Goering that nearly thirty-six thousand prisoners were working in industries producing equipment for the air force. In virtually every major German concentration camp, prisoners were deployed six days a week between nine and eleven hours a day producing airplane motor parts, artillery shells for antiaircraft guns, radio equipment, flak ammunition, and bombs. Himmler assured Goering that the SS was "helping with all available resources."[55]

To judge whether the deployment of prisoner labor effectively assisted the Nazi war machine is difficult. In the summer of 1944 nearly four hundred thousand prisoners worked in the armaments industry, scarcely more than 1 percent of the entire labor force in this field.[56] Nevertheless, the Nazi capacity to wage war would certainly have declined much more quickly had the vast pool of foreign labor both inside and outside the camps not been available to replace millions of German soldiers fighting on the front. Just as Hitler squandered the lives of the German soldiers for his dream of world conquest, Himmler, Pohl, and the camp commandants squandered the prisoners' lives by ruthlessly deploying them at hard physical labor or stressful assembly line work without adequate food, clothing, sleep, and simple peace of mind to perform at top effectiveness. The very nature of the forced-labor system in the concentration camps served as an obstacle to its own rationalization in the production process, for forced labor is useful primarily in performing manual labor; a highly trained technical work force that might have made for a more efficient and rational restructuring of the German war economy could be neither trained nor maintained under conditions prevailing in Himmler's camps. Indeed, although the death rate of working prisoners seems to have dropped during 1943, it climbed again in 1944 and continued to rise toward the catastrophic proportions of early 1945. Given the lack of the physical and spiritual prerequisites for life itself—let alone a full day of effective labor—the use of forced labor from the concentration camps "amounted to a ruthless waste of prisoners, because the depressing psychological and physical working conditions of these prisoners generally obstructed any real increase in productivity."[57]

The summer of 1944 inaugurated a fourth and calamitous phase in the development of the camps. The last year of the war saw a general breakdown in supply and communications, which in turn stimulated a higher than usual rate of corruption among SS personnel and prisoner functionaries in the distribution of the minimal food supplies among the prisoners. Individual camp commandants had more leeway to return to the old policy of "extermination through labor," blaming inadequate supplies for high death rates. Untreated illness and infection, coupled with exhaustion, caused thousands of prisoners to perish. Allied bombing of armaments plants, both inside and outside the camps, resulted in further deaths. Finally, in the last months of the war, thousands of prisoners were murdered either to prevent them from being liberated by enemy troops— thereby eliminating witnesses to the crimes committed in the camps—or out of pure revenge and hatred on the part of the old-guard camp staff members, who could not bear the thought that the "subhumans" had in fact triumphed over Nazi Germany. Due to a combination of these factors, prisoners in the camps died at faster rates during the last months of the war. Broszat estimates that out of a camp population of 714,211 prisoners in January 1945, at least one-third lost their lives.[58]

In the period 1942–44, a major restructuring of forced labor deployment in the camps took place, largely due to the inspiration of Himmler, Pohl, and the economic staff at the WVHA. Originally the purpose of hard labor at the camps had been to educate errant members of the German Volk to reenter the Nazi fold and to intimidate those who were "uneducable" into leaving the area of German control. With the outbreak of the Second World War, the purpose of intimidation was replaced by one of "annihilation through work" and was practiced on an extensive scale. As the war made more demands on the German economy, however, an enterprising faction in the SS leadership sought to enhance the economic power and influence of the SS by offering concentration camp labor to the German war effort at prices that the armaments industry could not afford to reject. Himmler's concern that the slave labor purpose of the camps would overshadow the educational purpose was well founded; one reads little about education in the camps after 1942. Pohl's efforts to alleviate the harsh conditions in camps as a necessary condition for more effective production, however, ultimately had little effect. Camp commandants and guards generally never moderated their attitudes toward the prisoners. Guaranteed that the Gestapo, which cast an ever-widening net to catch enemies of the state, would replenish the horrendous loss of prisoners through mistreatment, malnutrition, and disease, the commandants had no real incentive to keep the prisoners alive. In effect, they ceased to be educators, even in Himmler's terms, and never became Pohl's entrepreneurs. They did remain killers; and under their rule, forced-labor programs contributed to the well-deserved reputation of the camps as centers for the physical extermination of unwanted life.[59]

NOTES

1. Radio speech of Himmler, January 29, 1939, reproduced in part in Bradley F. Smith and Agnes F. Peterson, eds., *Heinrich Himmler, Geheimreden 1933 bis 1945 und andere Ansprachen* (Frankfurt am Main, 1974), p. 111. The emphasis on "education," however, should not obscure the fact that many opponents of nazism, Jews and Germans alike, were killed while being "reeducated."
2. Rudolf Hoss, *Kommandant in Auschwitz: Autobiographische Aufzeichnungen* (Munich, 1963), p. 58, emphasis added.
3. Circular of Chief of Security Police and SD, January 2, 1941, Record Group 238, 1063-a-PS, National Archives, Washington, D.C. (NA).
4. Circular of Himmler to State Police Offices, March 8, 1940, Record Group 238, Document R-148, NA; circular of Reichsführer SS and Chief of German Police, February 20, 1942, in RSHA Erlasssammlung, Section 2 A III f, pp. 15–37, RD 19/3, Bundesarchiv, Koblenz (BAK).
5. Within 14 months of the 1942 decree, nearly 2,000 Soviet civilians, more than half of whom were under twenty years of age, were sent to the Mauthausen

camp system alone. See Hans Maršálek, *Die Geschichte des Konzentrationslagers Mauthausen* (Vienna, 1980), p. 137. During the first six months of 1943, 2,790 Soviet civilians arrived in Dachau. See Dachau Prisoner Registry, January–June 1943, Record Group 242, NA.

6. Marsalek counted at least 2,500 Polish arrivals at Mauthausen-Gusen during 1940 (see *Mauthausen*, pp. 120–21). Eight hundred fifty-four Polish clergymen and divinity students arrived in Dachau alone in December 1940. See Dachau Prisoner Registry, December 1940, RG 242, NA. The first 750 prisoners arriving at Auschwitz in the spring of 1940 were Polish. See Jozef Busko, ed., *Auschwitz, Faschistisches Vernichtungslager*, 2d ed. (Warsaw, 1981), p. 16.

7. At least 1,800 Spanish Republicans, captured in France, arrived in Mauthausen in January 1941 (Marsalek, *Mauthausen*, p. 121); Neuengamme received a large influx of French, Belgian, and Dutch political prisoners during 1941 (Werner Johe, *Neuengamme* [Hamburg, 1981], p. 19).

8. Circular Decree of the Reichsführer SS and Chief of German Police, August 27, 1941, RSHA Erlasssammlung, Section 2 F VII a, p. 15, RD 3/19, BAK.

9. Enno Georg, *Die wirtschaftlichen Unternehmungen der SS* (Stuttgart, 1963), p. 145.

10. "Niederschrift über eine Besprechung im Büro Saur am 16 März 1942," signed Saur, March 17, 1942, Berlin Document Center (BDC). Hitler was kept informed and approved of these initiatives. See Albert Speer, *Infiltration* (New York, 1981), p. 17.

11. Johe, *Neuengamme*, p. 23.

12. Speer, *Infiltration*, p. 17.

13. See cables from Glücks to Himmler, April 2, 1942, BDC; Himmler to Pohl, July 7, 1942, BDC; Pohl to Himmler, September 8, 1942, BDC. According to Speer, not one single carbine had been produced in Buchenwald as of mid-July 1942. See *Infiltration*, p. 19.

14. Pohl to Himmler, April 30, 1943, with attached order of Pohl, April 30, 1943, Record Group 238, Document R-129, NA.

15. Ibid., Himmler to Pohl, May 29, 1942, Record Group 242, T-175/75/2592896, NA.

16. Pohl to Himmler, September 16, 1942, Record Group 238, NIK-15392, NA.

17. Speer, Reich Plenipotentiary for Labor Allocation Fritz Sauckel, and Commander of the Reserve Army General Friedrich Fromm won Hitler's support for their opposition to the takeover of armaments firms by the SS. See Speer, *Infiltration*, pp. 21–24.

18. Meindl (General Director and Chairman of the Board, Steyr-Daimler-Puch) to Himmler, July 14, 1943, Record Group 242, T-175/19/2522899–900, NA; and Reichsführer SS, Personal Staff to Meindl, July 22, 1943, Record Group 242, T-175/19/2522898, NA.

19. See Amtsgruppe D WVHA to Administration, Reichswerke AG für Erzbergbau und Eisenhütten, "Hermann Göring," October 2, 1942, Record Group 238, NID-14435, T-301/117/563, NA; Arbeitseinsatzführer (Buchenwald) to Com-

mandant's Headquarters, Concentration Camp Buchenwald, October 30, 1942, Record Group 238, NO-2106, NA.

20. Johe, *Neuengamme*, pp. 24–29; Ino Arndt, "Das Frauen-Konzentrationslager Ravensbrück," in Martin Broszat, ed., *Studien zur Geschichte der Konzentrationslager* (Stuttgart, 1970), p. 117; Toni Siegert, "Das Konzentrationslager Flossenbürg," in Martin Broszat and Elke Fröhlich, *Bayern in der NS-Zeit*, vol. 2 (Munich-Vienna, 1979), p. 452.

21. Secret Order of Chief of Security Police and SD, December 17, 1942, Record Group 238, 1063-d-PS, NA.

22. Chief of Security Police and SD to Pohl, December 31, 1942, Record Group 238, NO-1523, NA.

23. Circular of WVHA Amtsgruppe D to camp commandants, February 26, 1943, Record Group 242, T-175/218/2756230, NA.

24. Circular of chief of WVHA to camp commandants, November 22, 1943, Record Group 238, NO-1290, NA.

25. Secret Order of Reich Ministry of Air Transportation and High Command of the Air Force, September 4, 1940, Record Group 242, T-175/218/2756385–86, NA; secret letter of Chief of Security Police and SD to Inspector of Concentration Camps, September 7, 1940, Record Group 242, T-175/218/2756384, NA. These details were referred to as "Ascension Detachments" (*Himmelfahrtskommandos*).

26. Pohl to Himmler, September 16, 1942, Record Group 238, NIK-15392, NA.

27. Secret circular of the Inspector of Concentration Camps, November 15, 1941, Record Group 242, T-175/218/2756109–10, NA.

28. Top secret circulars of WVHA Amtsgruppe D to camp commandants, March 26, 1942 and April 27, 1943, Record Group 238, 1151-P-PS and 1933-PS, NA.

29. Secret circular of WVHA Amtsgruppe D, January 20, 1943, Record Group 238, NO-1523.

30. Himmler to Müller and Glücks, October 29, 1942, Record Group 238, NO-1514; Himmler to Pohl, December 15, 1942, Record Group 242, T-175/80/2600604, NA.

31. Secret letter of Pohl to Himmler, September 30, 1943, Record Group 238, NO-1010, NA.

32. Circular of Pohl, May 15, 1943, Record Group 238, NO-400.

33. Reichswerke AG fur Erzbergbau und Eisenhütten, "Hermann Göring" to Concentration Camp Subsidiary Drütte, November 17 and 23, 1943, and December 2 and 20, 1943, Record Group, NI-4771, T-301/35/585–89, NA.

34. Himmler to Pohl, March 5, 1943, Record Group 242, T175/73/2590812–14, NA.

35. Secret circular of Himmler, December 5, 1941, Record Group 238, NO-385, NA; circular of Maurer to camp commandants, November 27, 1942, Record Group 238, 3685-PS, NA. The RSHA, which controlled the duration of a prisoner's incarceration, permitted only about thirty such releases. See Georg, *Unternehmungen*, p. 112.

36. Himmler to Pohl, March 5, 1943, Record Group 242, T-175/73/2590812–14, NA.

37. Pohl to Himmler, September 16, 1942, Record Group 238, NIK-15392, NA; Himmler to Kruger, July 19, 1942, Record Group 238, NO-5574; Himmler to Glücks, January 25, 1942, Record Group 238, NO-500, NA.

38. Globocnik to Himmler, January 5, 1944, Record Group 238, NO-057, NA.

39. Memorandum of Opperbeck, January 13, 1944, Record Group 238, NO-1036, NA; memo of Baier, January 19, 1944, Record Group 238, NO-1036, NA.

40. Secret order of the SS Garrison Commander at Auschwitz, February 14, 1944, Archive of the Auschwitz Museum, Oswiecim.

41. In 1942, 14,293 deaths were recorded in the Mauthausen system. See Maršálek, *Mauthausen*, p. 157; Pohl to Himmler, September 30, 1943, Record Group 238, NO-1010, NA.

42. Wincenty Hein, *Lebens- und Arbeitsbedingungen der Häftlinge im Konzentrationslager "Dora-Mittlebau"* (Warsaw, 1969), p. 45. In January 1944 alone, 800 of the 10,000 inmates of Dora died. See testimony of Dr. Karl Kahr, April 10, 1947, *Trials of War Criminals Before the Nuremberg Military Tribunals* (Washington, 1950), 5:398.

43. Secret circular of WVHA Amtsgruppe D, December 2, 1942, Record Group 242, T-175/218/2756682–83, NA.

44. Secret Circular of WVHA Amtsgruppe D, April 11, 1944, Record Group 242, T-175/218/2756482.

45. Circular of General Inspector of the Reinforced Death's Head Regiments, January 22, 1940, Record Group 242, T-580/88/Order 437, NA.

46. Circular of chief of WVHA Amtsgruppe D, July 27, 1943, Record Group 242, T-175/218/2726563–70, NA.

47. Pohl to Himmler, September 30, 1943, Record Group 238, NO-1010, NA. In August 1944, one year later, 524,286 prisoners were in the camps. See Burger to Lorner, August 15, 1944, Record Group 238, NO-1990, NA.

48. Maršálek, *Mauthausen*, p. 145.

49. Dachau Prisoner Registry, Record Group 242, NA. German prisoners made up 10.46 percent of the prisoner arrivals during this time; west Europeans accounted for only 4 percent.

50. Fritz Bringmann, *KZ Neuengamme: Berichte, Erinnerungen, Dokumente* (Frankfurt am Main, 1982), p. 151. Scandinavians made up 6 percent of the camp population; Dutchmen, Frenchmen, and Belgians, 22 percent; and Germans, 9 percent.

51. Arndt, "Ravensbrück," pp. 118–119. Poles, 24 percent; Soviet civilians, 19.1 percent; Czechs and Yugoslavs, 3.2 percent. Other well-represented groups were Germans (19.9 percent) and Jews (15.1 percent). Most of the Jews arrived after the summer of 1944.

52. Manfred Bornemann and Martin Broszat, "Das KL Dora-Mittelbau," in Broszat, *Konzentrationslager*, p. 168.

53. Himmler to Speer, June 1943, Record Group 242, T-175/80/2600562–65, NA.

54. Pohl to Himmler, April 5, 1944, Record Group 238, NO-020, NA; Himmler to Pohl, April 22, 1944, ibid.
55. Himmler to Goering, March 9, 1944, Record Group 238, 1584-PS, NA.
56. Falk Pingel, "Die Konzentrationslagerhaftlinge im nationalsozialistischen Arbeitseinsatz," in Waclaw Dlugoborski, ed., *Zweiter Weltkrieg und sozialer Wandel* (Gottingen, 1981), p. 162.
57. Martin Broszat, "The Concentration Camps," in Helmut Krausnick, et al., *Anatomy of the SS State* (New York, 1968), p. 482. See also p. 493.
58. Ibid., p. 504.
59. Ibid., p. 400.

CHAPTER 5

Germans and Serbs: The Emergence of Nazi Antipartisan Policies in 1941

Christopher R. Browning

During World War II, roughly 1.5 million Yugoslavs—10 percent of the population—lost their lives. The demographic catastrophe occurred in many forms, but three were most prominent: (1) the genocidal massacres of the Nazi-sponsored Ustash regime in Croatia, (2) the veritable civil war between various ethnic groups and political movements in Yugoslavia unleashed by the German dismemberment of the country, and (3) the occupation policies of the German military itself aimed at crushing partisan resistance. If the German occupiers were indirectly responsible for the first two forms of bloodletting, they were directly responsible for the third.

This essay will focus on the third factor, and in particular on the question of the emergence of Germany's antipartisan policy in response to the uprising in Serbia in the summer and fall of 1941. I will argue that this response was not simply a programmatic deduction from Hitler's racial ideology but was produced by a more complex combination of causes: (1) the negative stereotype of Serbs that permeated German society; (2) the political culture of the Nazi regime, which spread other racial stereotypes and set a premium on ruthlessness; and (3) the occupiers' shifting perceptions of political expediency and military necessity.

How in general were Serbs perceived by Germans? Several anecdotes are illustrative. On July 24, 1914, British Foreign Secretary Edward Grey informed the German ambassador in London that if Serbia accepted the Austro-Hungarian ultimatum, it "would really cease to count as an independent nation." Upon reading the report of his ambassador, Kaiser Wilhelm II scribbled one of his famous marginal comments: "This would be very desirable. It is not a nation in the European sense, but a band of robbers."[1] Field Marshal Wilhelm List, a deeply religious and culturally refined Bavar-

64

ian who served as the first German occupation commander of the Balkans in 1941, was asked at his postwar trial in Nuremberg if the Serbs were actually different from other people. He replied that the Serbs were "far more passionate, hot blooded and more cruel" because of the prominent non-European aspect of their history. "The individual in Serbia is obviously like every other peasant under normal conditions, but as soon as differences arise, then, caused by the hot blood in their veins, the cruelty caused by hundreds of years of Turkish domination erupts." [2]

Neither Kaiser Wilhelm nor Field Marshal List were Nazis expressing the doctrinaire racial views of a Hitler-inspired ideology. Rather their comments, separated by more than 30 years and two world wars, reflected a negative stereotype that was pervasive in German society, namely that European civilization ended with the boundaries of the old Austro-Hungarian empire and that the Orient began in Serbia. According to this negative stereotype, a special "Balkan mentality" prevailed in this region. Balkan peoples in general and the Serbs in particular could not really be considered true members of the European community of civilized nations.

This stereotype was only reinforced by Yugoslavia's rejection of its alliance with Nazi Germany in March 1941 and the partisan uprising against German occupation in the following June. Both of these actions—like the Sarajevo assassination in 1914—were viewed by the Germans as typical examples of Serbian "treachery." The Waldheim affair all too clearly indicates that the ensuing antipartisan policies of the German occupiers in the Balkans are even today viewed by most Germans and Austrians as having been legitimate or at least understandable military measures provoked by the insidious tactics of a particularly cruel and brutal native population—thus quite distinct from Nazi crimes by racial ideology. Therefore, the treatment of the inhabitants of Serbia under German occupation must be seen, at least in part, as a manifestation not of National Socialism but of a negative stereotype far more widespread and enduringly held in German, and perhaps even more, in Austrian society.

Of course, that is only part of the explanation. Many of the Germans and Austrians who served in the Balkans in World War II were ardent Nazis and devoted followers of a man who considered all the Slavic peoples of eastern Europe to inhabit a relatively lowly position in his imagined hierarchy of races. However, this belief in Slavic inferiority did not inhibit Hitler from allying with Slovaks, Bulgarians, and later Croatians when it suited him, nor did it deter him from initially offering both the despised

Poles and the Serbian-dominated Yugoslav state the privileges of junior partnership with the Third Reich.

It was the spurning of these offers that exposed first Poland and then Yugoslavia to the full fury of German aggression and occupation, exemplified in the latter case above all by the terror bombing of defenseless Belgrade followed by the total dismemberment of the country.

If the fate of the Yugoslav state was sealed, the future of the Serbian remnant was not. Were the Serbs Balkan Untermenschen whose anti-German attitude from Sarajevo to the Belgrade *Putsch* proved them so unreliable that only a vengeful policy of population decimation and total subjection held out the prospect of eventual pacification? Or did at least some Serbs, if properly cultivated and offered the prospect of a future role in the New Order, have the potential to become useful junior partners and collaborators, facilitating political control and economic exploitation of Serbia on behalf of the German war effort? Hitler's emotional and ideological inclination tended toward the former alternative, but the priority given the eastern front and the resulting German manpower shortage in Serbia required pragmatic toleration of some Serbs. Without a definitive decision from Hitler, this question of the future position of Serbia in the New Order continued to divide the German occupiers of all stripes—diplomats, bureaucrats, military professionals, party loyalists, and even SS-men—throughout the war.

If Nazi ideology provided no explicit program for the fate of Serbia, how did it most influence German behavior there? I would suggest that its impact was felt most importantly in two ways. First, the Nazi proclivity for racial stereotyping proved quite contagious. From the beginning of the German occupation, the widely held negative stereotype of the Serbs was quickly intermingled with other racial stereotypes. Of course, the Jews were assumed to be Communists and would hence bear the murderous brunt of the Germans' antipartisan policies even before the Final Solution as a specifically anti-Jewish policy was initiated. Gypsies in turn were equated with Jews in the basic racial legislation decreed in Serbia.[3] When the Communist partisans were characterized as "outlaw bands," the Gypsies faced double jeopardy, for they were also seen as criminally inclined nomadic bands. When the partisan resistance reached its peak in 1941 and was perceived as a "national uprising" involving the entire population, then all Serbs faced the same fate as Communists, Jews, and Gypsies. One stereotype merged into another, creating a widening circle of victims.

Intensifying the potential for havoc was a second Nazi contribution to the German occupation regime in Serbia, namely a political culture that placed a premium on ruthless behavior free of traditional moral norms and inhibitions. Hitler's punitive terror bombing of Belgrade set the tone even before the partisan uprising, and thereafter the German documents are filled with shrill exhortations for policies and measures that were "ruthless, harsh, and draconic." In such an atmosphere, only violence and brutality, not moderation and restraint, could flourish.

We must now see how these factors—the pervasive negative stereotypes and the Nazi cult of ruthlessness—shaped German antipartisan policy in the face of the outbreak of a Communist-led uprising in Serbia after June 22, 1941. Initially, the Germans were inclined to avoid using army troops, for the three divisions in Serbia were the dregs of the German army— understrength, overaged, poorly equipped, and still in training. Instead the Germans intended to use police measures and terror. The former involved the use of not only German but also Serbian police. The latter meant above all reprisal shootings of arrested "communists and Jews." The identity of the two was assumed from the beginning, and the number of reprisal victims in these two categories totalled 111 by July 22.[4] At that point the German commander formulated new guidelines for reprisal executions, which also permitted measures against the local population if they had made themselves "co-responsible" by passively resisting the investigation or by offering fertile soil to anti-German activity.[5] In addition to suspected Communists and Jews, all Serbs found in the vicinity of partisan activity and deemed coresponsible were vulnerable to German reprisal measures.

Neither police measures nor reprisal terror stemmed the rising tide of the insurgency. The German occupiers, however, could not agree on countermeasures. The High Command of the Armed Forces (OKW) exhorted even more drastic terror, especially hanging rather than shooting so-called saboteurs; Field Marshal List, visiting from his headquarters in Saloniki, wanted the army troops to take a more active role; and a number of local occupation officials advocated a strengthened and better-armed Serbian police.[6]

All three policies in fact failed. By August the collaborating Serbian police force was demoralized and disintegrating—a process accelerated no doubt by the practice of forcing Serbian policemen at gunpoint to carry out reprisal shootings of their own countrymen.[7] The organization of army pursuit commandos was ineffective, for the troops were too few and too immobile to cover the territory assigned.[8] Reprisals, which increased nearly tenfold in August, proved to be not only ineffective but also counterproductive. As one German report noted, "Even with the most unrestricted reprisal measures—up until the end of August a total of approximately 1,000 communists and Jews had been shot or publicly hanged and the houses of the guilty burned down—it was not possible to restrain the growth of the armed revolt."[9] Many German observers frankly concluded that rather than deterring resistance, reprisal policy was driving hitherto peaceful and politically indifferent Serbs into the arms of the partisans.[10]

For the Germans the situation in Serbia reached crisis proportions in early September. They had just installed a new collaboration regime under General Nedic in the hope that he would have the prestige and popularity to mobilize anti-Communist sentiment against the partisans. But the Nedic experiment produced no immediate dividends; in the first test case after the installation of the new government, 450 Serbian police sent to Sabac refused to fight.[11] More disastrous for the Germans was the growing threat to their own troops. In all of August the German army in Serbia had suffered 30 dead, 23 wounded, and 1 missing. Suddenly, on the first of September, 100 men were captured at Losnica, and three days later another 175 were captured in a breakout attempt from Krupanj.[12] The thinly stretched German troops in Serbia were therefore not only unable to suppress sabotage and ambush but were now threatened with piecemeal defeat and capture by increasingly large and emboldened partisan units. Thus, the partisan uprising was not just an embarrassment to the professional pride of the German Army; if not checked, the increasing display of German military impotence and vulnerability would hearten Germany's enemies and stimulate yet further resistance that could snowball into disaster. In this crisis-ridden atmosphere, the Germans formulated new measures.

List's chief of staff, Hermann Foertsch, concluded quite simply: "Downright violence still remains the last resort." His boss concurred and issued blistering directives from Saloniki not only for "ruthless and immediate measure against the insurgents" but also for "increased pressure upon the population" because he was convinced the entire population was implicated in the uprising.[13]

List also dispatched frontline units, capable of going on the offensive, for a punitive expedition into the partisan-controlled Sava Bend region around Sabac. The guiding principle of this expedition was simple: "The entire population had to be punished, not only the men." All men between the ages of fourteen and seventy were to be interned in a concentration camp; all inhabitants who participated in resistance or who attempted to flee were to be shot and their houses burned down; all women and children were to be driven off the land and into the mountains. Once cut off from their food supplies from the valley and faced with feeding the women and children, the insurgents would it was hoped experience a "food catastrophe." The new commanding general in Serbia, Franz Böhme, exhorted his troops as follows: "Your mission lies in . . . the country in which German blood flowed in 1914 through the treachery of Serbs, women and children. You are the avengers of these dead. An intimidating example must be created for the whole of Serbia, which must hit the whole population most severely."[14]

Between September 23 and October 2, troops of the 342d division cut a swath of destruction through the Sabac region, executing 1,126 suspected Communists, interning over 20,000 men, burning villages considered sympathetic to the partisans, and relenting from driving off the women and children only at the last moment when it became clear that no one would be left to take care of the cattle and harvest.[15]

Rather than deter resistance, the expedition merely provoked counteratrocities. The Germans knew that the partisans held more than 300 German prisoners, and military intelligence eagerly tracked their whereabouts in the hopes of rescue. On October 2, however, the partisans ambushed a communications unit near Topola and executed by machine-gun fire at close range the troops who had surrendered, killing a total of 21 men.[16] Though this was a small fraction of what the Germans had just done in Sabac, Böhme immediately responded by escalating his terror policy another quantum leap. The head of the OKW, Wilhelm Keitel, had recently ordered that for every German soldier killed by insurgents in occupied territories, 50 to 100 "Communists" were to be executed in retaliation. He justified this order on the grounds that "a human life in these countries often counts for nothing and a deterrent effect can be achieved only through unusual harshness."[17] Keitel's view struck a responsive chord among the Germans in Serbia, where it was considered axiomatic that "[w]ith the people of the Balkans, the life of others means nothing, one's own life only very little."[18] Thus, Böhme immediately grasped the maximum ratio of 100:1, expanded the order to cover Jews as well as Communists, and let loose his firing squads on 2,100 "Communists and Jews" interned in camps at Belgrade and Sabac.[19] At the latter camp these executions were particularly absurd and grotesque, in that predominantly Austrian troops gunned down central European Jewish refugees mostly from Vienna in retaliation for Serbian partisan attacks on the German army.

The 100:1 reprisal ratio was then established as standard operating procedure for all subsequent casualties.[20] When the 717th Division of Major General Hoffman, operating south of Belgrade, suffered losses in mid-October, it had no access to a convenient reprisal pool of interned Jews. Instead the Germans conducted roundups in Kraljevo and Kragujevac, shooting 1,755 people in the first city and 2,300 in the second. In Kragujevac the victims included the students of the local high school and the workers of an airplane factory producing for the German war effort, though the Germans had never suffered a single casualty within the city.[21] This random roundup and massacre of over 4,000 Serbs in Kraljevo and Kragujevac between October 17 and 21 was criticized by various German occupation authorities, by Nedic, and even by the OKW, causing Böhme to reconsider his reprisal policy. "Arbitrary arrests and shootings of Serbs are driving to the insurgents circles of the population which up to now did not participate in the insurrection," Böhme's new order explained. "It must be . . . avoided, that precisely those elements of the population are seized and shot as hostages who, being nonparticipants in the insurrection, did not flee before the German punitive expedition." Thus the Germans reverted to what might be called the proximity principle, and henceforth reprisal victims were to be taken from those found in the vicinity of partisan attacks or from villages considered focal points of the insurgency.[22] If Serbs in the countryside were still at high risk, those living in urban areas that remained peaceful were relatively more secure.

While the Serbs received a partial reprieve from German terror, this was no help to the Jews and Gypsies. If the Germans could conceive that not all Serbs were Communists and that the random shooting of innocent Serbs would damage German interests, they had no doubt that all Jews were anti-German and that the Gypsies were no different than the Jews. And if more care had to be exercised in selecting Serbian hostages, the pressure to find hostages elsewhere to meet the 100:1 quota was that much greater. The new German policy stated succinctly: "As a matter of principle it must be said that the Jews and Gypsies in general represent an element of insecurity and thus a danger to public order and safety. . . . That is why it is a matter of principle in each case to put all Jewish men and all male Gypsies at the disposal of the troops as hostages."[23] The fate of the male Jews and Gypsies in Serbia was sealed, and their execution by army firing squad was completed by early November.[24]

At the same time the tide of battle in Serbia turned in the Germans' favor, and by December the partisans had retreated to the mountainous regions of Bosnia and Croatia beyond the Serbian border. They would continue their struggle against the Germans elsewhere but would not return in force to Serbia until 1944. With the first phase of the partisan war in Serbia at an end, the reprisal body count stood at about 15,000, of which some 4,500-5,000 were Jews and Gypsies.[25] In contrast, on December 1, 1941, the Germans rescued 319 prisoners whom the partisans had held since September but not executed.[26]

The Germans were convinced that the reprisal measures had made a major contribution to their success.[27] The antipartisan policies developed in Serbia—mass shootings as well as mass internments and deportation of the population in insurgent areas—would therefore be expanded upon elsewhere in Yugoslavia in the following years. Although the partisan war became increasingly vicious on both sides, this cannot alter the historical record that the deadly escalation was initiated by the Germans in Serbia in 1941. In doing so, the Germans were not reacting in kind to atrocities committed by savage partisans, as their postwar apologists would have it. Rather the Germans perceived the local population through a series of negative stereotypes and formulated policy in accordance with a political culture that exulted in violence and brutality. In doing so, they drowned their initial opposition in a sea of blood but ultimately provoked an unrelenting resistance that plagued them for the rest of the war.

NOTES

1. Immanuel Geiss, *July 1914* (New York, 1969), p. 183.
2. American Military Tribunal, Case 7 (hereafter cited as AMT 7), transcript, 3427-8, List testimony.
3. Jevrejski Istorijski Muzej Belgrade, 21-1-1/20, "Verordnung betreffend die Juden and Zigeuner" of May 30, 1941.
4. Bundesarchiv-Militararchiv Freiburg (hereafter cited as BA-MA), Anlage 33, report of July 22, 1941 (NOKW-1091). An additional 412 "communists" rounded up by the Germans on June 22 were immediately shot with no pretense of its being in reprisal for partisan activities. BA-MA, RW 40/5, Anlage 1, Commanding General in Serbia, Ia, to Military Commander Southeast, Ic, August 2, 1941 (NOKW-1128).

5. BA-MA, RH 26-104/8, Anlage 156, Edict on deterrent and reprisal measures of the military commander in Serbia.

6. BA-MA, RW 40/4, entries of July 22, 24, and 29, 1941; Anlage 33, Gravenhorst to 65th corps, July 21, 1941; Anlage 35, Kiessel to List, July 23, 1941; and Anlage 48, List to Danckelmann, July 29, 1941. Politisches Archiv des Auswärtigen Amtes, Bonn (hereafter cited as PA), Staatssekretär-Jugoslawien, Bd. 3, Benzler to Foreign Office, July 23, 1941.

7. BA-MA, RW 40/4, entry of August 9, 1941, and Anlage 61, Ehrman report of August 1, 1941; 40411/7, Bader to List, August 28, 1941. PA, Staatssekretär-Jugoslawien, Bd. 3, Benzler to Foreign Office, August 1, 1941.

8. BA-MA, 40411/7, Bader to List, August 28, 1941.

9. Paul Hehn, *The German Struggle Against Yugoslav Guerrillas in World War II: German Counter-Insurgency in Yugoslavia 1941–1943* (New York, 1979), pp. 28–29.

10. PA, Staatssekretär-Jugoslawien, Bd. 3, Benzler to Foreign Office, July 23 and August 1, 1941; Inland IIg 401, Benzler to Foreign Office, August 8, 1941. BA-MA, RW 40/5, Anlage 59, Ic report of Picht for July; 14 749/18, reports of Wehrmachtverbindungsstelle, July 31 and August 8, 1941 (NOKW-1114); 40411/6, Bader report of August 23, 1941.

11. BA-MA, RW 40/11, Anlage 33, report of September 12, 1941.

12. Hehn, *The German Struggle*, p. 31.

13. Ibid., 30. BA-MA, 14 749/5 Anlage 58, List to Danckelmann and Bader, September 4, 1941 (NOKW-453); and RW 40/11, Anlage 7, List to Danckelmann, September 5 1941 (NOKW-625).

14. BA-MA, 14 729/4, Anlage 17, Turner to Böhme, September 21, 1941 (NOKW-892); Anlage 20, Böhme order of September 22, 1941 (NOKW-183); Anlage 22, Böhme order of September 23, 1941 (NOKW-194); Anlage 17, Pemsel to Turner and 342d division, September 27, 1941 (NOKW-193); Anlage 31, Böhme order and message to the troops, September 25, 1941 (NOKW-1048).

15. For the records of the 342d division, see BA-MA, 15 365.

16. BA-MA, 17 729/2, entries of October 2 and 3, 1941; RH 26-114/2, October summary. AMT 7, Transcript, 8433-4, testimony of Topola survivor, Johann Kerbler.

17. BA-MA 17 729/9, Anlage 48, Keitel order of September 16, 1941 (NOKW-258).

18. BA-MA, RW 40/87, Turner Situation Report of October 6, 1941.

19. BA-MA, 17 729/8, Anlage 24, draft order to Turner and 342d division, October 4, 1941 (NOKW-192). According to later correspondence, the victims totaled two thousand Jews and two hundred Gypsies. NO-5810, Turner to Hildebrandt, October 17, 1941. Three hundred "suspicious" Gypsies had been interned in Belgrade in late September. BA-MA, RW 40/11, Anlage 76, Gravenhorst to Böhme, September 20, 1941.

20. BA-MA, 17 729/9, Anlage 48, Böhme order, October 10, 1941 (NOKW-891 and 557).

21. BA-MA, RH 26-117/3, entries of October 15–17, 1941; RH 26-104/16, Anlage

486c, König report of October 27, 1941 (NOKW-904); RW 40/12, Bischofshausen report, October 20, 1941 (NOKW-387).

22. BA-MA 17 729.9, Böhme order, October 25, 1941.
23. Ibid.
24. The most graphic description is the report of firing squad leader Lt. Hans-Dietrich Walther. BA-MA, RH 26-104/16, Walther report, November 1, 1941 (NOKW-905).
25. German statisticians calculated that 11,164 reprisal shootings had been carried out since early October under the 100:1 ratio, though this figure was admittedly low since not all units had reported (including those involved in shooting more than 1,000 Jews at Sabac). BA-MA, RW 40/23, Aktennotiz of December 20, 1941. In addition to the more than 1,000 "communists and Jews" shot during the summer and the 1,126 shot at Sabac by the 342d division, some 570 reprisal executions were carried out by other units in September.
26. BA-MA, 17 729/2, entry of December 1, 1941.
27. BA-MA, 17 729/2, entry of October 25, 1941; Anlage 202, ten-day report of October 30, 1941 (NOKW-199); ten-day report of December 10, 1941 (NOKW-660).

CHAPTER 6

Genocide in Satellite Croatia during the Second World War

Menachem Shelah

The state of Croatia, the subject of this essay, no longer exists. It was a short-lived German satellite, set up by the Germans and the Italians after the collapse of Yugoslavia in April 1941. It encompassed the former provinces of Croatia, Bosnia, and Herzegovina. The number of its inhabitants was approximately 6.5 million, of whom 3.3 million (51 percent) were Croats (Roman Catholics); 2 million (30 percent), Serbs (Pravoslavs); 0.7 million (11 percent), Moslems; 45,000 (0.7 percent), Jews; 27,000 (0.3 percent), Gypsies and other minorities, such as Germans, Hungarians, etc.

The leaders of the so-called Independent State of Croatia were members of a prewar Croatian ultranationalistic terrorist organization called "Ustasha." The Ustasha movement, because of its uncompromising and violent attitude toward the Yugoslav state, had been outlawed. Many of its members found refuge in fascist Italy, which gave them some political and military backing, depending on the fluctuations of Italian Balkan policy.

A prominent intellectual and Ustasha ideologue, A. Seitz, proclaimed that "the bell tolls. The last hour of those foreign elements, the Serb and the Jew, has arrived. They shall vanish from Croatia. It shall be done by the army and the Ustasha movement."[1] Similarly, a Ustasha priest, the Reverend Dijonizije Jurichev, said,

In this country, nobody can live except Croatians. We know very well how to deal with those that oppose conversion [to the Roman Catholic faith]. I personally have put an end to whole provinces, killing everyone—chicks and men alike. It gives me no remorse to kill a small child when he stands in the path of the Ustasha.[2]

No wonder the local press coined this slogan (it rhymes in the original): "Serb, crawl or perish!" (*Ili se pokloni ili ukloni*).

There is usually a certain discrepancy between ideology and praxis, between words and deeds. But alas, it was not so in this case. The Ustasha acted brutally and shamelessly on their declarations. Genocide of Serbs, Jews, and Gypsies was the first, foremost, and most consistent item on their political agenda. Wholesale massacres of the Serbian population commenced in Croatia even before the consolidation of Ustasha power, and continued until its collapse in May 1945. It began in the mixed regions such as Lika and Kordun. There the local Croatian inhabitants, led by Ustasha members, killed their Serb neighbors, pillaged Serb property, burned Serb houses, and raped Serb women. It is almost unbelievable that people of the same ethnic origin, speaking the same language, living together for generations, could turn on one another in such a terrible way. Despite the religious discord between the Serb Pravoslavs and the Croat Roman Catholics, and despite the pent-up political grievances from the Yugoslav period, the intensity and brutality are inexplicable in rational terms. As the French historian Jacques Sabille wrote:

The Ustasha bands spread terror throughout the countryside, directed against Serb Orthodox Christians and Jews. Whole families were murdered, towns were completely gutted, terrible acts of sadistic cruelty were perpetrated. . . . The Ustasha chapter written in the summer of 1941 was one of the most gruesome in the history of the World War II, which is saying a lot.[3]

Today there are Croat emigrant circles whose members claim such statements are sheer Communist propaganda intended to smear the Croat nation and hamper its fight for liberation. As a professional historian I can assure you that the account set forth in this essay is based on massive documentation and contemporary evidence, most of it from Nazi German, Fascist Italian, and Ustasha Croat sources.[4]

It is very difficult to give the precise number of Serb men, women, and children killed by the Croats. It depends very much on whom you include among the victims. Do you count only those killed outright in the murder orgy of the first months: those butchered by knife, thrown into deep ravines in the mountains, burned alive in Pravoslav churches and their homes? Or do you also include the thousands who died in the big expulsions, perished from hunger, exposure, and epidemics and in the camps on their way into exile? By a rough calculation, the number of Serbs killed in Croatia reaches the 200,000 mark in the first year of the Ustasha rule, about 10 percent of the Serb population in Croatia. During that period, special attention was given by the Ustasha to members of the Serbian elite. The percentage of murdered Serbian doctors, lawyers, teachers, priests, and intellectuals was much higher than the average. In that manner the Ustasha tried to destroy potential Serbian leadership.[5]

As a consequence of the widespread terror, in many parts of Croatia total anarchy prevailed. The Serbs, with whatever arms they had, tried to defend themselves and the country was plunged into a state of civil war. It was perfectly clear, at least to the Germans and the Italians stationed in Croatia, that continuation of the Ustasha rampage could jeopardize their rule and encourage the growing resistance movement.

Moreover, the Italians took advantage of the situation and helped the Serbs against the Ustasha to enlarge their territorial domain in Croatia. Hitler, in his meetings with Minister of War Slavko Kvaternik in July 1941, and with the Ustasha "Führer" Ante Pavelitch in June 1941, encouraged them in their genocide of Serbs, and of course, Jews. Hitler said that if Croatia wanted to exist, her policy in the next fifty years must be one of "national intolerance."[6]

The Germans stationed in Croatia were aware that the Ustasha rampage and anarchy could damage German interest in Croatia and push the harassed Serbs into the resistance movement. In their messages to Berlin the Germans emphasized the "unorganized" and "uncivilized" manner of the Ustasha killings while at the same time firing squads of the German Army stationed in Serbia executed thousands of Serbs and Jews in a much more "civilized" way.[7]

After a few months of indiscriminate killings, even the Ustasha government realized that the so-called Serbian question in Croatia could not be solved by total annihilation. They started to look for other ways and means, including legal harassment. In an avalanche of laws (many of them affecting Jews and Gypsies as well), the Ustasha tried to isolate, pauperize, and collectively outlaw the Serb minority.[8] By prohibiting the Serbs from taking part in most economic enterprises, appointing Croat commissars in Serb factories and shops, imposing collective fines on the community, and so on, they denied the Serb minority their livelihood. Other laws prohibiting Serb residence in certain neighborhoods and imposing restriction of movement and curfews turned the Serbs into pariahs without any legal protection. But even then the Serbs into pariahs without any legal protection. But even then the Serbs didn't vanish from Croatia. "Let the Serbian horde run to Serbia," decided the Ustasha leadership. But the Ustasha couldn't simply drive hundreds of thousands of people into territory governed by their German allies. The German military administration in Serbia vehemently opposed that plan on practical grounds, such as lack of food and accommodations. At last some sort of agreement was reached. The Croatians agreed to take in a few hundred thousand Slovenes from annexed Slovenia, and the Germans would accept the expelled Serbs.[9] The eviction campaign commenced, and whole districts (mainly in northwestern Bosnia, near the Serb border) were made *Serbrein*.

These forced expulsions were carried out in an especially unpleasant manner. Thousands upon thousands of women, children, and elderly people were cruelly herded into transit camps without proper arrangements for food or hygienic facilities. Epidemics such as typhus raged and killed thousands. The people were totally denuded of their belongings and, on arrival in Serbia, were left on their own. During the first year of Ustasha rule, around 200,000 Serbs were expelled from their homes and thrown into Serbia. Then in the beginning of 1942, the German authorities in Belgrade, for their own reasons, stopped this appalling exodus.[10] Another solution to the Serbian question was blocked. And all that time, some of the Ustasha leaders and "intellectuals" had kept an ace up their sleeves. Mladen Lorkovitch, the Croat minister of foreign affairs, formulated it like this: "In Croatia, we can find few real Serbs. The majority of Pravoslavs are as a matter of fact Croats who were forced by foreign invaders to accept the infidel faith. Now it's our duty to bring them back into the Roman Catholic fold."[11] In short, the Ustasha decided that whoever might fight them must be forced to join them. With tacit local (and Vatican) ecclesiastical approval, a most energetic and brutal conversion campaign began.[12] Catholic priests, escorted by armed Ustashas, descended on Serb towns and villages and in a matter of hours converted hundreds of "lost" Pravoslav souls. Taking into account that the alternative was death or imprisonment, the outstanding success of the crusade is perfectly understandable. Those "dedicated" Catholic priests were ordered to deny the benefit of conversion to Serb intellectuals and community leaders and instead to hand them over to the proper authorities to be killed or incarcerated in concentration camps. In this manner about a quarter of a million Serbs were converted during 1941 and 1942.

As a result of Ustasha genocide, the local Serbs tried both to defend themselves and to take revenge. The country was plunged into civil war. Partisans and bands of resistance armies roamed the woods and mountains. Thus, a very complex situation developed in Yugoslavia during the Second World War. The Ustasha Serbophobia was transformed in that context into "the fight for Croat national independence."[13] The atrocities perpetrated by almost everybody in 1942 were part of the fighting that was going on among all kinds of groupings. For instance, the terrible genocide of the Serb civil population of the Kozara District during the summer of 1942, in which the current Austrian President Kurt Waldheim took part, was a collective Ustasha-German enterprise that was part of an antipartisan drive. The whole population of the district—about 60,000 persons—was driven on foot to the notorious Jasenovac concentration camp, where most of the men were killed outright, the women sent to Germany, and the children— 20,000 of them—killed or dispersed throughout Croat orphanages.

The Ustasha government of the Independent State of Croatia undoubtedly initiated, prompted, organized, implemented, and carried out a policy of genocide against the Serb population of Croatia. It did so by wholesale killings, massive expulsions, forced conversions, and deliberate forcing of unlawful legislation, imprisonment, and bodily and spiritual damage.

The Ustasha also took part in the extermination of a group whose tragic fate during the Nazi period has scarcely been mentioned in the history of this period. One reason is that the documentary and oral evidence is scarce. Only a few German and satellite documents specifically mention the murder of Gypsies; they are part of the whole picture, a nomadic, so-called asocial group that had no place in the New Order.[14] In Croatia the fate of the Gypsies was particularly cruel. The local Ustasha didn't need German help to do the job. They carried out the Gypsy killings on their own. By a rough estimate, out of 27,000 Croat Gypsies, more than 26,000 were murdered. Some of them tried to save their lives by cooperating with the Ustasha and serving as grave diggers and helpers in the mass killings, but in the end they too were murdered.

As a historian I am obligated to certain standards of objectivity. But in this case my objectivity was jeopardized by the fact that I am a Croatian Jew, one of the very few Jews of that country who escaped the Ustasha killers. Can I possibly present the case of genocide in that country without compromising the Croat side? It is for you to decide, but let me remind you that before me stood the modest maxim, "Facts are facts are facts." And in my opinion the facts are true, their historical and moral impact is clear, and their contemporary importance is enormous.

I would like to finish with these lines written by Auden:

Look at Brueghel's painting of Icarus for instance:
How everything turns away

Quite leisurely from the disaster; the ploughman may
Have heard the splash, the forsaken cry,
But for him it was not an important failure; the sun shone
As it had to on the white legs disappearing into the green
Water; and the expensive delicate ship that must have seen
Something amazing, a boy falling out of the sky,
Had somewhere to get to and sailed calmly on.[15]

Could we be like that ploughman? Can we sail calmly on?

NOTES

1. Hrvatski Narod, June 24, 1941, a speech in Dugo Selo.
2. Viktor Novak, *Magnum Crimen:* Pola Vijeka Klerikalizma u Hrvatskoj (Zagreb, 1948), p. 627.
3. Poliakov and Sabille, *Jews under Italian Occupation* (Paris 1955), p. 132.
4. There is extensive documentation about the Ustasha atrocities in the Italian Army Archives (Ufficio Storico, Roma), especially in the Seconda Armata files. Other sources are in the Yugoslav Army Archives (Vojno Istorijski Institut, Beograd) and in the Bundesarchiv in Koblenz and Freiburg.
5. F. Jelic-Butic, Ustase i N.D.H., p. 166.
6. A. Hilgruber, ed., *Staetsmaener und Diplomaten bei Hitler,* vol. 2 (Frankfurt am Main, 1970), pp. 611–12.
7. On German Army reprisals in Serbia see C. Browning, *Fateful Months: Essays on the Emergence of the Final Solution, 1941–42* (New York, 1985), pp. 39–56.
8. Jelic-Butic, op. cit., pp. 158–87, especially pp. 164, 165, 183.
9. A. L. Lisac, Deportacija Srba iz Hrvatske *Historijski Zbornik IX 1956,* pp. 125–45.
10. Jelic-Butic, op. cit., pp. 167–71.
11. Interview published in the German newspaper *Neue Ordnung,* September 7, 1941.
12. Jelic-Butic, op. cit., pp. 173–74.
13. Among the many books about the civil war in Yugoslavia, I would recommend J. Tomasevic, *Chetniks* (Stanford, 1975).
14. Regretfully, until now there has appeared only one pioneering (and very partial) study on the murder of Gypsies by the Germans and their accomplices; see Kenrick and Paxton, "On Jugoslav Gypsies," in *The Destiny of European Gypsies* (London, 1972), pp. 59–100.
15. W. H. Auden, "Musée des Beaux Arts," in *Selected Poems* (London, 1950), p. 19.

CHAPTER 7

German Occupation Policy in Belgium and France

Sybil Milton

The invasion and occupation of Belgium and France in May and June 1940 resulted in immediate administrative and territorial changes. Two countries were transected into four zones.

1. The provinces of Alsace-Lorraine in France and Eupen-Malmédy in Belgium were incorporated into the Reich.
2. Belgium, without Eupen-Malmédy, retained its monarchy and civilian administration but functioned under the supervision of a German military authority that also extended into the two northeastern French departments of Nord and Pas-de-Calais.
3. In France, defeat brought a change of system. The Fascist regime known as Vichy France replaced the Third Republic and signed the armistice with Hitler. The occupied north of Vichy France was under German military administration and included the northern three-fifths of prewar France; its French administration was directed from Vichy in the south, and its German rule was centered in Paris.
4. The unoccupied southern zone of Vichy France, south of the so-called demarcation line, was autonomous but subject to German scrutiny and approval.

Vichy retained administrative control over French North Africa (Morocco, Algeria, and Tunisia), as did Belgium in the Congo.

Control of the unoccupied zone of France subsequently changed. In November 1942, in response to the first Allied landings in North Africa, the Germans occupied most of the south, permitting Italian troops to occupy eight departments in southeastern France. When Italy surrendered in August 1943, the Germans assumed control of the entire unoccupied zone.

Thus, defeated Belgium and France were governed by a patchwork of administrations, covering the spectrum from incorporated Alsace-Lorraine and Eupen-Malmédy to the semi-independent collaborationist Vichy regime. They rapidly set about excluding large numbers of so-called undesirables, because they had no place in the envisioned New Order.[1]

Almost immediately the Germans imposed their social and political values on Alsace-Lorraine, dumping 105,000 undesirables into unoccupied France between July and December 1940:

They were in the main Jews [22,000], Gypsies, and other foreign racial elements; criminals, asocial and incurably insane persons, and also Frenchmen and Francophiles.[2]

The policy of expediting Jewish immigration by dumping people across borders had already been initiated with the forced expulsion of Russian, Rumanian, and Polish Jews from Germany in 1938.[3] These measures had been expanded to encompass non-Jews with the dumping of Poles from the incorporated Polish areas in the General Government in 1939.[4] Similarly, the expulsions from Alsace in July and October 1940 involved the dumping of Jews, Gypsies, and other French citizens.[5] These measures were only the precursor of broader deportations affecting wider categories of the population.

At a conference in 1942, *Gauleiter* Robert Wagner of Alsace reviewed the measures his administration had applied in Alsace. The long-range policies of expulsion were designed to "cleanse Alsace of all foreign, sick, or unreliable elements."[6] Wagner summarized his plans, which had received Hitler's authorization:

The following classes of people are to be affected by [deportations]: A) colored persons and their offspring; Negroes and colored hybrids; Gypsies and their offspring; Jews from half-Jews on; Mixed Jewish Marriages (*jüdische Mischehen*). B) People of foreign race and their offspring. C) The patois-speaking population. D) Asocial persons. E) Incurably insane persons.[7]

The list of undesirables followed the usual categorization applied by the Germans in all occupied territories. The inclusion of blacks, however, was unusual and reflected the paranoia of Germans from the regions that had been occupied by the Allies after World War I; there the French had employed some black colonial troops, and stories of miscegenation had become part of German postwar folklore.[8]

In France and Belgium the new rulers could not remove all undesirables with the ease that was possible in the incorporated areas. Nevertheless, they proceeded to move against large numbers of persons. These persecuted persons can be loosely divided into different categories for purposes of analysis.

The Racial Enemies: Gypsies   Alongside the Jews, whose fate in France and Belgium has been relatively well documented, the Gypsies stood as the group persecuted for its racial origins. Already before the war commenced in late 1939, French Interior Minister Albert Sarraut specified that Gypsies be included among those without fixed domicile to be interned in *camps de concentration* as so-called security risks.[9] Their situation did not improve when the Germans arrived. German policy vis-à-vis the Gypsies had already been fixed inside Germany during the 1930s. Viewed by German social scientists as imbued by reason of their race with permanent criminal and asocial tendencies, the Gypsies in Germany had been excluded and later incarcerated by the Nazi regime.[10] In the German plan, the Gypsies in France were to be exterminated like the Jews. As in the case of the French Jews, this plan was not fully implemented before the Allied armies liberated the territories. Available statistics only show the deportation to the killing areas of the East of around 15,000 Gypsies; the remainder of the 40,000 French Gypsies survived in the French camps under inhuman conditions.[11]

Far fewer Gypsies resided in Belgium before the war, but the percentage of those killed was far higher than in France. In Belgium the Gypsies had not been incarcerated prior to the war; there the persecution commenced with the occupation and was carried out primarily by the Germans. Eventually approximately 500 of the 600 Belgian Gypsies were deported to their death in the East.[12]

The Social Undesirables   Research has not progressed sufficiently at this time to permit discussion of the fate of these persons. The members of this category—criminals, prostitutes, homosexuals, mental patients—suffered incarceration and death in Germany. But unlike the occupied East, there is no evidence that the Germans imposed such persecution on these groups directly in the West. No doubt, the Vichy collaborationist regime imposed its own persecution on this group, but this part of domestic French history has not yet received the attention of French scholars.

The Political Enemies   Most of the group that has been categorized in this book as the "other victims" consisted of the political opponents of the Nazi and Fascist regimes. These included anti-Nazi refugees from Germany and Austria (particularly socialists, communists, and pacifists), members of the International Brigade, and Spanish Republican exiles.

The first group, anti-Nazi refugees, amounted to approximately 15,000 to 17,000 persons in Belgium between January 1933 and December 1938, and to about 55,000 persons in France during the same period. In 1939 an estimated minimum of 20,000 refugees from occupied rump Czechoslovakia crossed into both Belgium and France. There were thus around 90,000 anti-Nazi refugees in France and Belgium when the Germans occupied these countries; however, about 80 percent of these immigrants were Jews. In all probability, the number of non-Jewish political dissidents among the German and Austrian anti-Nazi refugees did not exceed 20,000; the number of illegal refugees cannot be firmly established but probably exceeded 10,000 persons.[13]

Belgian and French hospitality to these German refugees was reluctant at best. In Belgium, legal resident permits for foreigners were issued in limited quantities, and then only for periods of six months (white card) or two years (yellow card). Both cards required semiannual renewal and frequently prohibited salaried employment or political activity. In the late 1930s Belgian police increasingly applied the threat of repatriation and *refoulement* (police expulsion of illegal immigrants caught within a fifteen-kilometer border zone). In February 1936 the Belgian police expelled the German Communist functionary Heinrich Bell along with four Jewish illegal immigrants caught in the border zone; all were handed over to the Gestapo.[14]

In France, official identity cards were required if a refugee wanted to remain longer than two months, and they were issued only with proof of legal entry. New restrictions were added in February 1935, limiting the validity of any refugee identity card to the administrative district where the holder resided. Special police permits were mandatory if refugees changed their residence within France. (In addition to the German refugees, more than 50,000 refugees from Fascist Italy had fled to France during the 1920s, and they were subject to the same restrictions applied against those from Germany, Austria, and Czechoslovakia). Work permits were almost impossible to obtain; many refugees were employed on the black market (one was portrayed by Charles Boyer opposite Ingrid Bergman and Charles Laughton in the film based on Erich Maria Remarque's *Arch of Triumph*).[15]

German refugees, already apprehensive about their future, were also exposed to German surveillance and physical threats, exemplified by the kidnapping of Berthold Jacob in 1935.[16]

When the war started in September 1939, the French authorities interned all male German and Austrian anti-Nazi refugees (ca. 15,000). A second wave of internment in December 1939 affected both men and women. In May 1940 an additional 7,000 anti-Nazi refugees from the Benelux countries were added to those interned in more than one hundred camps in southern France.[17] These camps became depots from which one-quarter million Jews and non-Jews were later sent to their death in the east. But it is not known how many of the refugee victims—killed by a combination of French hysteria and German "blood lust"—were not Jewish.

The incarcerated former members of the International Brigades of the Spanish Civil War form a separate subgroup among the anti-Nazi refugees. These German and Austrian freedom fighters were automatically interned when they fled across the Pyrenees in February 1939. Arthur Koestler described in his memoirs the political and psychological process that transformed "the martyrs of Fascist barbarism" into "the scum of the earth."[18] Although the eventual fate of all members of the International Brigades interned by the French is not known, we do know some from individual stories. Thus Hermann Langbein, born in Vienna, fought in Spain, was interned in the French camps of St. Cyprien, Gurs, and le Vernet, and was eventually deported to Auschwitz.[19]

With the defeat of Republican Spain in early 1939, nearly one-half million refugees fled across the border to France. Almost one-third were women, children, and the elderly. Choosing exile over imprisonment in Spain, these Spaniards were herded into primitive beach concentration camps near the Mediterranean coast and thus imprisoned by the French. The arrival of the largest number of Spanish refugees in France coincided with the intensification of antiforeigner legislation in France and with Daladier's desire to reach accommodation with Franco. Most of the internment camps were located near small fishing villages whose indigenous population usually consisted of 1,000 to 2,000 inhabitants. The first camp of Argelès-sur-Mer initially held 65,000 to 75,000 Spanish refugees. A few miles to the north, the second camp at St. Cyprien—with ocean on one side and electrified barbed wire on the other—held between 72,000 and 95,000 Spaniards in 1939. The third camp, at Barcarès, held 13,000 Spanish internees. Nearly 50,000 Spaniards were housed without shelter on the beach and in the foothills of the Pyrenees, where the camp of Gurs was eventually built. These were the camps that later also housed the anti-Nazi German and Austrian refugees.

When the Germans occupied northern France and Belgium in June 1940, approximately 15,000 Spaniards who had fought in the regular French Army and the Foreign Legion were captured; approximately 9,000 reached the beaches of Dunkirk, but fewer than 2,000 were evacuated during the British withdrawal. These captured Spanish soldiers were initially interned in POW camps and forced-labor brigades, and many were subsequently deported to Mauthausen, Buchenwald, and Dachau. Spaniards in the southern French transit camps were also deported in the fall of 1940 to Mauthausen and other German concentration camps. It is believed that the Spanish foreign office and the Vichy regime pressured the Germans to receive and incarcerate these republicans. Of the 12,500 Spaniards imprisoned in Mauthausen, 10,500 perished.[20]

Spaniards were also deported by Vichy authorities after 1940 to internment and labor camps in Morocco and Algeria. The Spanish Republicans accounted for 50 percent of all prisoners interned in fourteen Moroccan camps; 1,000 Spaniards were held in five Algerian camps. The other inmates of the North African camps were members of the Foreign Legion, anti-Nazi refugees, and Polish and Russian Jews. When the Allies liberated North Africa in November 1942, relief agencies such as the American Friends Service Committee (AFSC), visited these camps. Leslie O. Heath, the AFSC representative in Casablanca, reported:

Of all the nationalities interned, the Spanish are perhaps the worst off, as there is no government to look out for them and no committee supplied with adequate funds to give aid even to the most needy.[21]

Apart from the autobiographical fiction of Jorge Semprun and Michel del Castillo, we know very little about the experiences of the Spaniards incarcerated in Buchenwald, Dachau, and Ravensbrück.[22] Since the Spaniards had fought in the first war against fascism, they had many contacts among the popular front against fascism, and this enabled them to obtain better conditions in the German camps through the aid of established Communist prisoners. It also placed them in a position to assist in the resistance inside the camps, especially at Buchenwald and Mauthausen.

This survey of the persecution of the non-Jewish victims in France and Belgium has not included those native French and Belgian citizens who joined the resistance and were captured by the Germans; they became an important part of the international population that filled the German concentration camps. But their story is part of the internal history of France and Belgium during World War II, and their inclusion here would require another paper.

Obviously, the fate of the non-Jewish victims in France and Belgium was both harsh and tragic. Nevertheless, we must remember that there as elsewhere their story must be placed in context: the story of deportation and mass murder of the Jews.

NOTES

1. See Robert O. Paxton, *Vichy France* (New York, 1972), and Robert E. Herzstein, *When Nazi Dreams Come True: The Horrifying Story of the Nazi Blueprint for Europe* (London, 1982).
2. Office of United States Chief of Council for Prosecution of Axis Criminality, *Nazi Conspiracy and Aggression* (Red Series), 8 vols., 2 suppls. (Washington, 1946–48) 8:122 (Doc. R-114). See also National Archives and Records Administration (NARA), Record Group 238, Documents NG-4933 and NO-1499.
3. Sybil Milton, "The Expulsion of the Polish Jews from Germany, 1938," in *Leo Baeck Institute Yearbook* 29 (1984): 169–99, and Jacob Toury, "Ein Auftakt zur Endlosung: Judenaustreibungen über nichtslawische Reichsgrenzen 1933–1939," in *Das Unrechtsregime: Internationale Forschung ueber Nationalsozialismus*, ed. Ursula Buttner, 2 vols. (Hamburg, 1986), 2:164–97.
4. See Richard C. Lukas, *The Forgotten Holocaust: The Poles Under German Occupation, 1939–1944* (Lexington, Ky., 1986).
5. See Pierre Crenesse, *Le Procès de Wagner, bourreau de l'Alsace* (Paris, 1946), p. 45.
6. Red Series, 8:123.
7. Ibid. The English version in the Red Series reflects both the speed with which these documents were translated at Nuremberg as well as the usage current in the late 1940s.
8. See Reiner Pommerin, *"Sterilisierung der Rheinlandbastarde": Das Schicksal einer farbigen deutschen Minderheit 1918–1937* (Duesseldorf, 1979).
9. Michael R. Marrus and Robert O. Paxton, *Vichy France and the Jews* (New York, 1981), p. 165. For more details, see Gilbert Badia, "Camps répressifs ou camps de concentration?" in *Les barbeles de l'exil*, ed. Gilbert Badia et. al, (Grenoble, 1979), pp. 289–332.
10. See my paper on "Non-Jewish Children in the Camps," chapter 15 of this volume.
11. Rudiger Vossen, *Zigeuner* (Frankfurt, Berlin, and Vienna, 1981), p. 85.

12. Ibid. Also see Jose Gotovitch, "Quelques données relatives à l'extermination des tsiganes de Belgioue," (Brussels, 1976), pp. 161–80.

13. Herbert Strauss, "Jewish Emigration from Germany: Nazi Policies and Jewish Responses, Part I," *Leo Baeck Institute Yearbook* 25 (1980): 354–55; Betty Garfinkels, *Belgique, terre d'accueil: Problème du réfugié, 1933–1940* (Brussels, 1974); and John Hope Simpson, *The Refugee Problem: Report of a Survey* (London, New York, and Toronto, 1939).

14. See Sybil Milton, "The Artist in Exile, Internment, and Hiding, 1933–1944," in *Art and Exile: Felix Nussbaum, 1904–1944,* ed. Emily Bilski (New York, 1985), p. 73.

15. See Timothy P. Maga, "Closing the Door: The French Government and Refugee Policy, 1933–1939," *French Historical Studies* 12 (1982): 424–42; and Helmut F. Pfanner, "Trapped in France: A Case Study of Five German Intellectuals," *Simon Weisenthal Center Annual* 3 (1986):107–20.

16. See Herbert E. Tutas, *Nationalsozialismus und Exil: Die Politik des Dritten Reiches gegenüber der deutschen politischen Emigration* (Munich and Vienna, 1975).

17. Barbara Vormeier, "Die Lage der Deutsche Emigranten in Frankreich während des Krieges 1939–1945," in *Deutsche Emigranten in Frankreich/Französische Emigranten in Deutschland, 1685–1945: Eine Ausstellung,* ed. Jacques Grandjonc and Klaus Voigt (Paris, 1984), pp. 155ff.

18. Arthur Koestler, *Scum of the Earth* (London, 1941), p. 67.

19. Hermann Langbein, *Die Starkeren,* rev. ed. (Cologne, 1982). See also Patrik von zur Muhlen, *Spanien war ihre Hoffnung* (Bonn, 1985), pp. 286ff.

20. Louis Stein, *Beyond Death and Exile: The Spanish Republicans in France, 1939–1955* (Cambridge, Mass., 1979). For the Spaniards in the French camps, see Rene Grando, Jacques Queralt, and Xavier Febres, *Vous avez la mémoire courte . . .* (Paris, 1981). For the Spaniards in Mauthausen, see Manuel Razola and Mariano Constante, *Triangle bleu: Les républicains espagnols à Mauthausen* (Paris, 1980), pp. 111–13, 137–39.

21. American Jewish Joint Distribution Committee Archives, New York, Files on North African internment camps, Heath Report on November 25, 1942. Other reports of a similar nature were also filed by the Unitarian Relief Committee on the liberation of North Africa. These records are located respectively in the Leo Baeck Institute Archives, New York, and at the National Archives, Washington, D.C.

22. Jorge Semprun, *The Long Voyage* (New York, 1964); idem, *What a Beautiful Sunday!* (London, 1984); Michel del Castillo, *Child of Our Time* (New York, 1959).

CHAPTER 8

The Polish Experience during
the Holocaust

Richard C. Lukas

One of the most common abuses of history is simply to deny that something
ever happened. This technique has a long and dishonorable past. It was
common, for example, for emperors of Rome to condemn individuals to
historical oblivion and public disgrace by issuing official decrees and removing all physical evidence of a person's existence.

Several years ago I received the first of several issues of what purported
to be a new scholarly journal, the *Journal of Historical Review*. Upon close
examination, this journal was nothing more than anti-Semitic propaganda,
a clumsy attempt to deny the fact that millions of Jews perished in the
Holocaust. The editors and contributors to this publication seem to want
history published in loose-leaf pages so they can extract what they dislike
and substitute their own mythical version of history.

We have been confronted for some time by a similar problem as it relates
to the Polish experience during World War II. A mythical version of the
Poles has dominated much of the popular and serious literature that has
appeared in this country, and it has obscured and even distorted the historical version of the Polish experience during the Holocaust.

Despite the plethora of literature that has been published in English on
the Holocaust, surprisingly little of it directly concerns the Polish aspects
of that tragedy. To be sure, most books on the Holocaust deal with the
tragedy of the Jews who, after all, were its primary victims. Yet when the
Poles are mentioned, their tragedy at the hands of the Germans is mini-
mized or ignored.

Without detracting from the particularity of the Jewish wartime experience, available historical evidence shows that Nazi racial cleansing policies
were first applied to the German people. When World War II broke out,

the Poles were the next major victims. Hitler told the Wehrmacht one week before the invasion of Poland to "kill without pity or mercy all men, women, and children of Polish descent or language. Only in this way can we obtain the living space we need."[1] To the Germans, the Poles were subhumans who occupied a land that was part of the living space coveted by the German race. As Hitler had made clear, "the destruction of Poland is our primary task. The aim is not the arrival at a certain line but the annihilation of living forces. Be merciless. Be brutal. It is necessary to proceed with maximum severity. The war is to be a war of annihilation."[2] Heinrich Himmler, the man who implemented the German war on the Poles, echoed Hitler when he said that "all Poles will disappear from the world. . . . It is essential that the great German people should consider it as its major task to destroy all Poles."[3]

During 1939–41, while the Jews were herded into ghettos and confined there, the Poles were the major victims of German racial policies. Round-ups, pacification operations, and deportations to labor and concentration camps were routine operations against the Poles. The first killing by poison gas at Auschwitz included 300 Poles and 700 Russian prisoners of war. So many Poles were sent to concentration camps that virtually every Polish family had someone close to them who had been tortured or murdered there.

When the Germans shifted their fanatical racial priorities to the Jews, this did not mean that they abandoned their objective of exterminating the Poles. While the Germans intended to eliminate the Jews before the end of the war, most Poles would work as helots until they too shared the fate of the Jews. German officials made this quite clear. Hans Frank, Hitler's viceroy in the General Government—the part of Poland not annexed by Germany but treated during the war as a gigantic labor camp—declared that Hitler had "made it quite plain that this adjacent country of the German Reich has a special mission to fulfill: to finish off the Poles at all cost."[4] In 1944, Frank reflected that when the war ended and Polish labor was not required, the remnants of the Polish people had a grim future. "As far as I am concerned," he said, "the Poles and the Ukrainians and their like may be chopped into small pieces. Let it be, what should be."[5] For his part, Justice Minister Otto Thierack dolefully told Martin Bormann that he was turning over criminal jurisdiction against Poles, other Slavs, and Jews to Himmler because "the administration of justice can make only small contribution to the extermination of these peoples."[6]

Even leading Wehrmacht commanders were convinced that Poles and other Slavs were to share the same fate as the Jews, though the methods would be varied. General Heusinger, who headed the operations section of the Army High Command, believed "the treatment of the civilian population and the methods of anti-partisan warfare in operational areas presented the highest political and military leaders with a welcome opportunity of carrying out their plans, namely the systematic extermination of Slavism and Jewry."[7] Jews who survived the war shared the conviction that the scale of Hitler's hatred and the logic of his wartime policies toward the Poles inevitably meant the Polish Christians would have been exterminated if the war had been prolonged.

Thus the conclusion is inescapable that had the war continued, the Poles would have been ultimately obliterated either by outright slaughter in gas chambers, as most Jews had perished, or by a continuation of the policies the Nazis had inaugurated in occupied Poland during the war— genocide by execution, forced labor, starvation, reduction of biological prop- agation, and Germanization. As it was, the Germans came perilously close to attaining their objective in Poland. During almost six years of war, Poland lost 6,028,000 of its citizens, or 22 percent of its total population, the highest ratio of losses to population of any country in Europe. Over 50 percent of these victims were Polish Christians, victims of prisons, death camps, raids, executions, epidemics, starvation, excessive work, and ill treatment.[8]

If the magnitude of the Polish Christian tragedy were fully understood, unrealistic and unhistorical judgments about Polish relationships with the Jews during the war years would not be made. Too often Poles have been depicted as a nation of anti-Semites who either passively observed the Jewish tragedy or actively assisted the Germans in the extermination of the Jewish people. Thus the Poles emerge as co-conspirators instead of co- victims of the Holocaust.

This mythical version of history reduces the Polish wartime experience to the simplistic and distorted proposition that the *raison d'être* of Poland and its people during the war was anti-Semitism — usually prefaced by such adjectives as pandemic, historic, or traditional — which is accepted and repeated with monotonous regularity without the need for documentation. This preoccupation with Polish anti-Semitism by writers of the Holocaust is, of course, nothing new. When General Wladyslaw Sikorski, head of the Polish government-in-exile, visited the United States early in the war, a delegation from the American Jewish Congress expressed more concern over a few cases of anti-Semitism in the Polish Army than it did with the mass slaughter of its kinsmen at the hands of the Nazis. Members of the Jewish delegation never asked the Polish premier about the tragedy of the Jews in German-occupied Poland.

The desperate need to correct this flawed understanding of the Polish wartime experience is illustrated by the observations of writer-critic John Gardner in a review of William Styron's *Sophie's Choice:*

Poland, occupied for centuries first by one cruel master, then another, pitifully devoted to both German culture and Nazi-style anti-Semitism . . . points to that Edenic world that master musicians, the Poles and Germans, thought in their insanity they might create here on earth by getting rid of a few million detectives.[9]

Little wonder that Leon Uris's leading character in *QB7,* Adam Kelno, became so credible in the minds of millions of readers.

Polish anti-Semitism has become so pervasive a stereotype that one of the reviewers of James Michener's novel *Poland* took issue with what he perceived as a lapse in the book by asking, "But what about Polish anti-Semitism?" Michener appreciated more than his reviewer that Polish-Jewish relations did not exclusively revolve around anti-Semitism or in the Jewish case, Polonophobia, and that Poles and Jews lived more in harmony and mutual tolerance for a longer time in their shared history than is understood today. Michener obviously understood what a British rabbi meant when he said, "As long as Poland was powerful, Polish Jewry enjoyed inner autonomy and freedom equaled by no other contemporary Jewry. Furthermore, it cannot be too often repeated that to Poland belongs the priority among European peoples in religious and cultural toleration."[10]

For most people, history is not something they find in scholarly monographs. For them history is found in paperbacks, magazines, television, and films. Unfortunately the journalistic history one finds in these sources is often distorted and exaggerated for dramatic effect. In one installment of Herman Wouk's "Winds of War," Heinrich Himmler informs Adolf Hitler that three thousand men and officers of the Einsatzgruppen are ready to kill the Jews in Russia. "They will be the organizers," says Himmler, "but the local population will execute the job and there are plenty of volunteers in Poland."[11] The same impression was conveyed in NBC's adaptation of Gerald Green's *Holocaust,* which focused almost exclusively on the Jewish tragedy and ignored the plight of the Poles who, when depicted, were seen in a negative light. Claude Lanzmann's film, *Shoah,* does much the same thing. The film dramatically speaks to the enormity of the tragedy of the Jewish nation and, in that sense, is a great movie. But it is a flawed achievement because it perpetuates a partial view of Polish-Jewish relations during a time of common suffering and tragedy.

One would hope for a more accurate picture of the Poles in the writings of historians. Unfortunately, many Holocaust writers rarely qualify their condemnations of the Poles. They fail to realize that good history does not consist of judging an entire nation by its extremists. It seems that we are confronted by double-standard scholarship; canons of objectivity are abandoned when the subject concerns the relationship of Poles to Jews during the war. If a more objective view prevailed in the historiography on the Holocaust, there would be less said about Polish anti-Semitism and more about the great tragedy that overwhelmed Polish Christians at the time of the German occupation of Poland.

I will focus on only a few specific areas in Holocaust writing that, in the interest of historical objectivity, need to undergo partial or substantial revision. One claim about Poles is that they were passive or indifferent to the Jewish tragedy because they were anti-Semitic. To be sure, anti-Semitism existed in wartime Poland. But philo-Semitism also existed, as abundantly documented by the fact that over 25 percent of the Yad Vashem heroes and heroines who helped save Jewish lives are Polish. Apparently it is still necessary to be reminded that over three million Christian Poles joined almost three million Polish Jews in death during the occupation of their country. All six million are a tremendous loss to Poland. Since the Poles were also victims, they were naturally preoccupied with their own survival. Yet, despite their own tragedy, they gave substantial aid to the Jews. Even though Poland was the only Nazi-occupied country where aiding a Jew was punishable by death, hundreds of thousands of Poles — some estimates go as high as one to three million — aided the Jews during the German occupation. Thus a significant minority of Poles were involved in helping Jews during the war years. Poles were no different from western Europeans where only minorities in much less threatening circumstances aided Jewish people. The Polish record of aid to the Jews was better than many other peoples in eastern Europe. As Walter Laqueur has observed, "a comparison with France would be by no means unfavorable for Poland."[12]

Another area that badly needs reevaluation is the depiction of the Polish Home Army *(Armia Krajowa)* as a military monolith, composed of reactionaries and anti-Semites who did not give adequate help to the Jews during the Warsaw Ghetto Uprising. The AK, as it was called, was a large organization comprising many diverse military groups with different political attitudes. There were some anti-Semites, but there were also large numbers of moderate and liberal elements in the organization who were also quite sympathetic toward the Jews. For example, Henry K. Wolinski, a Yad Vashem medal winner who headed the Jewish Bureau in the AK and was on excellent terms with most of the Jewish leaders of the Warsaw Ghetto, stated to me recently that officers of the High Command of the AK in Warsaw personally sheltered and looked after approximately three hundred Jews at the time of the Warsaw Uprising.[13]

The AK's military cohesion, however, is described by a former chief of the AK as "a conglomeration of commanders and detachments, whose attitudes to one another are frequently undisguisedly hostile, and who are held together by a badly frayed threat of formal discipline that may snap at the start of operations."[14]

Although a small part of the AK engaged in some sabotage and diversionary activities against the Germans, the primary purpose of the bulk of the organization was to prepare itself for an eventual uprising when German power crumbled and the Poles had a viable chance to assert their military and political authority over their own country. Understandably, leaders of the AK were reluctant to squander their resources on confrontations with the Germans, which invited savage reprisals. It was not possible for the AK to embark upon systematic operations to liberate large numbers of Poles and Jews from prisons and concentration camps. The AK, like the populace at large, was helpless in preventing German roundups of Poles for forced labor, reprisals, and executions. If the AK could do so little to prevent these tragedies from occurring to Polish Christians, it was even more at a loss to assist the Jews who, locked up in ghettos and concentration camps like animals, were difficult to contact, let alone liberate.

When some two thousand Jews of the Warsaw Ghetto rose up in the spring of 1943, General Stefan Grot-Rowecki worried that a general Polish uprising might be launched, a situation he deplored because such an event would have been suicidal. The Germans were a long way from collapse. Most Jewish leaders at the time did not and could not expect the Poles to commit national suicide for them. After all, when the Poles finally decided to launch their own insurrection in Warsaw more than a year later—a larger operation involving more people and resulting in greater casualties and destruction than the earlier Jewish rising—they found that even in the more favorable circumstances of that time, the Germans could not be overcome without substantial Allied assistance, which never came. As it was, the AK joined the Gwardia Ludowa in conducting over twenty-five combat, supply, and evacuation actions on behalf of the courageous Jews during the Jewish uprising.[15]

Finally, the AK is frequently charged with alleged attacks against Jewish partisans. Few of these attacks have ever been documented. Most of these attacks appear to have been initiated by members of the National Armed Forces of NSZ (the initials of the Polish words for the organization), who came mostly from the anti-Semitic right wing of the Polish political spectrum. The National Armed Forces were not part of the AK; they conducted their own operations, often killing Jews, Communists, and democratic elements of the AK. There is a great deal of confusion in the sources on this critical point: the AK is often mistakenly charged with crimes against Jews when, in fact the NSZ or some other group was responsible.

In conclusion, I hope that this book broadens our perspective and encourages Holocaust scholars to explore and analyze critically but fairly many of the controversial questions that beg for objective study. By confronting the past in this way, we shall in Elie Wiesel's words, "rescue from forgetfulness the suffering of the non-Jewish victims from the Nazis so that in one voice we can condemn inhumanity."[16]

NOTES

1. Janusz Gumkowski and Kazimierz Leszczynski, *Poland Under Nazi Occupation* (Warsaw, 1961), p. 59.
2. Eugeniusz Duraczynski, *Wojna i Okupacja: Wrzesien 1939–Kwiecien 1943* (Warsaw, 1974), p. 17.
3. Karol Pospieszalski, *Polska pod Niemieckim Prawem* (Poznan, 1946), p. 189.
4. Central Commission for Investigation of German Crimes in Poland, *German Crimes in Poland,* 2 vols. (New York, 1982), 2:18.
5. Ibid., p. 21.
6. Raul Hilberg, *The Destruction of European Jews* (Chicago, 1961), p. 644.
7. U.S. Office of United States Chief of Counsel for Prosecution of Axis Criminality, *Nazi Conspiracy and Aggression,* 10 vols. (Washington, D.C., 1946), 6:435.
8. Roman Nurowski, *1939–1945: War Losses in Poland* (Poznan: 1960), pp. 44ff. There is no agreement concerning the exact number of Polish Christians who

perished at the hands of the Nazis. Informed estimates place the loss in the range of 2.8 to 3.1 million people.

9. John Gardner, review of *Sophie's Choice* by William Styron, *New York Times Book Review*, May 27, 1979, 16–17.

10. Quoted in statement by Banaczyk at Meeting of the Council for Rescue of the Jews in Poland, May 25, 1944, in C11/7/3c/8, in Records of Board of Deputies of British Jews, London.

11. Television production, "Winds of War."

12. Walter Laqueur, *The Terrible Secret: Suppression of the Truth about Hitler's Final Solution* (Boston, 1980), pp. 106–7.

13. Richard C. Lukas, *Out of the Inferno: Poles Remember the Holocaust* (Lexington, Ky., 1989), p. 179.

14. Quoted in Reuben Ainsztein, *Jewish Resistance in Nazi-Occupied Eastern Europe* (New York, 1974), p. 402

15. Tadeusz Bednarczyk, "35 Rocznica Powstania w Getcie Warszawskim," *Zycie Literackie*, April 16, 1978, p. 9.

16. Letter, Elie Wiesel to author, October 6, 1986.

CHAPTER 9

The Victimization of
the Poles

Israel Gutman

The relationship between the independent Polish republic and Nazi Germany prior to the Second World War followed a complex course. The nonaggression pact between Poland and the Third Reich, signed on January 26, 1934, resulted mainly from Poland's complicated political position, which has been at the root of Polish vulnerability from the late eighteenth century until the present.

The Nazis and the Poles differed essentially in judgment and expectation regarding the agreement. While Hitler wanted only a short-term step, the Poles believed that the shift in policy promised stability and created a basis for a new political orientation and reconciliation. The failure to understand the meaning of the Nazi *weltanschauung* and the total Nazi program led the Polish political leadership to make many catastrophic mistakes between 1934 and 1939.

The intensification of Polish anti-Semitism in the late thirties was to a certain extent also a result of the strengthened German-Polish relations, as well as of the example set by German anti-Jewish policy and persecution. After Munich and the dismemberment of Czechoslovakia, in which Poland took an active role against the Czechoslovakian republic, the brutal German threat was directed against Poland. The Poles did not hesitate to respond despite the risk of war. Their strong response marked a turning point in the prevailing policy of appeasement and submission toward Nazi expansionist designs. Once the war began, unfortunately, the Polish Army was defeated in a few weeks. After a mere twenty years of independence, Poland was again divided.

Nazi attitudes and policies toward the occupied countries were guided by two factors: race and utility. However, the ideological principle of a racial hierarchy was paramount. Scandinavians, for instance, were said to have a close blood relationship to the Germans; they were therefore entitled to a high status in the hierarchy of the Nazi New Order. The Slavs were considered far down the racial scale.

The second factor in the Nazi attitude toward the occupied countries was their political and military status and their usefulness to the Nazi's strategic plans. Unfortunately, the Poles did not score well on either account. They were marked as racially inferior by the Nazis, and Poland was neither politically nor strategically useful to them. Two other factors doomed the Poles. Poland had been the traditional target of German political expansion, and Hitler personally disliked the Poles. He could not forgive them for refusing to submit to his conditions and for imposing a great war upon him three or four years ahead of his original plans.

Even within the small ethnic Polish conclave established by the Germans on Polish soil, the so-called General Government, the Poles were denied national autonomy and individual rights as citizens; they were given no self-rule in internal affairs. In Poland and certain areas of the Soviet Union, the Germans established a regime of absolute occupation.

During the war the general outline of the German policy toward the Polish people was as follows: (1) to absorb a small part of the superior Polish strata into the German *Volksgemeinschaft;* (2) to prevent the intelligentsia from playing a major role in national life even if this required that members of this group be killed; and (3) to turn the masses of the Poles, mainly the peasantry, into a reservoir of cheap or slave labor. Actually, Poland became a kind of a German colony. As Dr. Hans Frank, the head of the General Government, stated, all governmental authority, except for the very lowest levels, was transferred from Polish to German officials.[1]

In March 1941, just five months after taking his position, Frank reported for the first time that he had given audience to a native Pole, Alfred Wysocki, but even this gesture was an exceptional case. It occurred only because the Führer personally recommended him as the one and only trustworthy Pole.[2]

The regime planned and daily implemented economic exploitation of both private and state property. The domestic market was restricted to providing basic tools for the native inhabitants. Official daily food rations in Warsaw in 1941 were 2,613 calories for a German, 699 calories for a Pole, and 184 calories for a Jew.[3]

More than two million Poles were sent to Germany as forced laborers.

Only elementary schools were allowed to remain open. All higher education was forbidden. Polish culture was systematically destroyed and terror was directed against the intelligentsia, the teachers, and clergy.

The Nazis' intention was to stifle national life and spiritual development. Hundreds of thousands of Poles were uprooted and expelled from their homes. These harsh, destructive measures were challenged by a large and well-organized Polish underground movement. The Poles showed impressive solidarity and resistance. The Polish resistance organization was often referred to as an underground state.[4]

During the last stage of the war, Frank made attempts to moderate the regime and to bring the Poles into the Polish-German camp. The attempt failed because no high-level German leaders were ready to reconcile Polish and German needs and no authoritative Polish personalities were ready to negotiate any form of alliance with Nazi Germany. The Polish people were victims of Nazi aggression, terror, and cruelty, which condemned some groups in Poland to partial physical destruction.

The plight of Poland must not be forgotten. Yet, the suffering and the plight of the Poles—however grievous—are not identical with the Holocaust. Both Poles and Jews suffered, but in unequal measures; the two groups were *unequal victims*. The difference is basic. As a group the Jews were sentenced to death, whereas Poles had the chance, the possibility, and the *right* to remain alive.

According to official Polish records, the total number of people on Polish soil declined by six million during the war and occupation. This figure includes Poles, Jews, and smaller minorities. Of the six million civilians, three million were Jews. This sad figure demonstrates that non-Jewish losses in Poland were about 10 percent of their population, while the Jewish losses amounted to 90 percent of the Jewish population in Poland. This is more than just a quantitative difference. The Polish underground itself recognized the profound distinction between the fate of the Poles and that of the Jews, and stated so in numerous reports and publications.

Indeed many Poles were gripped by the fear that after the Final Solution of the Jewish question, they would be the next in line. More precisely, the supreme commander of military Polish forces (AK) in the underground, Stefan Rowecki (grot), issued an order on November 9, 1942:

As to the operation of annihilating the Jews, [carried out] by the occupier, there are signs of disquiet amongst the Polish public, lest after this operation is completed, the Germans will begin the liquidation of the Poles, in exactly the same manner.

I order self-control and action to calm the public. However, if the Germans do indeed, make any attempt of this sort, they will meet with active resistance on our part, without consideration for the fact that the time for our uprising has not yet come. The units under my command will enter armed battle to defend the life of our people. In this battle we will move over from defense to offense by cutting all the enemy channel transports to the eastern front . . . .[5]

From this order we are able to learn something about the attitude of the Polish underground toward the Jewish victims, and about the difference between Jewish and Polish fate. The Polish underground did not enter into a comprehensive battle against the occupier until the last stage of the war. Political considerations propelled the underground into this battle. When in 1943 a few transports of deportees from the Zamosc area came to Auschwitz, the SS was prevented from liquidating the children, the elderly, and the ill people; they received explicit instructions not to treat the Poles the same way the Jews were treated.

Even Dr. Wetzel, the cocreator of the general plan for the long-range solution of the Slavic nation, stated in April 1942, "It must be quite obvious that the Polish question cannot be solved by liquidation depots like the Jews."[6]

Several major elements show why and how the Poles fared differently from the Jews. First, Jews were not rivals of the Germans. No real conflict existed between the two parties. The source of hatred and the goal of total destruction stemmed from the Nazis' image of the Jews as a racial, biological, and political threat to German civilization. Surely this sort of perverted ideological view could not appear without deep roots and a long history of anti-Semitism in Europe. Widely shared and deeply held anti-Semitic beliefs among the native population contributed to the adoption of Nazi racialism and anti-Jewish actions in Germany and some occupied countries.

Second, there is the scope and breadth of the destruction. Whole families were killed and entire Jewish communities were wiped out. Yet this was only one aspect of the totality. Perhaps more significant was the scope of the attack upon the Jews, who were targeted everywhere, even in unoccupied Europe. The Nazis did not hunt down Poles or Polish intelligentsia in France, Belgium, or Hungary.

Third, the so-called Final Solution of the Jewish question became a major world goal. A special bureaucratic network was created to identify and search for Jews, to transport them from all parts of Europe to the death camps, which were established for the purpose of killing Jews.

The German scholar Eberhart Yatkin speaks about two definite goals of Hitler: conquest and the elimination of Jews. The English historian H. Trevor-Roper stated:

Hitler's anti-Semitism was much more than an opportunistic device. It was a deep-rooted conviction and integral part of what he called "the *granite-firm* foundation" of his ideology. . . . He declared again and again that the Jews should be exterminated. Even victory in the war was deemed less essential than the completion of this macabre operation to which essential resources, even in 1944, were still being diverted from the German armies now fighting desperate battles for the defence of the Reich.[7]

In conclusion, I would like to warn against confusing the Holocaust with other painful events, even all genocidal policies, because this constitutes reshaping a historical phenomenon by hindsight. Any such attempt to change the precise meaning of the Holocaust is either a deliberate distortion or is based on misinformation. Furthermore, we ought not distort our view of the period and consequently abandon the basic principles of historical evaluation.

NOTES

1. *Das Diensttagebuch des deutschen generalgouverneurs in Polenu 1939–1945* (Stuttgart, 1975), p. 128.
2. Ibid., p. 130.
3. Czestaw Manojczyk, *Polityka III Rzeszy w okupowaney Polsce,* vol. 2 (Warsaw, 1970), p. 71.
4. See for example Stefan Korboniski, *The Polish Underground State: A Guide to the Undergroup 1939–1945* (New York, 1978).
5. Jreneusz Caban and Zygmunt Mankowski, *Zwiazek Walui Zbrojnej w okrsgu lubelskim 1939–1944,* vol. 2 (Warsaw, 1971), p. 60.
6. Biuletyn Gtonsnej Kornisji, *Bandania Zbrorlm Niemieckich w Polsce* vol. 5 (Warsaw, 1949), p. 223.
7. Hugh Trevor-Roper, "The Will to Exterminate," in *Times Literary Supplement,* January 28, 1983.

CHAPTER 10

Slavs and Jews: Consistent and Inconsistent Perspectives on the Holocaust

Bohdan Vitvitsky

A number of years ago, after the publication of my brief monograph on the Slavic and Gypsy victims of the Nazi Holocaust,[1] I delivered a lecture on the subject of the Nazi Holocaust and its impact upon intergroup relations before various university, professional, and community audiences in the United States and Canada. During these lectures I expressed concern that the Nazi Holocaust had managed to bequeath to the future what I then described as an acrid cloud composed in part of memories, and in part of myths and misunderstandings, that had, ironically and tragically, come to poison relations between two of the categories of peoples whom, in addition to the Gypsies, the Nazi Holocaust had been intended to damage the most, namely the Jews and the Slavs.[2]

What began for me as a source of some concern has in the intervening years escalated into a full-fledged anxiety that the portrait of the Nazi Holocaust, which has evolved into a kind of orthodoxy, has not only contributed to an ongoing poisoning of intergroup relations, but also constitutes —in regard to the portrayal of the status of the Slavs during the Nazi Holocaust—a fundamental distortion of the historical record.

Before I focus on the inconsistencies in perspectives on the Nazi Holocaust between Slavs and Jews, I think it valuable to focus on a very important consistency in perspectives. Lucy Dawidowicz and others have in the past criticized various official histories of the Nazi era that have been published in Communist Eastern Europe and that distort or minimize what Dawidowicz had referred to as Hitler's "war against the Jews." That distortion, brought about chiefly by political considerations, is an aberration pertaining to the general perception among Slavs, or at least of those living in the West, of what happened to the Jews during the Holocaust.

In the years since the publication of my monograph, I have come in contact with many hundreds of people who have engaged me in conversation about the Nazi Holocaust. Many of these have been Slavs who themselves witnessed the events of the Holocaust, including some who witnessed it from inside concentration camps. A striking aspect emerging from these conversations has been the virtually unanimous agreement regarding the basic fact about the Holocaust, namely that only the Jews were slated for total extinction and that six million Jews had in fact been gassed, starved, machine-gunned, or burned to death.

This unanimity has caught my attention for two reasons. First, concerning who did what to whom—whether within their respective national groups or between the national groups—I have found that there is very little else about which Slavs who survived the war agree. Second, they, who are among the best informed, are the most steadfast adherents to the accurate version of events that constituted the mass victimization of the Jews. In my experience the Slavs, second alone to the Jews, have expressed the greatest astonishment and indignation that so-called historical revisionists now deny that the Nazis intentionally murdered six million Jews. The source of this response is unrelated to whatever sentiments these Slavs may have toward Jews and is simply based on their collective experience of the Nazi Holocaust. They, with their own eyes, saw the Jews branded and deported or killed, and for them anyone who now denies any of that is a madman or a liar. Whatever their other differences in perspective, the Slavs and Jews agree wholeheartedly about the scope and character of the terrible suffering endured by the Jews during the Holocaust. And in an era when some are trying to deny the extraordinary victimization of the Jews, and many others prefer to remain in blissful ignorance of it, perhaps that might be a significant point of commonality.

Recently a letter to the editor appeared in a New York daily that said that "Hitler and the Ukrainians and the Poles killed six million Jews." On the one hand, the allegation that the Holocaust was a project of Hitler, the Ukrainians, and the Poles is nothing short of extraordinary. On the other hand, however, the statement is also notable because it is probably as candid and succinct an expression of the views of a significant segment of the Jewish community as one is likely to find. Claims, suggestions, and inferences with a similar content abound. In remarks responding to my book that were printed on its back cover, Dr. Michael Berenbaum made the equally remarkable claim that the Slavs shared the Nazis' "most central goal—the extermination of the Jewish people."[3] In a November 1981 article in the *New Yorker*, Lawrence Weschler reported being asked by a Jewish acquaintance whether it could have been a coincidence that the Nazis had located so many of the major concentration camps in Poland. He was told that the Poles were allegedly "only too pleased to accept things that even the Germans wouldn't stand for." The Polonophobic suggestion that the Poles had something to do with the placement of Auschwitz and the other camps on Polish soil is one that I have encountered on numerous occasions. And even Elie Wiesel, on a more philosophical plane, has suggested that, in regard to their collective behavior during the Holocaust, the Poles and Ukrainians showed themselves to be worse human beings, less humane, less heroic, and less concerned with ethical imperatives than others in Europe.

Statements of the type referred to above raise the following issues of overriding importance regarding the Nazi Holocaust, Were the Slavs principally victims or victimizers? And it is here that the perspectives of Slavs and Jews differ most radically. Although what follows is of necessity an oversimplification, it is probably fair to say that a significant segment of the Jewish community believes that during the Nazi Holocaust every second Ukrainian or Pole was either a killer or a betrayer of Jews. On the other hand, many Ukrainians seem to think or want to think that no Ukrainians ever harmed Jews and that in fact many tried to shelter or save Jews. The frequently encountered view among the Poles about their posture toward the Jews seems closely to resemble that which Ukrainians ascribe to themselves.

Quite frankly, I do not have much confidence in either of these perspectives. But before raising the factual issue of real and alleged collaboration, I shall address a methodological issue. The determining factor in the inquiry about whether Slavs were principally victims or victimizers is *not* the character of the relationship between Slavs and the Jews but rather the character of the relationship between the Germans and the Slavs. And, what was the character of this relationship? I will focus briefly on the Ukrainians.

According to the Nazi racial taxonomy of peoples, Ukrainians as Slavs were considered *Untermenschen*, or subhumans. The Ukrainian elite was to be exterminated and the remainder of the population either dispersed into

Asia or enslaved as part of the German policy of *Drang nach Osten,* or "Drive to the East," which was the means by which the Nazis were planning to attain appropriate Lebensraum or living space for the Aryan superman.

As a result of these racist Nazi fantasies, millions of Ukrainian civilians were deliberately burned, shot, starved, and worked to death. Millions of others were pirated off for slave labor in Germany, and untold numbers were frozen or starved to death as Soviet POWs, whom the Nazis treated as common criminals. And these figures do not even touch upon the military casualties sustained, since such figures are of course outside the scope of any discussions of the Nazi Holocaust.

Tens of thousands of Ukrainians perished at places later made famous because of the earlier executions of Jews there, such as Babi Yar in Kiev, as well as at various places that have never escaped obscurity. Some perished at the Nazi concentration camps in Germany or Poland. Two brothers of the Ukrainian nationalist leader Stepan Bandera died in Auschwitz; the famous Ukrainian poet Oleh Olzhych was tortured and killed at Sachsenhausen.

The dominant feature of the Germans' relationship with the Ukrainians and other Slavs was racism. Erich Koch, the brutal Nazi administrator of a large portion of occupied Ukraine, referred to Ukrainians as Negroes and held the position that they stood "far below us and should be grateful to God that we allow them to stay alive."[4] During the occupation, the Kiev ballet theatre displayed a sign that announced "No Ukrainians or dogs admitted." Ukrainians were also restricted to the rear sections of tramcars in Kiev. Nazi racism was so pervasive that even in some of the concentration camps (whose populations included a mosaic of victims), when it came to standing in line for something that was being distributed, Ukrainians as Slavs had to line up behind everyone else—except of course the Gypsies and the Jews.

To summarize, the Slavs, along with of course the Jews and Gypsies, were victims of the Nazis' intense racist campaign to remake Europe, and particularly eastern Europe. Although no people suffered during the Nazi Holocaust as did the Jews, and although only the Jews were slated for total extermination, given the Nazis' ideology and their murderous and ruinous practices toward the Slavs, there can to no doubt that the Slavs too were among the major victims of the Nazi Holocaust.

Books about the Nazi Holocaust by such leading authors as Raul Hilberg, Lucy Dawidowicz, and Martin Gilbert are not about the Nazi Holocaust as a whole but more specifically and explicitly about its most important story, namely, the Nazi campaign to annihilate the Jews. It is difficult to find fault with this approach since scholars are obviously free to mark off the scope of their historical analyses however they choose, and each of the aforementioned authors explicitly announces in the title or subtitle of his or her major work that the subject is the Nazi campaign to annihilate the Jews.

Might there not be some connection between such highly regarded histories of the Nazis' murderous campaign against the Jews and the reversal of the record that occurs when Slavs are characterized as principally victimizers rather than victims? I believe that one possible source of the problem may be that in the histories that are exclusively focused on the victimization of the Jews, the only actors that appear on the stage are of course the Jews and those Gentiles whose activities somehow had a bearing upon the plight of the Jews. Thus, only those Slavs who collaborated with the Nazis in victimizing the Jews fall within the scope of such books.

Ukrainians or Poles who had no relationship to the victimization of the Jews and who themselves happened to be victims of the Nazis are irrelevant to the Jewish story and are therefore invisible on the pages of such books. As a result, the Ukrainians or Poles who usually appear in the standard treatments of the Nazi Holocaust are only those who may have collaborated. The historical record is thus distorted and the Slavs are represented principally as victimizers rather than as victims.

What about the issue of Slavic collaboration? Once again, I will restrict my remarks to the Ukrainians. A claim frequently heard in the Ukrainian community, to the effect that no Ukrainians brutalized any Jews but that instead Ukrainians tried to shelter Jews, is naive, disingenuous, or both.

The only statistical estimate of collaboration I have encountered, one based on the records of Israel's War Crimes Investigations Office, suggests that 11,000 Ukrainians were involved in some type of anti-Jewish measures, such as massacres or deportations.[5] Some Ukrainians have denounced this figure as being wildly inflated.[6] For the purposes of this paper, however, I am willing to accept it as accurate.

What is important is that we construe this estimate within the proper context. Given the dramatic decrease in the Ukraine's population between the beginning and the end of the German occupation, it is very difficult to estimate the population's size at any given point. For our purposes, however, let us postulate a figure that some believe to be a reasonable wartime estimate, namely 36 million.[7] In relation, then, to a total population of 36 million, 3 million Ukrainian Gentiles perished at the hands of the Nazis, another 2.4 million were pirated off for slave labor in Germany, additional hundreds of thousands were murdered as Soviet POWs, and last, 11,000 collaborated.[8] As should be patently obvious, the number of Ukrainians who collaborated with the Nazis is dwarfed by the number of Ukrainians who were victimized by the Nazis. The number of collaborators simply disappears in significance when compared with the total population. Once again we see that the portrayal of Slavs as principally victimizers rather than as victims constitutes a profound distortion of the historical record.

The fact that Slavs were principally victims rather than victimizers does not, however, resolve the question of whether or not the response to the Nazis' genocidal campaign against the Jews was more reprehensible in the Ukraine or Poland than it was in other countries in Europe. Was the behavior of the Ukrainians or the Poles truly less humane, less heroic, less concerned with ethical imperatives, as suggested by Professor Wiesel? Unfortunately, very little reliable evidence exists that could authoritatively resolve this question.

Numerous factors, however, must be taken into account in any serious attempt to analyze this issue. First, it is crucial to bear in mind that the conditions under which the Ukrainians and Poles lived during the Nazi Holocaust were radically different from those experienced by the Danes, Belgians, or French. The Ukrainians and Poles were being brutalized on a massive scale. This naturally had a major impact on these peoples' interest in or ability to be concerned about someone else's suffering.

Second, the size of and relationship to the Gentile populations of the Jewish communities in Poland and the Ukraine were very different from those in any of the western European countries. Since most of the western European countries had much earlier expelled most Jews, their Jewish populations were a fraction of the size of the Jewish populations in Poland or the Ukraine. Concomitantly, due in part to their own volition and in part to historical accident, the Jewish communities in the West were much more integrated into the fabric of their respective societies. To some extent this explains why a few of the western European peoples may have found both the inclination and the opportunity to shelter their comparatively small communities of Jews. This factor may reveal that logistics probably had more to do with the location of the death camps in Poland than anything else. It seems fairly obvious that, from the German perspective, transporting several hundred thousand Jews from western Europe to Poland made much more sense than trying to transport 3 million Polish Jews to France.

Third, there is what might be called the problem of proportions. The Ukrainian Catholic Metropolitan Sheptytsky needed to employ a network of some 550 Ukrainian monks and nuns to provide shelter during the German occupation for 150 to 200 Jewish children. On an infinitely more modest scale, my father had to go through a fair amount of terrifyingly bureaucratic rigmarole to help shelter a single Jewish friend by helping to establish that his friend was a Christian. On the other hand, one Ukrainian collaborator could single-handedly, in an hour or a day, undo that which some good samaritans had so laboriously achieved, and could probably do so with a fraction of the effort exerted by the good samaritans. A single Ukrainian or Polish collaborator could easily brutalize a hundred Jews in a couple of hours while it might require an extended commitment by several Ukrainians or Poles to shelter a single Jew. Surely this may explain at least some of the psychology behind the belief by some in the Jewish community that every second Slav was a collaborator. But was the above-described state of affairs prevailing in eastern Europe during the Holocaust a reflection of the Slavs' moral inferiority, or simply of the demonic conditions created by the Nazi regime?

At least one other issue needs to be raised, namely that of misidentification. During the war in Poland and to some extent since the war, some of the official Polish and Soviet publications commonly refer to anyone originating from the Soviet Union and accused of some wrongdoing during the war as a "Ukrainian," regardless of whether that person was in fact a Ukrainian or a Russian or a Byelorussian or something else entirely. Thus, for example, the Russian forces of the Russian collaborator General Vlasov have frequently been referred to in Polish and Soviet accounts as "the Ukrainians."[9] This is, in some sense, similar to the anti-Semitic impulse to allege that Lenin and most of the other leading Bolsheviks were all Jewish. One would hope that any serious attempt to analyze the question of Slavic collaboration would eliminate all such misidentifications.

To conclude, there is no incompatibility between telling the full story of the genocidal—and incomparable—victimization of the Jews and giving an honest accounting of the roles of the various collaborators and providing an accurate portrayal of the victimization of various collaborators. To portray the former, one must understand the latter.

NOTES

1. Bohdan Wytwycky (Vitvitsky), *The Other Holocaust: The Many Circles of Hell* (Washington, D.C., 1980).

2. For the purposes of this paper, I am using the term *Slavs* to refer to Poles, Ukrainians, and Byelorussians, the three peoples among the Slavs who suffered the longest, most extensive, and most destructive German occupations.

3. Dr. Berenbaum made this statement in the following context:

> Bohdan Wytwycky has written a most interesting and in many senses pioneering study of the fate of the many victims of Nazi oppression. Despite some philosophical and methodological reservations, one cannot fail to be impressed by the seriousness of its tone, the power of its central image of the many circles of hell, and the importance of his undertaking. Wytwycky has shared with the general reader in the English-speaking world, additional dimensions of Nazi oppression and its impact upon the many cultures and the many peoples of Eastern Europe. He has also raised anew in a serious and somber way the question of the universality of the Holocaust and the centrality of the Jewish experience under nazism. I would have liked to have seen his keen intellect probe the critical and unavoidable question of the collaboration with the Nazis of the other victims of their oppression in murdering Jews, sharing with their enemy the most central goal— the extermination of the Jewish people. But this must await some future work by Wytwycky and others. With *The Other Holocaust*, Wytwycky has begun a critically important task.
>
> —Wytwycky, *The Other Holocaust*, back cover

4. Alexander Dallin, *German Rule in Russia, 1941–1945* (London, 1957), p. 149.

5. Stefan T. Possony, "Anti-Semitism in the Russian Area," *Plural Societies* (Winter 1974), pp. 91–92.

6. Such views have been conveyed to me orally.

7. Possony, "Anti-Semitism," pp. 91–92.

8. Sources for these estimates of civilian victims, slave labor deportations, and POW victims are gathered in Wytwycky, *The Other Holocaust*, p. 91; the estimates of collaborators is in Possony, "Anti-Semitism," pp. 91–92.

9. See, e.g., Central Commission for Investigation of German Crimes in Poland, *German Crimes in Poland*, 2 vols. (Warsaw, 1946–47).

CHAPTER 11

The Holocaust and
the Ukrainian Victims

Aharon Weiss

The expansion policy of Nazi Germany based on ideological, geopolitical, and economic reasons created many victims in the enslaved nations. Some of them were defined as "inferior nations"; the Slavs, including the Ukrainians, belonged to this category.[1]

As a result of the war and during the German occupation the Ukrainians suffered heavy losses: tens of thousands were killed in the prisoner-of-war camps, many were sent to forced labor, and entire villages were burned down because of the peasants' refusal to supply a quota of agricultural products.[2]

Specific groups of Ukrainians became the object of persecution, and their lives were endangered because they did not go along with the anti-Jewish policy of the Germans and their collaborators. I am referring not to an organized group, but only to individuals who disagreed with the collective death sentence imposed upon the Jews and tried to help rescue them. To define those Ukrainians, I use the term *victims* because they had to stand opposite the enormous exterminating apparatus during a time when the traditional anti-Semitism supplemented by elements of racial theories reached its climax.

However, those Ukrainians had to stand not only against the Germans, but also against the Ukrainian collaborators who identified themselves with the Nazi policy and participated in carrying out crimes against the Jews.

The research of the behavior of these Ukrainian victims should focus on the following questions: (1) What was their motivation when helping Jews? Was it for humanitarian considerations, or for materialistic, religious, or political reasons? and (2) What was the attitude of the Ukrainian leadership and the Church to the Jewish Holocaust, and to those Ukrainians who attempted to assist the Jews? I will try to refer, even if partially, to these questions; the issues will be illustrated mostly by the events that occurred in western Ukraine.

The approach of the Ukrainian leadership to the Jewish question can be seen in the resolution adopted in April 1941 by the Second General Congress of the Organization of Ukrainian Nationalists–Bandera faction. In that resolution the Jews were defined as "the most faithful support of the ruling Bolshevik regime and the vanguard of the Muscovite imperialism in the Ukraine."[3] In those decisive days when the preparations for the Final Solution reached their climax, this approach had a tragic influence on the attitude of the Ukrainian population and on the local leaders. Immediately after the Germans invaded Soviet territories, they started to settle accounts with the Jews, who were presented by the Ukrainian nationalists as the sole and only supporters of the Soviet regime.

Actually anti-Jewish riots broke out right after the withdrawal of the Soviets in the summer of 1941. A wave of pogroms spread throughout the area, resulting in about 24,000 Jews killed in fifty-eight cities and towns and in many villages.[4] The main reasons behind the pogroms and the further consistent hostile measures against the Jews were rooted in two sources: (1) the traditional anti-Semitism among various layers of the Ukrainian population, and (2) the fostering of some elements of the Nazi ideology by the Ukrainian nationalists. Kost Pankyvsky, the chairman of the Ukrainian regional committee in Lviv, defines the OUN as "people who for many years were connected with the Fascist and Nazi ideologies, preached totalitarian ideas and acted to realize them.[5] J. Armstrong writes: "The theory and teachings of the Ukrainian nationalists were close to Fascism, and in some respects, such as the insistence on 'racial purity' even went beyond the original Fascist doctrine."[6]

In some places the leaders of the Ukrainian communities either initiated or joined the riots. These took place in Stanyslaviv, Ternopil, and other localities.[7] In Skalat, for instance, a local Ukrainian priest participated in a delegation that demanded severe restrictions be imposed on the Jews.[8] In Kosiv, Ukrainian youth were mobilized to dig mass graves for Jews before their execution.[9] And these are only a few examples.

The Ukrainian militia was an important factor in those cruel events. Some Ukrainian sources have ignored these facts, claiming that only marginal groups were involved in the atrocities.

The anti-Jewish riots, however, took on a mass character. A remarkable part of the Ukrainian population welcomed the German army as liberators and cooperated with German authorities. The public atmosphere favored the actions against the Jews. It is therefore important to present some cases of help and rescue by Ukrainians, which had occurred as early as the summer of 1941. In Tovste and its surroundings, about 200 Jews were killed in a pogrom, but many were saved due to the intervention of a Ukrainian priest, Izvolski.[10] In Lapatyn and Melnytsia Ukrainian priests also prevented pogroms.[11] In Yaniv, near Lviv, a pogrom was avoided due to the actions of some members of the Ukrainian intelligentsia.[12] In Korostkiv, the Ukrainian mayor tried to prevent a pogrom, but ultimately the extremists prevailed.[13] In Wolhynia, Ukrainian Baptists and Sabbatarians consistently helped rescue Jews.[14] These cases prove that tension existed between the anti-Semitic forces and those individuals who opposed the inhuman deeds, thus becoming victims of heavy pressure.

Even after the cooling off of relations with the Germans in July 1941, the Ukrainian leadership still persisted in looking upon the Jews as the main supporters of the Soviet regime. This strategic point of view prevented them from opposing the German policy of the Final Solution. Let me quote a slogan referring to Bandera's people after animosity was aroused toward the Germans: "Long live a greater independent Ukraine without Jews, Poles, and Germans; Poles behind the river San, Germans to Berlin, and Jews to the gallows."[15]

Alas Sanchuk initialed an editorial in the newspaper *Volhynia* dated September 1, 1941, which said, "The Jewish problem is on the way to solution and will be solved within the framework of the general reorganization of the New Europe."[16] This attitude of the Ukrainian official circles and of the Ukrainians in the underground shaped public opinion and legitimized the anti-Jewish activity of the general population.

We can generalize three different patterns of behavior exhibited by the Ukrainian population. Some persecuted Jews, handing them over to the Germans and actively participating in murder. Others were indifferent to the fate of their Jewish neighbors. Still others assisted Jews; I have termed these people the *victims*. Shmuel Spector, in his research on Volhynia mentions that

the German Civil and Police establishments in Volhynia were relatively small. Those German forces could not cover all the towns and communities. Scarce forces and convenient topographic conditions could facilitate hiding, but the hostility of the Ukrainian national underground and the Ukrainian population prevented it. The

Ukrainians helped to capture the remaining Jews in fields and forests. Those Jews were either killed directly by the Ukrainians or handed over the Germans. . . .[17]

According to Spector, the same evaluation refers to some UPA (Ukrainian insurgent army) units that persecuted and murdered the last of the Jews in the forests of western Ukraine. Even Pankivsky noted that very few of the Jews who hid in the forest survived.[18] He did not indicate who caused the death of those Jews.

As we have seen, the attitude of the Ukrainian clergy toward the Jews during the Holocaust was not uniform. In this context it will be worthwhile to assess the behavior of Metropolitan A. Sheptytsky. His ties with the Jews went back many years and were based on mutual understanding and respect. In July 1941, when a pogrom against the Jews was carried out by the Ukrainians in Lviv, Rabbi Levin appealed to Sheptytsky to help stop the slaughter of the Jews. Sheptytsky promised to restrain his compatriots from committing acts of robbery and murder. (Rabbi Levin was killed in this pogrom.)[19] But at the same time Sheptytsky greeted the German army that delivered the Ukrainians from the Soviet enemy.[20] He viewed the Germans as "liberators" even while he expressed reservations about the crimes they committed against the Jews. Thus, Sheptytsky experienced a contradiction between his political orientation and his fundamentally humanitarian feelings. This tragic contradiction characterized his position in the following months. In fact, in February 1942 Sheptytsky sent a letter to Himmler demanding that he put an end to the activities of the Ukrainian police in all the outrages against the Jews.[21] But in the same month Sheptytsky, together with three other Ukrainian leaders, signed a declaration to Hitler expressing the hope that the Ukrainian state would find its place within the frame of the New Order in Europe.[22] Sheptytsky should have known that a New Order in Europe meant a Europe without Jews. In November 1942 Sheptytsky published a pastoral letter, "Thou shalt not kill."[23] It may well be that the letter also refers to the Jewish issue. The hiding and rescue of about 150 Jews by Metropolitan Sheptytsky with the assistance of his relatives and monks was the climax of his humanitarian deeds.[24]

Yet other aspects of Sheptytsky's behavior indicate that he did not change his political orientation to Germany. According to Armstrong, Sheptytsky favored the creation of the SS Galicia Division.[25] The fact that the Waffen-SS was one of the main pillars of the Nazi regime cannot be ignored. Therefore the position taken by Sheptytsky regarding the SS Galicia Division was a most unfortunate one.

Thus, the situation of those Ukrainians whom I call "victims" was most difficult, if we bear in mind the background, the hostility of a remarkably large part of the Ukrainian population, the consistent anti-Jewish position of the Ukrainian leadership, and the German measures against anyone who attempted to rescue Jews. Indeed, about 100 Ukrainians from all the strata of the population were executed by the Germans in eastern Galicia due to their attempts to hide Jews.[26]

Itzhak Levin, the son of the murdered Rabbi Levin of Lviv, expresses in his memoirs deep appreciation for those Ukrainian victims: "Among the Ukrainian black clouds which covered the Jews it is necessary to mention the noble minority of Ukrainians, who did their utmost to help Jews during the Holocaust."[27]

But unfortunately, one fact should be emphasized: only about 17,000 out of 870,000 Jews survived in western Ukraine—namely 2 percent of the whole Jewish population in that region.[28] Some of these survivors were saved by their own efforts, and others by Polish, Czech, and Ukrainian righteous.

The full responsibility for these crimes falls on the Nazis, but if the attitude of the Ukrainian population toward the Jews had been different, the number of survivors would have been larger by far. Then, also, those Ukrainian victims about whom I have spoken here would have suffered much less, and those who extended help would have been able to do so more effectively.

The debate on the other Nazi victims is particularly important if we want to learn from the past to avoid similar crimes in our days and in the future. To achieve this aim, it is necessary to engage in a detailed study of the conditions that enabled the realization of the Final Solution of the Jews in Europe, and of the Nazi attitude toward other nations.

While researching these issues, however, we have to be aware of some dangerous tendencies, including attempts to attach to the Holocaust a more extended meaning and interpretation. Actually, the intention is to extricate the Holocaust from its unique character and thus consider it as part of a universal process.

We are to condemn all crimes against either individuals and/or masses, but when speaking about the Holocaust of the Jews, we must bear in mind that it was based on an until-then unknown principle in the history of mankind—the principle of genocide. A total biological war was conducted against the Jews. This definition should be remembered when referring to the Holocaust.

To attain their political aims, the Nazis never hesitated to use extreme cruelty toward their enemies. They established a scale determining the dimension and character of the treatments applied to the various enemies. However, since the Jews were victims of racial anti-Semitism, they received very "special treatment"—the result of which is well known. This distinction must not be blurred if we wish to understand the real essence of nazism.

Another tendency is the attempt to exonerate some important individuals or groups involved in the Holocaust from criminal responsibility. In German historiography, for instance, efforts have been made to absolve Hitler from the responsibility for the Final Solution.[29]

The above-mentioned tendencies have prevailed among the Ukrainians too. After the war in the Soviet Ukrainian republic, references were made to the Soviet citizens killed by the Nazis. I appreciate the principle of equality, but in this case such an approach blurs the fact that the Jews were exterminated because of their being Jews and not merely Soviet citizens.

As for some circles of Ukrainians in the West, we can detect a deep feeling of embarrassment when discussing the Holocaust of the Jews: often they deny that the pogroms executed by the Ukrainians took place at all; when it is difficult to disregard the riots and murders, the Ukrainian sources claim that the number of Jewish victims was minimal. According to them only marginal elements committed these crimes. They also totally disqualify any sources—whether German, Polish, Soviet, or Jewish—that prove such acts. But the same sources are credible when cases of help and rescue by the Ukrainians are described.

Such Ukrainians in the West try to include some of the tragic chapters in their history in the term *Holocaust*. They exonerate important Ukrainian groups from any responsibility for the terrible acts committed against the Jews. These trends should be rejected.

As researchers we are compelled to do our utmost to present a complete, accurate, and reliable picture, and thus fulfill our duty toward both the Jewish and the non-Jewish victims. We hope this will also contribute to preventing further tragic events in the future.

NOTES

1. Heinz Hohne, *The Order of the Death's Head* (London, 1969), p. 42.
2. John Armstrong, *Ukrainian Nationalism 1939–1945* (New York, 1955), pp. 118–24.
3. Litopys UPA, vol. 6, *UPA v svitli nimetskyh dokumentiv*, (Toronto, 1983), p. 41.
4. The total of eastern Galician victims is obtained by adding all figures appearing on the *Pinkas Hakehillot* eastern Galicia, Poland, Jerusalem, 1980, entries; Shmuel Spector, *The Holocaust of Volynian Jews* (Jerusalem, 1982), pp. 3, 349–51. The Ukrainian sources for the most part do not refer to the number of Jewish victims, especially when Ukrainians were involved in the events. The pogroms are either generalized or completely ignored. In most Ukrainian sources the responsibility for the pogroms in July–August 1941 is laid on the Germans.
5. K. Pankivsky, *Roky nimetskoi okupatsii* (New York, Toronto, 1965), p. 13.
6. Armstrong, *Ukrainian Nationalism*, p. 279.
7. *Pinkas Hakehillot*, pp. 245, 369.
8. A. Weisbrod, *Thus Died a Town* [in Yiddish] (Munich, 1949), pp. 20–21.
9. T. Fuchas, *Wanderings through the Occupied Territories* [in Yiddish] (Buenos Aires, 1947), pp. 221–24.
10. *Pinkas Hakehillot*, p. 269.
11. Ibid., pp. 300, 321.
12. Ibid., p. 283.
13. Ibid., p. 230.
14. Spector, *Holocaust of Volynian Jews*, pp. 217–18.
15. Einsatzgruppen report no. 24, July 16, 1941, p. 5, YVA 051/ER-24.
16. "Zavoiuiemo mista," Volyn, September 1, 1941, p. 2.
17. Spector, *Holocaust of Volynian Jews*, p. 184.
18. Pankivsky, *Roky nimetskoi okupatsii*, p. 72.
19. David Kahana, *The Diary of the Lviv Ghetto* [in Hebrew], (Jerusalem, 1978), p. 29.
20. Armstrong, *Ukrainian Nationalism*, p. 80; Roman Ilnytzkyj, *Deutschland und die Ukraine* (*1934–1945*) (Munich, 1958), 2:274.
21. Kahana, *Diary of the Lviv Ghetto*, p. 155.
22. Ilnytzkyj, *Deutschland und die Ukraine*, vol. 2.
23. Kahana, *Diary of the Lviv Ghetto*, pp. 173–85.
24. Phillip Friedman, "Ukrainian-Jewish Relations during the Nazi Occupation," in *YIVO Annual of Jewish Social Science*, vol. 12 (New York, 1958–59), p. 293.
25. Armstrong, *Ukrainian Nationalism*, p. 172.
26. Friedman, "Ukrainian-Jewish Relations," p. 293.
27. Itzhak Levin, *Ukrainskyi Samostiinyk* (June 1966), p. 32.
28. Pinkas Hakehillot, p. xii, xxix; Spector, *Holocaust of Volynian Jews*, pp. 3, 349–51.
29. Hans Mommsen, "Nationalismus," in *Soviet System und demokratische Gesellschaft: Eine vergleichende Enzyklopadie*, Bd. IV (Freiburg, 1971).

CHAPTER 12

The Ukrainian Losses
during World War II

Taras Hunczak

Almost immediately after the Nazis were driven out of the Ukraine, the American journalist Edgar Snow went to that country to get firsthand information about the consequences of Nazi occupation and about the destruction caused by war. Mr. Snow published his findings in an article that appeared in the *Saturday Evening Post* on January 27, 1945, under the title "The Ukraine Pays the Bill." In his report Snow stated:

This whole titanic struggle, which some are apt to dismiss as "The Russian Glory" has been, in all truth and in many costly ways, first of all a Ukrainian war. And greatest of this republic's sacrifices, one which can be assessed in no ordinary ledger, is the toll taken of human life. No fewer that 10,000,000 people . . . have been lost to the Ukraine since the beginning of the war. . . . No single European country has suffered deeper wounds to its cities, its industry, its farmlands and its humanity. [1]

Snow's report was not a flight of poetic fancy or overdramatization of the conditions he observed in the Ukraine. If anything his observations were an understatement of the tragic conditions the Ukrainian people experienced as a result of the life-and-death battle that was fought by the two leviathans on the Ukrainian soil. That the Ukraine was the center stage of the war is attested to by the fact that already in 1941 the entire country, with a population of 41.9 million, was occupied by the Germans. By contrast, at the same time only some 17 percent of the Russian territory, which had a population of 27 million, was occupied by the enemy. [2]

The Ukrainian human and material losses were not, however, solely the result of purposeful Nazi policy of genocide and the Soviet extermination operations between 1939 and 1941. Upon entering the Ukrainian territory, the German authorities initiated a policy of economic exploitation and ruthless oppression. This was very much in accord with Hitler's plans for eastern Europe, which he articulated with unmistakable clarity during a conference at his headquarters on July 16, 1941. Referring to the Soviet Union, Hitler stated that his objective was first, to dominate it, second, to administer it, and third, to exploit it. [3]

Erich Koch, Hitler's henchman in the Ukraine, followed the dictates of his master very closely. During his inauguration speech in September 1941, Koch very candidly stated his policy for the Ukraine:

I am known as a brutal dog. Because of this I was appointed as Reichskommissar of the Ukraine. Our task is to suck from the Ukraine all the goods we can get hold of, without consideration of the feelings or the property of the Ukrainians. . . . I am expecting from you the utmost severity towards the population. [4]

Similar sentiments concerning the eastern European population were expressed by Governor General Hans Frank in a speech delivered on January 14, 1944:

"Once we have won the war, then for all I care, mincemeat can be made of Poles and the Ukrainians and all the others who run around here." [5]

As can be expected, the Nazi officials did not need much exhortation from their leader; they were ready to do their duty and more to secure the area for future German colonization, to secure the much promised Lebensraum for the German people. Already in 1932 an influential Nazi argued in favor of a ruthless German colonization policy:

All this, however, would remain an idle dream unless a planned policy of colonization and depopulation are carried out. Yes, a depopulation policy. . . . It [will be] necessary to bring agriculture lands predominately into the hands of the German Herren Class. [6]

What should, perhaps, be clearly understood is that the Nazi policy of genocide was not an aberration of the war conditions, but rather a conscious and purposeful effort on the part of the Nazi leadership to provide the eastern European territories for German colonization. [7] This was to be done by whatever means, including mass murder if necessary.

The colonial objective of the Nazi party in eastern Europe was expressed in a more concrete form in May 1942 in the *Generalplan Ost*. The plan states that some of the natives would be left behind to serve their German masters, while the rest of the population would be moved eastward. Those who stayed behind as slaves would not be permitted to own land or possess any capital. [8]

The implementation of the German plans gave rise to a growing popular opposition that, aside from the Communist partisans, escalated into an armed national resistance movement. It is interesting to note that Hitler saw a certain advantage in the escalating partisan warfare. He thought that fighting against the partisans[9] would provide the Germans with the opportunity to eradicate all those who opposed them.[10] That these were not empty dreams is attested to by the evidence given at the Nuremberg trials. SS-Gruppenführer Erich von dem Bach-Zelewski, who was in charge of antipartisan warfare in eastern Europe, testified that "the warfare against bandits" was used to achieve Himmler's goal of reducing the Slavic population to 30 million.[11]

Orders, suggestions, and memoranda concerning the exploitation of the Slavic population came from a variety of sources; principally, however, they originated in the higher offices of the Nazi machine. Thus, for example, Martin Bormann stated his views in an official memorandum of the Ministry for the Eastern Territories, which were to be adhered to in the actual governing of the population of those territories. He stated that

the Slavs are to work for us. In so far as we don't need them, they may die. Therefore compulsory vaccination and German health services are superfluous. The fertility of the Slavs is undesirable.[12]

The documentation on German policies in eastern Europe is voluminous, but for our purposes the few examples of the attitudes of Hitler and several of the leading individuals provided thus far should shed sufficient light on the problem. It is probably no exaggeration to say that the Germans were true to their policies. They depopulated the Ukraine through mass executions, deportations, and famine.

Hitler's expectations that fighting the partisans would provide the Germans with an opportunity to eradicate wide segments of the eastern European population were completely fulfilled in the Ukraine, which, besides Byelorussia, was the main battlefield between the various partisan groups and the Germans.[13] The two principal groups were the Soviet partisans[14] directed from Moscow and the Ukrainian Insurgent Army (UPA), which was a nationalist force fighting for the establishment of an independent Ukrainian state.[15] To the Germans they were all the same. Therefore not only the partisans, but also anyone suspected of dealing with them, were to be killed and the villages destroyed.[16]

Very revealing, as far as the consequences of antipartisan warfare in the Ukraine is concerned, is the report to Alfred Rosenberg of February 12, 1943. This report, covering the period from November 1942 to January 1943, informs the minister for the occupied eastern territories that in the course of these two months 108 villages were destroyed in the district of Zhytomyr. The report states further that 2,336 people were executed, but it doesn't say how many people perished during these punitive operations. [17] One might ask how many villages were destroyed altogether and how many people perished in the process. The historians record the Czech tragedy of Lidice, but hundreds of Ukrainian Lidices remained unnoticed by the Western scholars. All those women and children perished in anonymity, as if they were not part of humanity.

Available evidence suggests that the principal victims in the partisan-Nazi confrontation were the civilian population. Thus, for example, when 9,902 partisans were killed or executed between August and November 1942, at the same time the Germans executed 14,257 civilians whom they suspected of aiding the partisans. [18]

A Polish scholar, Ryszard Torzecki, views the mass extermination of civilian population as the greatest drama of the Ukraine during World War II. According to him there were 250 sites of mass extermination of Ukrainian people together with detention camps in which thousands of people perished. [19]

In a great many cases, mass murder was related to partisan warfare. H. Kuhnrich estimated that as a result of the antipartisan war 5,909,225 people were killed. Since the Ukraine was the center of partisan activity, it was there that the greatest losses occurred. According to Kuhnrich some 4.5 million people, both partisan fighters and civilians, lost their lives in the Ukraine, as did 1,409,225 in Byelorussia. [20]

Wanton German behavior toward the Ukrainian population is recorded in some detail in a lengthy document that Volodymyr Kubijovych submitted to Governor General Hans Frank. Each case of that report presents the corrupting influence of power given to individuals who become intoxicated with self-importance. Recognizing no moral or ethical boundaries, their behavior was characterized by a complete absence of human understanding or human decency. To put it in other terms, the behavior of the German occupation authorities betrays the tragedy of moral degeneration. Taking of innocent life became a daily routine.

Listing examples of wholesale shootings, Professor Kubijovych wrote:

On 29 January 1943 in the village of Sumyn . . . 45 Ukrainians, including 18 children between the ages of 3 and 15 were shot, and on 2 February 1943 in the villages of Pankow and Scharowola . . . 19 Ukrainians were shot, including 8 children, aged 1 to 13 years. [21]

Aside from the civilian population, the group that suffered the greatest consisted of the prisoners of war. According to the German military records, by May 10, 1943, the German Army took 5,405,616 prisoners. [22] How many of them survived the German camps, no one really knows. What we do know, however, is that life in the German prisoner-of-war camps was extraordinarily difficult. Many prisoners died of hunger and exposure and a great many were executed. A report for December 1941 states that 89,693 Soviet prisoners died or were executed. In January 1942, 87,451 prisoners died or were executed. [23] Since there was no change in German policy one can assume that, at least until spring of 1943, these tragic losses continued, ultimately running into millions.

Historians have thus far shed some light on another group of victims of World War II: the forced laborers who were sent to Germany by the millions, where they—particularly the Ostarbeiter—were subjected to all kinds of indignities and harsh treatment. According to an estimate by Soviet scholars some 2.2 million Ukrainians were sent to Germany. [24]

Certainly the most innocent victims of the Nazi regime were the juveniles and children of the Ukraine and other eastern European countries. Thousands of them were either kidnapped or rounded up during various operations and sent with their mothers to prisoner-of-war camps, such as Trawniki, [25] or to specially prepared camps just for children or juveniles where they were expected to learn to work and obey the commands of the master race. [26] The treatment of those children was harsh and, according to a Soviet source, at least on one occasion the Germans killed in the Ianiv camp some 8,000 of those innocent victims. [27]

Although the Germans were the chief perpetrators of heinous crimes against the Ukrainian people, the Soviet government was not far behind in its brutal abuse of power. The main victims of the Soviet regime were the inhabitants of the western Ukrainian lands occupied by the Soviet Army in September 1939. In three successive waves—December 1939, April 1940, and June 1941—the Soviet Secret Police (NKVD) arrested and, without trial, shipped hundreds of thousands of innocent people in cattle cars to Siberia. Many of these later perished. [28] Sometimes entire families were deported. Ostensibly the people deported were "enemies of the people," but in reality they were victims of a vicious regime that sought to terrorize the population in order to facilitate its lawless rule.

The people deported were mostly Ukrainians and Poles but also included some wealthy Jews, particularly those who were members of the Zionist movement. In a letter to the Vatican of November 7, 1941, Metropolitan Andrei Sheptytsky reported that as many as 200,000 Ukrainians of the Lviv eparchy were either sent to Siberia, jailed, or executed, and that the Ukrainian losses in Galicia were probably as high as 400,000. [29]

With the German invasion of the USSR, the Soviet rule of violence entered a particularly bloody phase. Unable to evacuate the Ukrainian political prisoners, the NKVD (a predecessor of the KGB) proceeded to massacre them. Some died while being tortured. The evidence of this heinous crime is incontrovertible.

From the reports of the German Security Police, we learn the following of the murders of the NKVD: in Stryi, 150 dead; Lviv, 5,000; Dobromyl, 82; Sambir, 520; Lutske, 2,800; Zolochiv, 700; Lublin, 100; Kremianets, 100–150; Dupno, a "severe blood bath" *(ein schweres Blutbad);* Ternopil, 600. [30] These are but a few examples of mass murder perpetrated on an unprecedented scale in the western Ukraine. [31]

The mass murder in Vinnytsia, sometime between 1936 and 1941, is a special case. The extent of the atrocity can be compared to the Kaytn forest massacre of the Polish officers. The mass graves unearthed in Vinnytsia in the spring of 1943 revealed that the NKVD murdered 9,432 Ukrainians, men and women from all walks of life, and tried to hide the atrocity by burying the victims secretly in a restricted area. [32] Among those murdered were also 28 Poles.

The tragic details of Vinnytsia have come to light since World War II. These are the eyewitness accounts of journalists who were present during the unearthing of graves and the medical examination of the corpses by an international body of physicians. One such witness was Anthony Dragon, who referred to the scene as "the valley of sorrow and tears, ruin and death." [33] Equally informative and interesting are the observations of Zenon Pelenskyi, which he conveyed to the U.S. Congress committee investigating Communist aggression. The same congressional committee listened to the testimonies of three other men, natives of Vinnytsia, who essentially confirmed the veracity of Pelenskyi's statements and added some background information. [34]

In view of the above, it should be obvious that the Ukrainians were victims of a variety of factors: the Nazi policy of genocide, the Soviet rule of terror, and the military operations that were conducted without any restraint or concern for the civilian population. By the time the Germans were cleared from the Ukrainian territory more than 700 cities and towns, representing 42 percent of all urban centers devastated by the war in the entire USSR, and more than 28,000 villages had been destroyed.[35] The material losses were incalculable, although the Soviet authors estimate that they amounted to 1.2 trillion rubles, which was approximately 30 percent of the national wealth of the Ukraine.[36]

Certainly the most painful loss to the Ukrainian nation during World

TABLE 12.1

Estimates of Direct World War II Population Losses in the Ukraine

Source		Estimate
1. *Ukrains'ka RSR v velykli vitchyz'nianii viini,* vol. 3 (Kiev, 1969), p. 150.		
Civilian population losses		3,898,457
Military personnel killer or died as POW		1,366,588
Losses of Zakarpattia and Crimea		250,059
	Total	5,515,104
2.a. Iu. V. Arutiunian, *Sovetskoe krest'ianstvo v gody velikoi otechetvennoi voiny* (Moscow, 1963), pp. 390, 392.		
Losses in Ukrainian villages (working population)		2,500,000
b. Akademiia Meditsinskykh Nauk Ukrainskoi SSR, *Otchet komissii po obsledovaniiu poter i sanitarnykh posledstvii voiny* (Kiev, 1946), pp. 18, 19.		
Losses in Ukrainian towns		3,500,000
	Total	6,000,000
3. V. V. Shcherbyts'kyi, *Radians'ka Ukraina,* October 18, 1974.		
	Total	6,750,000
4. M. M. Palamarchuk, *Ekonomichna heohrafiia Ukrains'koi RSR* (Kiev, 1975), p. 80.		
	Total "more than"	5,000,000

Source: Stephen G. Prociuk, "Human Losses in the Ukraine in World War I and II," in *The Annals of the Ukrainian Academy of Arts and Sciences in the United States* (New York, 1973–77), 13:36.

War II was its people. The exact figures of those losses are not known; the best that we can do is to estimate on the basis of incomplete factual data. While doing that, we should keep in mind that when we speak of Ukrainian human losses, we speak of the decline of the population, which includes those who were killed as well as those who were evacuated or deported and never returned. Considering a total demographic picture of the Ukraine, we observe that in January 1941 the population was 41.9 million, of whom 14 million lived in the cities. By the end of the war in 1945, the total population had declined to 27.4 million and the city population consisted of only 7.6 million inhabitants. Hence, a loss of 14.5 million people. [37] Other sources give somewhat lower figures, 13,614,000 [38] and 11 million. [39]

As far as human losses in terms of those killed, most estimates range between 5.5 million and 7 million. This includes some 600,000 Jews who fell victim to the German extermination policy. [40]

Table 12.1 conveys the magnitude of the Ukraine's demographic losses. Proportionally the greatest losses occurred among the Ukrainian urban

TABLE 12.2
Ukrainian Urban Population, 1939 and 1942–43

| | Population in Thousands | |
City	January 17, 1939	1942–43
Kiev	846	330
Odessa	604	300
Dnipropetrovs'k	501	152
Zaporizhzhia	289	120
Mariupoi'	222	178
Kryvyi Rih	198	125
Mykolaiv	167	84
Dniprodzerzhyns'k	148	75
Poltava	130	75
Kirovahrad	100	63
Kherson	97	59
Zhytomyr	95	42
Vinnytsia	93	42
Melitopol'	76	65

Sources: *Deutsche Ukraine Zeitung* (Luts'k) February 2, 1943; *Novoe Slovo* (Kiev), July 22, 1942; and Stephen G. Prociuk, "Human Losses in the Ukraine in World War I and II," in *The Annals of the Ukrainian Academy of Arts and Sciences in the United States* (New York, 1973–77), 13:125–26.

TABLE 12.3
Losses of Population by Country

| Country | Number of Losses in Thousands | | | Losses As a Percentage of the Whole Population |
	Military	Civilian	Total	
Ukraine	2,500	4,500	7,000	16.7
Germany	4,500	2,000	6,500	9.0
Poland	123	4,877	5,000	19.6
Japan	2,000	350	2,350	3.4
Yugoslavia	300	1,400	1,700	10.6
France	250	350	600	1.5
Italy	400	100	500	1.1
Rumania	300	200	500	3.7
Greece	100	350	450	6.2
Hungary	136	294	430	4.6
Austria	270	104	374	5.6
Great Britain	290	60	350	0.7
Czechoslovakia	46	294	340	3.0
USA	300	—	300	0.2
Holland	12	198	210	2.4
Finland	84	16	100	2.7
Belgium	13	75	88	1.1
Canada	42	—	42	0.4
Bulgaria	25	10	35	0.3
Australia	35	—	35	0.5

Source: Wolodymyr Kosyk, "Die Opfer der Ukraine waehrend des zweiten Weltkriegs," *Jahrbuch der Ukrainekunde,* 1984 (Muenchen, 1984), pp. 125–26.

population. The fate of Kiev epitomizes the tragedy of the city population of some 900,000. By 1945 as a result of extermination of 195,000 people and deportation to Germany of another 100,000, the city had a population of 186,000.[41]

The decline of the Ukraine's urban population was reported on February 2, 1943, in the *Deutsche Ukraine Zeitung.* Those findings are reflected in table 12.2.

The full dimension of the Ukrainian tragedy can be comprehended only when we compare it with the losses of other nations that were directly or indirectly involved in World War II. Indeed, the single fact remains that, in sheer numbers, no nation lost as many people as did the Ukrainians. This is borne out by Table 12.3

The facts presented in this study tell only part of the story of the Ukrainian victims of World War II. For the most part it is presented in terms of statistical data; what is missing, however, is the dimension of suffering and anguish that left an indelible mark on those who survived.

NOTES

1. P. 18.
2. Wolodymyr Kosyk, "Die Opfer der Ukraine waehrend des zweiten Weltkriegs," *Jahrbuch der Ukrainekunde,* 1984 (Muenchen, 1984), p. 116.
3. *Nazi Conspiracy and Aggression* (Washington, 1946), 7:1087.
4. Ihor Kamenetsky, *Hitler's Occupation of Ukraine (1941–1944): A Study of Totalitarian Imperialism* (Milwaukee, Wis., 1956), p. 35.
5. John A. Lukas, *The Great Powers and Eastern Europe* (New York, 1953), p. 570.
6. Alexander Dallin, *German Rule in Russia 1941–1945: A Study of Occupation Policies* (New York, 1957), p. 278.
7. See Henry Picker, *Hitler's Tischgespräche* (Bonn, 1950), pp. 52, 73–74, 303. For Hitler's ideas on economic exploitation, see *Hitler's Secret Conversations,* translated by Norman Cameron and R. H. Stevens (New York, 1961), pp. 56, 61, 113, 581.
8. Dallin, *German Rule in Russia,* p. 282. For a detailed discussion of the project see "Der Generalplan Ost," in *Vierteljahrshefte fuer Zeitgeschichte,* 6 (1958) and 1 (1960). See also Czeslaw Madajczyk, *Polityka III Rzeszy w okupowanej Polsce* (Warsaw, 1970), 1:139–48, 320–21.
9. In June 1942 Himmler issued an order to the effect that henceforth the term *partisan* was to be replaced with the description *bandit.* The objective of this order was to reduce an individual fighting for a cause to the level of a common criminal. See Pawel Chmielewski, "Hitlerowski teror wobec ludnosci cywilnej okupowanych obszarow zwiazku Radzieckiego," in Piotr Lossowski, ed., *Zwialzek radziecki w latach Wielkiej Wojny Narodowej 1941–1945* (Warsaw, 1979), p. 167.
10. *Nazi Conspiracy and Aggression* (Washington, D.C., 1946), 7:1087.
11. Ibid., 6:427.
12. Ibid., 2:904.
13. For a map of the partisan-infested areas, see the National Archives, Washington, D.C., T78/489.
14. See Erich Koch's report of June 25, 1943, "Derzeitiger Stand delz Bandenlage," Bundesarchiv, Koblenz, NS 19/1433. See also D. Karov, *Partizanskoe dvizhenie w SSSR w 1941–1945 gg.* (Munich, 1954).
15. For the German documentation on UPA see Taras Hunczak, ed., *The UPA in Light of German Documents,* vols. 6 and 7, *Litopys Ukrainskoi Povstanskoi Armii* (Toronto, 1983).

16. See Erich Koch's telegram to H. Himmler, February 25, 1943, Bundesarchiv, Koblenz, NS 19/1433, pp. 121–23.
17. "Bandenbekämpfung in Generalbezirk Shiromir," Bundesarchiv, Koblenz NS 19/1433, pp. 132ff.
18. "Meldung Nr. 51, Russland-Süd, Ukraine, Bialystok. Bandenbekämpfungserfolge vom 1.9, bis 1.12.1942." Bundesarchiv, Koblenz, NS 19/2566.
19. Ryszard Torzecki, "Polityka hitlerowska wobec okupowanej Ukrainy" in Piotr Lossowski, ed., *Zwiazek radziecki w latach Wielkieg Wojny Narodowej 1941–1945* (Warsaw, 1979), p. 198. See also Instytut istorii partii, *Ukrainskaia SSR w velikoi otechestvennoi voine sovetskogo soiuza,* 3 vols. (Kiev, 1975), 3:152.
20. Heinz Kuhnrich, *Der Partisanenkrieg in Europa 1939–1945* (Berlin, 1963), p. 543; also Pawel Chmielewski, op. cit., p. 177.
21. For the entire report see *Trial of the Major War Criminals before the International Military Tribunal* (Nuremberg, 1948), vol. 27, pp. 298–324. A somewhat shorter version of the report can be found in *Nazi Conspiracy and Aggression* (Washington, D.C., 1946), 4:79–83.
22. National Archives, Washington, D.C., T78/489.
23. Ibid. For a perceptive insight into the Nazi-Soviet criminal activity see Eugene H. Methvin, "Hitler and Stalin—Twentieth Century Superkillers," in *National Review,* May 31, 1985, pp. 22–29.
24. V. S. Koval, *Mizhnarodnyi imperialism i Ukraina, 1941–1945* (Kiev, 1966), p. 153.
25. See "Geschlossene Unterbringung von Bandenfrauen mit Kindern in einem Sonderlager Trawniki," National Archives, Washington, D.C., T175/140/2668026.
26. See ibid., "Einrichtung von Kinderlagern," T175/140/2668061; "Behandlung der Bandenkinder," T175/140/2668026; "Uebersicht ueber bisherige Anordnungen und Anregungen betr. Bandenkinderunterbringung," T175/140/2668036.
27. *Nimetsko—fashystivskyi okupatsiinyi rezhym na Ukraini* (Kiev, 1963), pp. 340, 347, 353–54.
28. We don't really know how many people were deported from the western Ukraine. One Polish author suggests that as many as 1.8 million people were deported. This seems to be a rather high figure. See Wladyslaw Studnicki, *Rzady Rosji Sowieckiej we wschodniej Polsce 1939–1941* (Warsaw, 1943), p. 34.
29. Milena Rudnytska, ed., *Zakhidnia Ukraina pid bolshevykamy* (New York, 1958), p. 456.
30. This information is based on German archival material. For details see, Der chef der Sicherheitspolizei und des SD Berlin, der 12 Juli 1941. Ereignismeldung UdSSR, nr. 20, Bundesarchiv, R58/214, 4, for the situation in Stryi. SS Brigadier General Erwin Schul, commander of Einsatzkommando 5 (of Einsatzgruppe C), testified at Nuremberg that 5,000 inhabitants were murdered in Lviv. For his testimony, see *Trials of War Criminals before the Nuremberg Military Tribunals* 4:518–21. A report of July 16, 1941, states that about 20,000 Ukrainians disappeared from Lviv during Soviet rule. At least 80 percent of

them were members of the intelligentsia. The number of those murdered is estimated at between 3,000 and 4,000. See Der Chef der Sicherheitspolizei und des SD, Ereignismeldung UdSSR, Nr. 24, Bundesarchiv, R58/214, 10. For pictures of those murdered, see National Archives, Washington, D.C., T312/617/83082878308296. In Dobromyl the victims were thrown into the salt mines. See Der Chef der Sicherheitspolizei und des SD, Ereignismeldung UdSSR, Nr. 24, Bundesarchiv R58/214, 10–11, 13, 15. The figures for Lublin, Kremianets, and Dubno can be found in Der Chef der Sicherheitspolizei und des SD Berlin, den 20, Juli 1941, Ereignismeldung UdSSR, Nr. 28, Bundesarchiv, R58/214, 7–9. The German report most likely referred not to Lublin, which was under the Nazis in 1939–41, but either to the villages of Liuby or Luiblynets, both in Volhynia. The report also indicated that, following the Soviet occupation in September 1939, some 2,000 Ukrainians lost their lives, and about 10,000 Ukrainians disappeared from Ternopil.

31. For eyewitness accounts as well as reports from various parts of the western Ukraine, particularly from Sambir (Ivano-Frankivsk), where the NKVD tortured and murdered 1,200 Ukrainians, see Rudnytska, *Zakhidnia Ukraina pid bolshevykamy*, pp. 441–92. For corroborating information on Soviet occupation see Roy A. Medvedev, *Let History Judge: The Origins and Consequences of Stalinism* (New York, 1971), pp. 248–49.

32. The findings concerning the Vinnytsia atrocity are contained in *Amtliches Material zum Massenmord von Winniza* (Berlin, 1944).

33. Anthony Dragon, *Vinnytsia: A Forgotten Holocaust* (Jersey City, N.J., 1986).

34. For details of the testimonies, see *Select Committee to Investigate Aggression: Investigation of Communist Takeover and Occupation of the Non-Russian Nations of the U.S.S.R. House of Representatives,* 83d Congress (Washington, D.C., 1954), pp. 1–31.

35. Bodhan Krawchenko, "Soviet Ukraine under Nazi Occupation, 1941–44," in Y. Boshyk, ed., *Ukraine During World War II: History and its Aftermath* (Edmonton, 1986), p. 15.

36. Instytut istorii, partii, *Ukrainskaia SSR v velikoi otechestvennoi voine Sovetskogo Soiuza 1941–1945 gg,* 3 vols. (Kiev, 1975), 3:158. See also *Istoriia Ukrainskoi RSR* (Kiev, 1977), 7:512.

37. Kosyk, *Die Opfer der Ukraine,* p. 124.

38. *Ukrainskaia SSR v velikoi . . . ,* 3:158.

39. Stephen G. Prociuk, "Human Losses in the Ukraine in World War I and II," in *The Annals of the Ukrainian Academy of Arts and Sciences in the United States* (New York, 1973–77), 13:49.

40. Lucy S. Dawidowicz, *The War Against the Jews, 1933–1945* (New York, 1975), p. 544.

41. *Radianska Ukraina,* October 13, 1968.

The German Occupation Regime on Occupied Territory in the USSR (1941–1944)

Georgily A. Kumanev

The Second World War was the cruelest and most severe of all wars throughout history. More than fifty million people perished in that war, including twenty million Soviet citizens. Millions of people became ill, invalid, or were orphaned. The total damages incurred by the Soviet Union as a result of the Fascist invasion totaled an astronomical 2,569 million rubles (in prewar prices.)[1]

The civilized world has witnessed nothing else like the violence that was perpetrated against the occupied Soviet Union by the Nazi invaders. The actions of the occupying forces were not just a haphazard chain of cruelty and illegality, but the result of a planned, systematic state policy enacted by the German Fascist government.

The German occupation policy in the East between 1941–44 was racist and was conceived by Nazi leaders to further their far-reaching plans of invasion. Nazi propaganda fed to the people of Germany asserted that the Germans were a "higher race" destined to rule all other people, especially the Slavic people. The destiny of the Slavs was to be subjugated by the Germans. They were to serve "God's race" through their labor. The leaders and ideologies of fascism spoke openly of the necessity of acquiring "living room," i.e., taking other peoples' territories and enslaving the inhabitants. Hitler's followers considered the capture of eastern Europe and the Soviet Union and the subsequent enslavement of their peoples to be of primary importance. Hitler wrote, "When we speak of conquering new territories in Europe one can of course only have in mind Russia and those border nations which are subjugated by her."[2] The German occupation of almost all of western and southwestern Europe in a relatively short period of time was a prelude to its march eastward, toward the Soviet Union.

Hitler's variation of the Barbarossa plan approved in 1940 was a synthesis of German imperialist aggressive plans aimed at the Soviet Union. In its preparations for war against the USSR, the Fascist German invaders tried not only to acquire Soviet territory, but also to destroy the Soviet state. Moreover, they had carefully planned practical measures aimed at the dismembering of the Soviet Union, plundering and exploiting the national treasures and natural resources of the Soviet republics.

The fact that the predetermined nature of German occupation policies was planned was proven long ago by incontrovertible evidence, primarily by documents belonging to German leaders. These include the so-called "Instructions for Special Areas for Directive No. 21" dated March 13, 1941. This is a directive of the German High Military Command concerning the installation of an occupying regime in the Soviet Union. This directive leads one to believe that is was an inherent part of the Barbarossa plan to liquidate the Soviet state as a political entity and to break up the occupied territory into several large areas commanded by Reichs Commissars appointed by the Führer. I would like to point out that details of the governing system were worked out more than three months before the war began.

One other document is very typical: a protocol of a meeting between Hitler and the leaders of Wehrmacht sections concerning the organizational structure of the economic particulars of the Barbarossa plan, the so-called Oldenburg protocol. The meeting took place March 29, 1941, more than two months before the start of the invasion. The protocol mentions the appointment of Goering to control the economy of occupied Soviet territory, and also mentions the organization of centers for the occupation regime in areas far removed from the western border, such as Murmansk, Arkhangelsk, Leningrad, Vologda, Moscow, Yaroslavl, Rybinsk, Stalingrad, Krasnodar, Grozny, Tbilisi, Baku, and Batumi.

A similar document is the May 13, 1941, directive signed by Field Marshall Keitel, "On the Military Jurisdiction in the Region of 'Barbarossa' and on Special Military Powers." This directive mandated the timely implementation of certain "mass repressive measures" against the Soviet population in occupied territories and absolved the soldiers of the Wehrmacht of any responsibility for violent acts committed against peaceful citizens.

Unsurpassed in their cynicism and inhumanity are the "Twelve Commandments for German Behavior in the East and for Treatment of Russians," issued June 1, 1941, which openly proclaimed the occupation regime in the USSR as an "eternal" institution of German supremacy in the East.

It required the servants of the occupying administration "to conduct the cruelest and most merciless measures. It entreated the occupiers: "Do not be soft or sentimental" in dealing with the Russians. They "always want to be a mass which is ruled."

Appearing March 30, 1941, at a meeting of his top brass, Hitler said that when one talks about war with the USSR, "one is talking about annihilation."[3]

Finally, the determination of the Germans to dismember and plunder the Soviet Union is proven in the famous documents found in Goering's "Green Folder," the so-called "Directives for Managing the Economy," which called for maximum exploitation of resources in occupied areas to the benefit of Germany.

Germany's leaders had already solved the problem of what form of government they would establish in the occupied Soviet Union. The "Instructions for Special Areas for Directive No. 21" (the Barbarossa variation), dated March 13, 1941, determined a system of measures for these territories. German commanders in the corresponding areas and the Reichs commissars were empowered with the privileges of high military command, including unlimited rights concerning the civilian population. In the spirit of installing Nazi leaders, they drew up a general *Ost Politik* plan, which reflected the essence of Nazi extermination policies concerning the Slavic nations.

The Soviet press had already published several documents from the general *Ost Politik* plan, and in particular a circular written by Himmler that contained his thoughts on how one should treat the local population in occupied territories. On May 25, 1940, Himmler informed Hitler in writing of his ideas on this topic. These ideas were affirmed and approved by the Fuehrer in a directive known as "Several Ideas on Ways to Handle the Local Population in the Eastern Regions."[4] As this document shows, Hitler's policies were aimed at the physical destruction and complete annihilation of certain Slavic peoples, in particular the western Ukrainians, Byelorussians, and others. "We insist that every effort be made to prevent the people of the eastern regions uniting; we want to break them up into the smallest groups possible."[5] Himmler was adamantly against giving the people of the eastern regions the right to an education. Himmler considered the maximum amount of knowledge for these people to be the ability to "count to 500, to sign their names, and that the essence of God's Law was to be subservient to the Germans." He believed it unnecessary for them to learn to read. The cannibalistic document No. 3 is also interesting. It contains notes and suggestions for the general *Ost Politik* of the Reichs Führer's SS troops. It was signed April 27, 1942, by Dr. D. Wetzel, head of the colonization division of the first chief political directorate of the Eastern Ministry. These notes completely affirm the *Ost Politik* plans to remove thirty-one million people over a thirty-year period from Poland and the western sections of the Soviet Union and to settle the area with Germans. The Eastern Ministry suggested raising the number of people designated for removal to between forty-six and fifty-one million.

The notes of the Eastern Ministry paid particular attention to the question of the future of the Soviet state. This was not limited to routing the central Moscow government, as stated in this document:

Achievement of this historic goal would never completely solve this problem. One must destroy the Russians as a people, separate and alienate them. It is essential that the majority of people remaining on Russian territory be of a primitive, semi-European type. [6]

Hitler's politicians and the Gestapo were not the only ones to develop and implement cruel, terroristic policies against the population of occupied territories. The Nuremberg trials established that German generals actively participated in these activities; such men as Keitel, Brautchitch, Jodl, Warlimont, Colonel Hausiger (who at the time was chief of operations at headquarters), as well as many other generals and officers, were responsible for mass crimes against civilians. In carrying out their occupation policies in the East, the German Army, the Gestapo, and the SS acted as a single entity.

Perhaps the best expression of the essence of Fascist German occupation policy in the USSR can be found in the lead story of *Das Schwartze Kor* (the organ of the imperial leadership of the SS) dated August 20, 1942, with the headline "Should We Germanize?"

Arguing against the necessity and feasibility of Germanizing the native population of the occupied territories of the USSR, the newspaper reasoned:

A victory in the East is only a prelude to securing our future; this guarantee will be attained only when the land acquired at the expense of a holy, bloody victim becomes German to that degree to which it is suitable for colonization, becomes German by virtue of the fact that it is inhabited by Germans who work the land, becomes German by virtue of the fact that German ploughs are operating there at full steam.

Land reacquired by us should be filled with German blood and German lives, but never with Germanized people. (italics added)

Thus, the predatory goals of the occupation policy of the Germans toward the USSR were painfully obvious.

The occupation regime threatened the lives of tens of millions of Soviet people. Before the war approximately eighty-eight million people lived in the occupied Soviet territory; millions of them were evacuated; many men were drafted into the Red Army. Yet no less than seventy million were under the rule of the invaders and were subjected to the extermination policy of the occupying forces.

What was the nature of the occupation regime that carried out these goals? Having captured the Ukraine, the Baltic states, Byelorussia, Moldavia, part of the Finnish Karelian Republic, several *Blasts* and *Krais* in the Russian Federated Republic, Hitler's forces arbitrarily redrew the political map of these territories, paying no attention to the independence and territorial integrity of the Soviet republics.

The entire occupied territory of the Soviet Union was divided into two parts. The first part was the theater of military operations for infantry forces and included the territory from the front lines to the hinterland borders for army groups. This was subdivided into regions of military action and rear unit army regions. The entire power structure was in the hands of the military chain of command. The second part consisted of a military administrative zone, which included the remaining territory and had two Reichs Commissariats: Ostland and the Ukraine.

The first part included Estonia, Latvia, Lithuania, part of the Leningrad Oblast, and part of Byelorussia with Reichs Commissar Gauleiter Lose's headquarters in Riga. Part of the western Ukraine—Lvov, Drogobyk, Stanislav, and Ternopol Blasts—was included in the domain of the Polish General Government. The other part—the area west of the Yuzhniy Bug River, together with Moldavia (*Transnistriya*)—was given to the kingdom of Romania. The rest of the Ukraine was included in the Ukraine Reichs Commissariat with Reichs Commissar Gauleiter Koch living in Rovno.

Every Reichs Commissar had four main divisions in his area that were responsible for nationality and race policy, religious, legal, financial and tax, industrial, agricultural, transportation, and other questions.

The Ostland Reichs Commissariat was divided into four general commissariats—Lithuania, Latvia, Estonia and Byelorussia—each headed by General Commissariats.

As a result of Hitler's administrative reforms the Byelorussian republic was broken up into various sections. The northern part of the Brest Oblast was included in the region of eastern Prussia. The southern part of Brest Oblast—almost the entire Gomel Oblast, part of Pinsk and Polessk Blasts—was annexed to the Ukraine Reichs Commissariat. The northwestern regions of the Vileisk Oblast were included in the general Lithuanian Okrug. The Vitebsk, Mogilev, and eastern regions of the Minsk Oblast were considered the German Army's rear and were under military command. For all practical purposes, Byelorussia was reduced to the territory consisting of the Baranovich Oblast, the western part of the Minsk Oblast, and certain regions of the Vileisk, Pinsk, Brest, and Polessk Blasts.

All of the Baltic republics had self-governing status in Lithuania, Latvia and Estonia that was similar to the governing system of the Reichs Commissariat. The occupied Blasts were under the control of the military field command. The Military Administration of Eastern Karelia was set up in Berlin to manage the Reichs Commissariats. The first thing the new Reichs Minister did was hand out positions for future German colonies in the East. In a few short weeks, all the General Commissar positions were handed out (including Sverdlovsk and Baku).

The occupying forces destroyed all Soviet electoral organs. They introduced precincts *(Gebits)* headed by Gebit Commissars who resided mainly in Oblast centers. For 1,050 Gebit Commissar positions there were 114 applications from the SA Führers, 450 from civil servants in the Internal Affairs Ministry, and 261 from members of the Nazi Labor Front. The Rayon centers were controlled by Burgomasters. Other populated areas were headed by sergeant majors and councils of elders.

The entire local population in the occupied territory was closely scrutinized. New people who appeared in the cities or villages were required to register with the policy immediately. The inhabitants were not allowed to leave populated areas without special permission. It was forbidden to take water from the wells and reservoirs located near the German garrisons. People were permitted on the streets only during daylight hours. During evening and nighttime hours, Nazi patrols opened fire on passersby without warning. Thus, during the first days of the occupation of Kiev the German command announced an order to shoot anyone seen outside after 7:00 P.M. The city was littered with bodies with signs on them, "Walking at 7:10 P.M."

The economic policies of the invaders reflected their general political goals. In 1941, various joint-stock companies started to appear based on Goering's "Green folder"—the main administration of the eastern coal industry, the "East," "Hermann Goering Metal Works" and others. They also began to include Soviet industrial enterprises. Thus, the Voroshilov engine building works was first given to Hartman, the former owner of the factory; shortly thereafter Krupp representatives of the Goering concern made claims on the property, which ultimately resulted in the factory being divided.

Hitler's high command was very active in the plunder of Soviet industry. Keitel testified on this subject at the Nuremberg trials. There was yet another organ in Berlin in addition to General Tomas's agency, which coordinated all activities concerning the exploitation of occupied territories. This was the Ost Economics Headquarters (its code name was Oldenburg Headquarters), which was headed by Secretary of State Kerner and was under the direct supervision of Goering. The general quartermaster (rear chief), Rosenberg's ministry, the Food and Supplies Ministry (headed by Darre), and the Economics Ministry (headed by Funk) all had an interest in the plunder of the Soviet nation. The headquarters was controlled by General von Schubert, a senior officer of the Reichswehr. General Schubert had an appointed economics inspector in each army group at the front.

The Ost Economics Headquarters included representatives of the largest German monopolies. Every economics post was filled by people who were closely allied with one or another concern. In 1941 the headquarters established a general inspector for the collection and exploitation of raw materials in the occupied eastern regions. This position was filled by Lieutenant General Walter Witting, who was earlier in the administration of occupied France. Witting was closely allied with Friedrich Flick Company, the huge coal and metal works. It was Witting who brought Flick and Goering together, enabling them to take control of several Soviet factories and create the Dniepr-Stal and Berg und Huttenwerke Ost. Moreover, one of Flick's firms had captured factories in Dniepropetrovsk and Voroshilovgrad. Flick had more than its share of occupation booty. When Hitler's invaders began their mass exportation of labor forces to Germany, Flick's factories were the first to receive new workers.

During the war years, the connections between the monopolistic capital and the high command grew stronger. Wehrmacht Field Marshall Manstein wrote in his memoirs that during the fiercest fighting in the Donbass Region, he had been visited by General Director Pleiger, one of the "trump aces" of the Ruhr coal industry. Max Inger, the master of chemical espionage, also made a trip to the front.

By the end of the war, almost every major capitalist venture had its general. For example, the Flick Company had Witting, I. G. Farben had Mumentei, and the Stinnes Company had Brautchitch. Close contact between the generals and their firms ensured them swift plunder of the occupied countries.

The occupying forces imposed an inhumane system of exploitation and labor on the Soviet workers. At most factories, the workers were considered just nameless numbers without families. They were imprisoned in special hard labor camps if they refused to work. Those suspected of sabotage were executed by a firing squad. An announcement posted in Zaporozhye dated August 9, 1943, stated that those who left their place of work would be subject to the death penalty. The official workday lasted from ten to twelve hours. But factory owners were given the right to extend the hours at will and the workday usually lasted fourteen to sixteen hours. The pay was paltry. There was no overtime, Sunday pay, night, or other differential remuneration. Workers were given a miserly food ration. In the Donbass coal mines, where it was extremely difficult for the occupying forces to regulate the coal mining industry, the daily food ration for a miner was less than two hundred grams of poor quality food, and sometimes even this ration was not distributed for months at a time. Workers in all industrial cities captured by the Germans faced the same situation. Millions of Soviet citizens were doomed to die a torturous death of starvation.

In October 1943 Himmler cynically announced, "I do not care what happens to the Russians or the Czechs. I am interested in other people's prosperity or death from hunger only to the extent that these people can be used as slaves in our culture."

Soviet peasantry also bore a tedious burden under occupation forces. German agrarian policies were aimed at plundering the economy. The occupation forces destroyed agriculture, took the crops and livestock away to Germany, and left peasants to die of hunger. The land and possessions of the state farms (*Sovkhoz*) were made property of the Reich and labeled "government estates." These estates were run by German administrators. All agricultural products were put at the disposal of the German Army and the occupation forces.

Even before Hitler's armies invaded the USSR, they had planned to liquidate the collective farms (*kolkhoz*), but these plans were realized only in the western regions of the Ukraine, Byelorussia, and the Baltic republics, territories that right before the war were part of the Soviet Union. In other areas of the Soviet Union the German invaders met strong resistance expressed in various ways. Risking their lives and property the peasants often hid their livestock, grain and agricultural inventory, and equipment. Before experiencing widespread resistance among the majority of collective farms, the Nazis hoped to make good use of the collective farming system, its massive land plots, and the rich labor resources to plunder the agricultural products.

But in February 1942, the German government issued a directive, signed by A. Rosenberg, on a new order for land use. The essence of this directive was the gradual transfer to private land ownership in agriculture. Ostensibly, Rosenberg's agrarian law gave large groups of the peasant population private ownership of the land, but this was sheer demagoguery by which the occupying forces wished to convert the peasants to their side. In actuality, land was given to the kulaks and landowners. The peasants were turned into farm laborers forced to work for beggarly wages and subjected to the whims of the unlimited powers of German administrators and occupying forces.

The occupying forces burdened the peasants with many taxes. In several areas they imposed extortionist taxes encountered previously only during the Middle Ages: a tax on beards, on "extra" windows and doors, on "superfluous" furniture, on cats, dogs, etc. In 1943 the Ukraine collected more than ten types of taxes both in money and in payments in kind. A 50-ruble fine was imposed for grazing cattle in the forest without permission. A 150-ruble fine was imposed for grazing cattle in forbidden areas, a 250-ruble fine for nonpayment of taxes, etc. Even after payment of all taxes and various fines and delivery of their goods, the peasants still could not enjoy the fruits of their labor. For example, if a peasant dared to slaughter a cow or a pig, the meat was confiscated and his remaining livestock was taken away from him. The peasants gave their produce to the occupying forces and were unable to purchase anything for hard currency, so they starved, became ill, and died of epidemics.

The rural population could not travel beyond the borders of their territory nor could they sell their products. If peasants appeared at the marketplace without authorization, they faced fines of 5,000 rubles or sixteen days in jail. [7]

Everything stolen from Soviet citizens by the occupation forces went to supply the German Army or was taken away to Germany. During an inspection tour of the Ukraine at the beginning of 1943, A. Rosenberg demanded that the occupation forces increase the amount of agricultural products taken away to Germany.

The military command actively participated in the plunder of the Russian peasantry. On June 17, 1944, Dr. Huttenbraucker gave a report at a meeting of the German agricultural command for the central group armies in Bobruisk. He noted that in 1942–43 the German Army took 2.5 million tons of grain and 200,000 tons of meat; from the Ukraine in 1943–44, they took 1.5 million tons of grain and 67,000 tons of meat.

The German invaders gave top priority to taking Soviet citizens away to slavery in Germany. The general policy concerning slave labor was formulated on April 20, 1942, by Saukel, administrative officer for exploitation of labor forces:

It is absolutely necessary to make maximum use of the human resources in occupied territories. If we are unable to find the necessary number of laborers on a voluntary basis, then we must immediately put a forced labor plan into effect. Maximum use of all prisoners of war, as well as the implementation of huge numbers of foreign civilian workers—men and women—has become an absolute necessity if we are to solve the question of mobilization of a work force in this war. [8]

The forced evacuation to German labor camps was very difficult for unfortunate Soviet citizens. Hitler's men used every method they could to get the people from the occupied areas of the USSR to obtain the laborers they needed.

The Germans made much noise about the fact that they were taking these people to Germany on a voluntary basis. In reality, these people were forced to go to Germany against their will. The Germans conducted searches for people who were then taken to Germany in convoys as slaves. Thus, in February 1943 Hitler took reprisals against the people in the village of Osinka in Ternopol Oblast who had refused to go to Germany and work. Sixty elderly men were taken to a square in town and executed with machine guns. One hundred sixteen houses were burned, property was confiscated, and livestock was driven away.

An order was issued in Kiev requiring all people capable of working to register at the labor exchange. The list of registrants was checked daily, and noncompliance was treated as an act of sabotage. Those guilty of the charge were executed by firing squad. In spite of the threat, thousands of people did not show up at the exchange. The occupation powers and the police did everything they could to determine those capable of working who were living in the city. The police often conducted searches on the streets and in the markets, and all those deemed capable of labor were sent off to work.

In Zaporozhye the city's youth were forcibly mobilized for transport to Germany. A gray card, a notice of conscription, was delivered to the city's households. This meant that the family was required to supply slaves for Germany. The occupation forces sent 20,000 young boys and girls away to labor camps in Germany from Zaporozhye alone.

According to the January 14, 1943, order, "Administration of the Use of Labor Forces," published in the *Minsker Zeitung,* "in 1942 alone approximately two million people were sent to Germany away from the occupied territories in the East."[9]

Erich Koch, Reichs Commissar for the Ukraine, wrote that the occupation forces were able to send hundreds of thousands of Ukrainian workers to Germany, mostly to work in the military industry. The forced transport of Soviet citizens to Germany intensified. In April 1943 Hitler demanded that Saukel, the general administrator for the use of labor resources, send an additional million workers to Germany throughout the course of 1943, 800,000 of whom were from the occupied regions of the Soviet Union. As the invaders retreated, they tried to drive more and more of the population to the west not only to fill their need for workers, but also to leave the territory abandoned.

In Chernigova the occupation forces announced that people refusing to go to Germany would be shot on the spot.[10] The German command in Zhlebina issued a warning to the civilian population announcing that "the entire city has been surrounded by German troops. Anyone trying to hide or escape will be shot. Go outside and move where the German soldiers order you to go."[11] It was the same everywhere. Soviet people who refused to go to Germany were barbarically beaten and shot.

The forced transport of labor forces to Germany was conducted under the direct supervision of the Wehrmacht generals. A July 28, 1944, report signed by a general quartermaster stated that as of June 30, 1944, out of a total of 2,792,699 "eastern workers," the vast majority (more than two million) were sent from the rear regions of various army groups.[12]

One of the many ways the Germans acquired candidates for forced labor was during punitive raids against partisans. The Latvian chief of security for the police and SD issued the following orders: "On November 3, 1942 the SS Reichsfuehrer ordered that the remaining civilian population capable of labor in the occupied areas already searched be taken prisoner. They must be sent to Germany as workers."

Echelons of slaves were taken to Germany day and night from regions of Byelorussia, the Ukraine, and Russia. The people were transported like cattle, sixty to seventy people in each boxcar. The special "orders on dealing with foreign workers taken from the civilian population of the empire," which were developed by Hitler's slave owners, stated the following:

Eastern workers should be kept in closed camps which they can leave only to complete a job; they should be under constant guard. When these people are employed in small agricultural enterprises or on individual farms, where the use of eastern labor is permitted, the laborers can be kept outside the camp in a locked room where there is a German male who could keep his eye on the person. [13]

There were many letters written from Germany to the front that spoke of the unbearable conditions under which the Soviet people were driven into slavery. Wilhelm Bok, a soldier killed on the Soviet-German front, carried a letter written by his mother in Chemnitz. It said:

Many Russian women and girls are working at the "astrawerke" factories. They are forced to work 14 hours and more a day. Of course they receive no wages for their work. They are brought to and from work in a convoy. The Russians are so exhausted that they literally cannot stand on their own two feet. They are often whipped by the guards. They have no right to complain about the beatings or the bad food. [14]

Hitler's occupation forces transported more than five million Soviet citizens to Germany to work in the labor camps. The Germans forced Soviet civilians into slavery in Germany not only to fill their insufficient labor needs, but also as a way to deplete the Soviet population.

The Germans were determined to physically destroy a significant part of our population and to that end they knew no limits. They used various methods.

Their principal means of exterminating the civilian population as well as prisoners of war was systematic mass murder: they starved people to death, let them freeze or die of epidemics, and subjected them to many other tortures. Many documents in the hands of historians clearly describe the horrendous methods of mass human extermination resorted to by the Germans.

Nazi rule was arbitrary in the occupied territories. Since the population had no rights whatsoever, it is practically impossible to make an exact count of the victims of Nazi terror. After the Red Army liberated the occupied territories, they reviewed data from 55,162 documents compiled by a special state commission to examine the crimes committed by the Fascist German invaders and by other committees in various areas. Only then was it possible to give an estimate of the losses suffered by the Soviet people. The following numbers (which cannot be considered final or exact) give an indication of the scale of German extermination of the population of certain Soviet Republics:

Ukraine	4.0 million
Byelorussia	2.5 million
Occupied territories of the RSFSR	1.7 million [15]

Thus, facts and documents clearly prove that the occupation regime established by the Germans on the occupied territory of the Soviet Union was well thought out and contained a detailed plan for the enslavement and extermination of the indigenous population of our country, the plunder of its natural resources, and the destruction of its state. The occupation was a completely arbitrary regime in its rule, a regime of violence and lawlessness, which was even more fearsome because it was controlled by a misanthropic Fascist ideology based on racial supremacy, hatred of a conquered people, and the delirious idea of a "higher destiny" for the German race. The only possible response of the people of the USSR to this form of existence was all out war against the invaders. Tens of millions of Soviet citizens took up the call to a holy war for the fatherland against German fascism, which resulted in the latter's complete military and moral defeat and a great victory for the Soviet Union and the entire anti-Fascist coalition.

NOTES

1. *Vozrozhdeniye prifrontovykh i osvobozhdennykh rayonov SSSR v gody Velikio Otecheestvennoi Voiny, 1941–1945* (Moscow, 1986), p. 3.
2. Adolph Hitler, *Mein Kampf* (Boston, 1943).
3. *Voyenno-istoricheskii zhurnal*, 1959, no. 2, pp. 81–82.
4. *Voyenno-istoricheskii zhurnal*, 1969, no. 1, pp. 87–88.
5. Ibid.
6. *Voyenno-istoricheskii zhurnal*, 1960, no. 1, p. 96.
7. TsPA IML pri KPSS, F. 17, op. 1, d. 2303, 1. 41.
8. *SS v deistvii: Dokumentyi materialy* (Moscow, 1960), pp. 532–33.

9. *Nyurenbergskii protsess*, 1:809.

10. TsPA IML f. 17, op. 1, d. 2313, 1. 41.

11. *Sbornik soobshchenii Chrezvychainoi gosudarstvennoi kimmissii porassledovaniyu prestuplenii nemetsko-fashistskikh zakhvatchikov* (Moscow, 1946), p. 185.

12. A. Dallin, *German Rule in Russia* (London, 1957), p. 452.

13. *Nyurenbergskii protsess*, 1:799–800.

14. Ibid., p. 814.

15. TsGDOR, f. 7021, op. 125, d. 3, 1. 84–85.

CHAPTER 14

The Fate of the Soviet
Prisoners of War

Christian Streit

Among the different groups that fell victim to the Nazi politics of extermination, the Soviet prisoners of war must be accorded a special place. After the Jews, they were the numerically largest group of victims, and there are close ties between their fate and that of the Jews.

What happened to the Soviet prisoners of war in the years between 1941 and 1945 has been largely ignored. A total of approximately 5.7 million Red Army soldiers were taken prisoner between June 22, 1941, and the end of the war. In January 1945, there were some 930,000 Soviet POWs left in the prison camps of the Wehrmacht.[1] About 1 million more had been released from captivity, most of them as so-called *Hilfswilligen*,[2] that is, "helpers of the Wehrmacht." According to estimates from the German Army staff, another 500,000 of the prisoners either had escaped or were eventually liberated by the Red Army.

The remaining 3,300,000 or about 57 percent of the total number, had perished by 1945. To make these figures more meaningful, they should be compared with statistics on the British and American prisoners of war. Of the total of 231,000 such prisoners in German hands, 8,348, or 3.6 percent, died before the end of the war.

The losses of the German prisoners of war in the hands of the Red Army by far exceeded those of the British and American soldiers. Some 3,250,000 Wehrmacht soldiers were taken prisoner by the Red Army and about 1,200,000, or 36 percent, perished in Soviet camps. The number is huge if compared to Anglo-American losses, but still almost three times as many Soviet soldiers lost their lives in German captivity.

Before I go into the reasons for the death of more than half of the Soviet prisoners, I want to outline briefly the development of the mortality rate.

How rapidly their numbers were decimated is shown by the example of those in occupied Poland. In the fall of 1941, 361,000 Soviet prisoners vegetated in the camps there. Of these, only 44,000 were still in the camps by 1942. Approximately 7,500 had escaped, but 310,000—more than 85 percent—had perished, and a sizable number had been shot. [3]

The mortality rate in the camps seems to have been relatively low in July and August 1941, but in August epidemics like typhoid and dysentery broke out in a number of camps in the East. The increase in mortality did not bother the German authorities at this point. In October, however, the rate shot up to dreadful levels in the General Government areas of occupied Poland. Fifty-four thousand Soviet prisoners had died before October 20, 1941, but in the next ten days another 45,690 died, almost 4,600 persons a day. The peak of mortality seems to have been reached between October and December, and signs indicate that even the German authorities were surprised by the extent of the deaths.

From December 1941, the death rate dropped slowly to between 8 and 9 percent for the month of March 1942; this decrease was due to the fact that by the end of October 1941, the German leaders had realized that they needed the Soviet prisoners as workers in the German war industry. The measures taken—slightly raised rations, slightly improved housing—were, however, still far from sufficient to force the mortality rates down to a level comparable to that of the other prisoners of war in German custody. [4] The rate was reduced in the summer of 1942, but in late 1943 it started climbing again, and in 1944 there were again camps with dozens, if not hundreds, of deaths every week.

There are four main reasons for the death of so many prisoners. The most obvious is hunger. The others are lack of shelter, the methods used in transport, and the general treatment meted out to the prisoners. Supplying provisions for the vast number of the Soviet prisoners certainly posed immense problems for the German Army, but that was not the true cause of starvation.

Obtaining foodstuffs from the East was one of the principal objectives of the German Reich in the war against Soviet Russia. The breakdown of Germany in November 1918 had been a traumatic experience for the German leaders, and it was still remembered by Hitler and his generals. The merciless exploitation of the food resources in the East was designed to make it possible for the German people to enjoy food consumption as in peacetime and, thus, to stabilize wartime morale.

The bureaucrats involved in planning this exploitation were perfectly aware of the fact that this implied "without doubt the starvation of umpteen million people."[5] From the very beginning, the rations handed out to the Soviet prisoners of war were far below the minimum required for subsistence. For example, the prisoners who during the summer of 1941 were marched through the rear area of the army group center in White Russia received daily rations of "one ounce of millet and three ounces of bread, no meat"; or "three ounces of millet, no bread."[6] These rations supplied less than a quarter of what an average man needs for survival.

The consequences soon became evident. In August reports reached the Wehrmacht High Command that often only 20 percent of a transport of prisoners arrived at its destination. In that month the Wehrmacht High Command decreed fixed rations for all Soviet prisoners: those who worked were to receive an equivalent of 2,100 calories a day, which fell below the minimum required for existence, but the records indicate that usually the prisoners received much less.[7]

The state of health among the prisoners became desperate in September 1941. Numerous reports show that the despairing prisoners turned to eating raw grass and leaves.[8] In spite of the rapidly climbing death rates in the camps, Army Quartermaster General Eduard Wagner, following the demands of Hermann Goering, ordered the drastic reduction of rations for the prisoners in the front areas. This reduction particularly hurt the weaker prisoners, because nonworking prisoners were to receive no more than 1,500 calories a day.

The decimation of large numbers of prisoners was accelerated by winter because the prisoners were without any protection. Even in the Reich area and in occupied Poland, the prisoners had often been left for months to vegetate in trenches, dugouts, or sod houses.

When daily death rates climbed above 1 percent in October, authorities improvised winter shelters in unused factories and prison buildings, but they were not able to put all the prisoners in such shelters before December.

In occupied Soviet areas, conditions were even worse. For example, in many camps in White Russia only roofs were available to protect the prisoners from snow and cold. Even in January 1942 there were camps where many of the prisoners still lived in dugouts.

Tens of thousands, if not hundreds of thousands, lost their lives on the way from the front to the prison camps. Most of the prisoners taken in 1941 had to march for hundreds of miles to the rear areas, even if winter had started. During these marches, thousands of exhausted prisoners were shot. Again and again, such instances were reported even from the centers of cities like Smolensk and Minsk.[9]

There were army commanders who repeatedly issued orders trying to stop these shootings, but only in May 1942 did the army and Wehrmacht high commands call for a change. Earlier, in the fall of 1941, however, there were army commanders who had entirely different notions. Field Marshall Walter Von Reichenau, commander of the Sixth Army—the one that later perished at Stalingrad—ordered guards "to shoot all prisoners who collapse."[10]

If prisoners were carried by train, an order from the Army High Command permitted only the use of open freight cars. This order did not merely limit the transportation available; it also caused enormous losses when temperatures began to drop below the freezing point. In the rear area of the army group center, transportation in closed freight cars was not permitted until November 22, 1941, after more than three weeks of severe frost. The immediate cause for the change was the fact that out of the transport of 5,000 prisoners, 1,000 had frozen to death.

But even transportation in closed but unheated freight cars was no decisive improvement. A December 1941 report to the Ministry of Labor said that "between 25 and 70 percent of prisoners" died during transportation. In some cases the prisoners had been left without food for several days."[11]

In 1941 the German soldiers were led to think that the life of a Soviet prisoner of war had very little value indeed. This evaluation was not only a result of Nazi propaganda, which depicted Soviet citizens as "subhuman," it was also the result of the basic Wehrmacht directives issued for warfare in the East. The most notorious of these was the so-called Barbarossa Directive of May 13, and the Commissar Order of June 6, 1941.

The Barbarossa Directive limited the military jurisdiction to the maintenance of discipline. In accordance with Hitler's demands, the troops were expected to deal ruthlessly with any "criminal attacks" committed by Soviet civilians. Crimes that Wehrmacht soldiers committed were to go unpunished if the perpetrator claimed political motives for his actions.

The Commissar Order charged the troops to shoot all political commissars of the Red Army upon capture. Recent research has established beyond doubt that during the summer and fall of 1941, Red Army commissars usually were shot by frontline troops. [12]

From the very beginning, the orders for the treatment of the Soviet prisoners were more than harsh. The orders stressed that bolshevism was the deadly enemy of Nazi Germany. They called for ruthless and forceful action in order to break any resistance. Guards were told to shoot escaping prisoners without warning and to use their weapons to implement their orders. One of the basic directives for the treatment of Soviet prisoners concluded, "the use of arms against Soviet prisoners of war is generally considered lawful." [13] That was clear license to kill.

This order, however, did not go unchallenged. On the initiative of Helmuth James von Moltke, one of the most impressive minds of the German opposition to Hitler, Admiral Wilhelm Canaris, chief of the Wehrmacht High Command Counterintelligence Department wrote to the commander in chief, Field Marshall Wilhelm Keitel, demanding the repeal of this order.

Canaris not only drew Keitel's attention to the violation of international law, but also made serious military and political objections. Keitel's response rejecting the protest left no doubt about his own attitude: "The objections reflect the soldierly concept of chivalrous warfare! What we are dealing with here is the destruction of a worldview (Weltanschauung)! Consequently I approve of measures as ordered and I support them." [14]

Keitel's endorsement of the policies of destruction included actions that have not yet been mentioned. With the killing of the Red Army commissars, the Wehrmacht had accepted a share in the liquidation of the Soviet political system, but the Wehrmacht's involvement in the war of extermination went even beyond that.

About three weeks after the attack on the Soviet Union had started, General Hermann Reinecke, the general responsible for prisoners-of-war affairs in the Wehrmacht High Command, and the chief of the Reichssicherheitshauptamt, Reinhard Heydrich, negotiated an agreement stating that special units of the SS, so-called Einsatzkommandos, were to "sort out" and do away with "politically and racially intolerable elements" among the Soviet prisoners.

Immediately the number of victims multiplied, because such "intolerable elements" consisted not only of "all important state and party functionaries," but also "all fanatical communists," "the intelligentsia," and "all

Jews."[15] Several hundred thousand prisoners became victims of the ensuing selections, which continued to the end of the war.

The connection between these murderous activities and the so-called Final Solution is obvious, but it is more than a purely factual connection. For one thing, the Wehrmacht collaborated very intimately with the Einsatzgruppen. Furthermore, both Auschwitz-Birkenau and the Majdanek extermination camps were originally built to shelter Himmler's share of the Soviet prisoners. He wanted to use them as slaves in the industrial complexes he planned together with major corporations such as I.G. Farben.

Of the 15,000 prisoners taken to Birkenau and Majdanek in 1941, only a few hundred survived in January 1942. Since no more Soviet prisoners could be expected, six days after the Wannsee Conference Himmler decided to fill these two camps with 150,000 German Jews. The camps built for Soviet prisoners of war became part of the infrastructure needed for the destruction of the Jews.

In dealings with the Soviet prisoners of war at Auschwitz, Camp Commandant Rudolf Hoess, and his deputy, Karl Fritzsch, discovered the means that made industrialized murder feasible. In early September 1941, some 600 Soviet prisoners who had been selected for execution by the SS arrived at Auschwitz.[16] Anxious to avoid the task of shooting such a large group, Fritzsch decided to use the pesticide Zyklon B to gas them and another 250 camp inmates selected as "unfit to work." He thus found the way to kill thousands with a minimum effort.

There are many reasons why so many prisoners died, but one reason in my opinion has not been given enough attention. After all, it was not part of the tradition of the German Army to kill defenseless prisoners of war by the thousands and to deny them shelter and food. The popular explanation is that the entire Wehrmacht had adopted the Nazi concept that all Soviet citizens were "subhumans" and that German soldiers acted accordingly. There is some truth in this statement, but I do not think that it was the single most important reason. Were this the case, it would be very difficult to explain why a significant number of senior officers, who were committed opponents of Hitler, and who later had a share in the 1944 movement, participated in the policy of destruction in 1941. Their behavior may be explained only if we identify antibolshevism as a powerful motive.

It is very significant that the first murderous activities that the military leaders were asked to accept were designed to eliminate Communist leaders. When the army leadership permitted the employment of the SS Einsatzgruppen in the rear army group and army areas, they did so because these Einsatzgruppen would destroy the party infrastructure.

The same motives made them accept the Commissar Order. It is equally significant that the first Einsatzgruppen massacres were labeled "retaliatory measures for Bolshevist crimes" or "punitive actions."[17] It seems that most German soldiers, if they ever learned about such massacres, accepted them because the Einsatzgruppen succeeded in identifying them as an integral part of the fight against what was called Jewish bolshevism, or as retaliation against real or alleged crimes of the Soviet regime.

The following example demonstrates how this mechanism worked even with officers for whom the concept of soldierly honor, or chivalrous warfare, was not just a meaningless slogan. On June 30, 1941, one week after the attack had started, Lieutenant General Lemelsen, commanding general of an armored corps, issued an order sharply criticizing the fact that many Red Army soldiers had been shot upon capture in his command area. "This is murder!" The Soviet soldier who had fought bravely, Lemelsen continued, was entitled to decent treatment.[18] These sentences were quite exceptional in an order pertaining to the treatment of Soviet prisoners of war. I have not been able to find anything comparable. But Lemelsen went on to say that this did not apply to commissars and partisans. They were to be led aside and shot on the order of an officer. It was quite obvious that even for Lemelsen, who adhered to the traditional military code of honor, the long-cherished military principle of giving quarter to an enemy who surrendered did not apply to Communists.

NOTES

1. For a more detailed account, see my book *Keine Kameraden: Die Wehrmacht und die sowjetischen Kriegsgefangenen 1941–1945*, vol. 13 of *Studien zur Zeitgeschichte*, ed. the Institut fuer Zeitgeschichte, Munich, (Stuttgart, 1980), pp. 244–46. The number for January has been taken from the monthly POW statistics that the High Command of the Wehrmacht (OKW) sent to the International Red Cross at Geneva (Bundesarchiv/Militaer-Archiv, Freiberg [BA/MA], RW 6/v. 453).

2. This is an estimate. Up to May 1944 a total of 816,000 Soviet POWs had been released from captivity (Nuremberg doc. NOKW-2125). Most of them served as ammunition carriers, grooms, etc., in Wehrmacht units or as auxiliary police. More POWs were released in 1944–45 to serve in the Vlassov units, but no definite number can be established.

3. See Streit, *Keine Kameraden*, p. 134.

4. Before January 31, 1945, a total of 1.6 percent of the French, 1.2 percent of the British, and 0.3 percent of the American POWs had perished. (In the last months of the war, the mortality rates for these POWs rose sharply, too, due to the chaos that developed in the Reich area); cf. Streit, *Keine Kameraden*, pp. 246, 293f.

5. Memo about a conference of undersecretaries of various departments on May 2, 1941 (Nuremberg Document 2718-PS).

6. See Streit, *Keine Kameraden*, p. 131.

7. Ibid., pp. 137–62.

8. Ibid., pp. 135, 152; Szymon Datner, *Crimes Against POWs. Responsibility of the Wehrmacht* (Warsaw 1964), p. 229.

9. Streit, *Keine Kameraden*, pp. 168f.

10. Nuremberg document NOKW-3147.

11. Streit, *Keine Kameraden*, p. 166.

12. Ibid., pp. 83–89; Juergen Foerster, "Die Sicherung des 'Lebensraumes,' " in *Das Deutsche Reich und der Zweite Reich und der Zweite Weltrieg*, ed. Militaergeschichtliches Forschungsamt (Stuttgart, 1983), pp. 1069–70.

13. Nuremberg Document 1519-PS; see Streit, *Keine Kameraden*, pp. 181f.

14. Nuremberg Document EC-338; see Streit, *Keine Kameraden*, pp. 231f.

15. Nuremberg Document NO-3414; see Streit, *Keine Kameraden*, pp. 231f.

16. My account follows Stanislaw Klodzinski, "pierwsze zagazowanie wiezniow i jencow w obozie oswiecimskim," in *Przeglad Lekarski*, 1972, no. 1, pp. 80–94.

17. Streit, *Keine Kameraden*, p. 125. Dozens of examples can be found in the "Ereignismeldungen USSR," which the Reichssicherheitshauptamt compiled from the reports of the Einsatzgruppen (Bundesarchiv, Koblenz, R 58/214–217).

18. Lemelsen's order is printed in Ortwin Buchbender, *Das toenende Erz: Deutsche Propaganda gegen die Rote Armee im Zweiten Weltkrieg* (Stuttgart, 1978), p. 104.

CHAPTER 15

Non-Jewish Children
in the Camps

Sybil Milton

The general subject of non-Jewish children in the camps has received no systematic coverage in the growing literature, in part because the number of such children was statistically insignificant. The obvious must also be stated at the outset: children were seldom the targets or victims of Nazi violence because they were children. They were persecuted along with their relatives for racial, religious, or political reasons. Furthermore, it is difficult—probably impossible—to conceptualize persecuted children as a single or unified group, because of the enormous and complex variations in their backgrounds and the distinct needs of different age groups from infants to teenagers.

This essay will thus examine selected case studies as a way of opening several windows into the historical experiences of non-Jewish children. I have selected material about the abduction and deportation of Polish children from the Zamosc region (eastern General Government), 1942–43; the development of a policy toward the abandoned children of partisans in occupied Latvia and White Russia during the first half of 1943; and several examples from the persecution of children of Gypsies, Jehovah's Witnesses, and Spanish Republican refugees. Although it is still too early to understand the contours or common aspects of this subject on a pan-European basis, it is clear that the fate of non-Jewish children must always be placed in the context of the fate of Jewish children of similar nationality and background.

Let me digress for a moment. The term *children* covers at least three distinctive age groups irrespective of gender: first, infants and toddlers up to age six; second, young children ages seven to twelve; and third, teenagers from thirteen to eighteen. Their chances for survival and their ability to perform physical labor varied enormously by age, as did other factors such as the place and date of deportation and Nazi ideological tenets about the national, group, or ethnic identity of the children. [1]

Let us begin with the first case: the treatment of Polish children. We must remember that in Hitler's well-known speech to his military commanders at Obersalzburg on August 22, 1939, there was not only the famous reference to the Armenian genocide, but also a discussion essentially authorizing the killings without pity or mercy of all men, women, and children of Polish race or language. [2]

Nearly one year later, Heinrich Himmler elaborated his views about "The Treatment of Racial Aliens in the East" in a top-secret memorandum with limited distribution, dated May 25, 1940. That document also outlined the administration of incorporated Poland and the General Government, where Poles were to be assigned to compulsory labor and racially selected children were to be abducted and Germanized:

Regarding the treatment of alien racial groups in the East, it is important that we cultivate and recognize as many individual groups as possible. . . .

A fundamental issue in the solution of these problems is the question of schooling and thus the question of sifting and selecting the young. For the non-German population of the East, there must be no higher school than the fourth grade of elementary school. The sole goal of this schooling is to teach them simple arithmetic, nothing above the number 500; writing one's name; and the doctrine that it is divine law to obey the Germans. . . . I do not think that reading is desirable.

Obviously, Himmler's plan combined the cultural with the physical enslavement of occupied Poland. But let us continue with the text of his May 1940 memorandum:

Apart from this schooling, there are to be no [other] schools at all in the East. Parents, who from the start want to give their children a better education . . . must apply to the Higher SS and Police Leaders. The [outcome of such] application will depend on whether the child is racially above reproach and conforms to our conditions. If a child is recognized to be of our blood, the parents will be notified that the child will be sent to school in Germany and will remain permanently in Germany.
. . .

Apart from examining such parental applications, there will be an annual screening of all children, ages 6 to 10, in the General Government to separate racially valuable and non-valuable juveniles. The racially valuable will be treated in the same way as children admitted by approved parental applications. . . . The population of the General Government during the next decade, as a result of the consistent implementation of these measures, will be composed of the remaining inferior population supplemented by those deported from the eastern provinces. . . . This population at our disposal will consist of laborers without leaders, and will furnish Germany annually with migrant workers and labor for special tasks (roads, quarries, construction of buildings). . . .[3]

The racial and geographical consolidation of Nazi-occupied eastern Poland thus involved colonization by German settlers, de-Polonization with the forced resettlement of the original inhabitants, and the kidnapping and forced Germanization of Polish children. In a letter of June 18, 1941, Himmler wrote Arthur Greiser, Reich Plenipotentiary and Gauleiter of the Wartheland:

I would consider it proper if young children of Polish families with specially good racial characteristics were collected and educated in special children's homes which must not be too large. The seizure of these children would have to be explained by danger to their health. . . . Genealogical trees and documents of those children who develop satisfactorily should be procured. After one year, such children should be placed as foster children with childless families of good race. . . .[4]

In late July 1941, Himmler visited the districts and towns of Lublin and Zamosc (the latter to be renamed Himmlerstadt) and selected four districts for de-Polonization and the "search for German blood." That operation was directed by SS Lieutenant Hermann Krumey, who opened in Zamosc a branch office of the Central Resettlement Office Litzmannstadt. In mid-October 1941, SS and Police Leader Odilo Globocnik suggested that operations commence, since the proposed zone of German settlements in the eastern part of the General Government would consolidate German control from the Baltic in the north to Transylvania in the south.[5] From November 1941 to August 1943, mass expulsions affected 110,000 native inhabitants, including 30,000 Polish children, from 297 villages in the Zamosc region. This was 31 percent of the Polish population of the region. (In Poland as a whole, an estimated 200,000 Polish children were kidnapped between 1939 and 1945.)

The expellees were forced to leave all property behind except for hand luggage and twenty zlotys. One of the deported children later recalled:

They began to rap at windows and doors. Chattering in German proved that we were surrounded and there was no escape. . . . I also had a package with a doll, but when the Germans rushed into the dwelling they gave us only five minutes to prepare and to take some things and immediately pushed us out of the house, disregarding the weeping of children and the requests of our parents. My parents took only the bundles with bedding.[6]

After the initial trauma of loss and separation from their homes and familiar milieus, the evicted Polish families in the General Government were transported to transit camps at Zamosc (as well as an auxiliary overflow facility at Zwierzyniec). Although there are no complete statistics available for the entire period, it is believed that the highest number of prisoners at Zamosc was 12,079 in July 1943. The average number of children hovered around 1,000 at all times.

At Zamosc, all new arrivals were confined to the overcrowded barracks, where they slept on floors and were vulnerable to exposure, malnutrition, and disease. Each barracks building was surrounded by barbed wire. After initial registration, the expellees were processed into one of four possible racial groups: (1) ethnic Germans; (2) those with German blood or racial features; (3) those assigned to compulsory labor in Germany or the General Government, ages fourteen to sixty; and (4) the sick and disabled, the very young and very old (under fourteen and over sixty years). The first two groups were considered *wiedereindeutschungsfaehig* and comprised approximately 5 percent of those examined. The third group, classified as either *Arbeitseinsatz Altreich* or *Arbeitseinsatz Generalgouvernement*, made up 74 percent. The fourth category comprised 21 percent, and frequently members assigned to this category were transferred directly to Auschwitz or Maidanek.

After the racial examination and categorization, housing was assigned by group and the prisoners stayed at Zamosc for two to six additional weeks. After racial examination, children selected for Germanization were also separated from their mothers. A similar facility existed for the incorporated Wartheland in Lodz. Located adjacent to the Jewish ghetto, it was opened in 1942 and processed children of both genders, ages twelve to sixteen. [7]

Although we do know that the abducted Zamosc children were separated from their parents and kept in *Sammellager*, we do not know their ultimate fate. However, there are some indications. The Auschwitz *Kalendarium* informs us that thirty-nine boys, ages thirteen to seventeen, arrived from Zamosc in the Auschwitz *Stammlager* on February 23, 1943, and were murdered almost immediately by phenol injections to the heart. [8]

Let us now turn to the second case, the abandoned children of partisans in occupied Latvia and White Russia during the first half of 1943. After the SS Einsatzgruppen had killed most Jews and Gypsies in the Baltic and Russia, they were regrouped as so-called *Bandenkampfverbaende* to engage in pacification and antipartisan operations. These operations killed large numbers of adults; the orphans posed a problem for the killers. A summary of interoffice correspondence, part of the Nuremberg documentary evidence, shows the evolution of Nazi policy toward these children. The correspondence was conducted among Heinrich Himmler; SS Lieutenant General Erich von dem Bach-Zelewski, who headed the antipartisan operations; the heads of Einsatzgruppen B and D; and the commanders (BdS) of the Sipo and SD for Ostland and the Ukraine. The first entry in the file is a Himmler order of January 6, 1943:

The racial and political sifting of juveniles is to take place in collection centers [Sammellager]. Male and female children without racial value are to be assigned as apprentices to factories in concentration camps. Such children have to be raised and educated for obedience, diligence, unconditional subordination, and honesty toward their German masters. They must be able to count to 100, know traffic signs, and be trained as farmers, blacksmiths, masons, carpenters, etc. Girls are to be trained as farm hands, spinners, knitters, and for similar jobs. [9]

Notice the parallels in language and policy to Himmler's May 1940 memorandum mention earlier. The next significant entry in the file is a request on April 21, 1943, from SS Lieutenant Colonel Dr. Brandt that 3,735 unsupervised orphans from Soviet territory held by Army Group North be seized. He further reported that 266 of these children were under the age of two; 1,006 were between the ages of two and five; and 2,463 were between six and fourteen years old. Von dem Bach's response noted that no housing was available for 2,500 of these children under the age of ten. [10] Further, on May 15, 1943, Einsatzgruppe B reported that children were "continuously turning up" with their mothers and recommended that mothers and children not be separated, since housing them together in the camps was expedient:

One of every 10 or 20 women could always take over the supervision of the children in order to let the others work undisturbed. Women with children do not try to escape as quickly and this would simplify the transfer of partisan families. [11]

The file closes with a June 21, 1943, request from Dr. Brandt:

The Reichsfuehrer SS [Himmler's office] wants monthly reports about the number of children in the camps in the East, their ages, and data about their education, care, and feeding. [12]

The surviving historical record provides us with only scattered material about the detailed fate of these children.

For the third case let us now turn to an entirely different facet of the subject: children of German political dissidents, Jehovah's Witnesses, Spanish Republicans, and Gypsies. Obviously, the repressive apparatus of the early Nazi state, commencing shortly after the Nazi seizure of power in 1933, extended incidentally to the family life and child-care arrangements of arrested dissidents, a precursor of later Nazi policies of using immediate family members as hostages and for reprisals. Women were often made hostages for the political activities of male relatives who had been arrested or had fled Germany, and this in turn affected the children of such families. For example, when Gerhart Seger published his account about his experiences in, and escape from, the Oranienburg concentration camp in Czech exile in 1934, his wife and daughter were arrested in reprisal and were released only after international protest. [13] Similarly, when the Socialist Franz Mueller fled to Czechoslovakia, his wife was arrested in June 1935 and held in custody for eleven months. Their four minor children, ages six to twelve, were left bereft of parental support. [14] Moreover, in November 1935, the Cologne Gestapo mailed notices to all police stations nearby that both spouses in Jehovah's Witness families were not to be arrested simultaneously, since "their children would become a burden on public welfare and also suffer emotional as well as economic damage." [15] These few examples suggest the need for further research about the families of political opponents and religious dissidents.

The first children in concentration camps arrived in the late 1930s, usually with their parents. This was the case with Austrian Gypsy female children included in the first Gypsy transport to Ravensbrück in June 1939 and the Spanish republican refugee children interned in the French transit camps after 1939 and deported with their fathers to Mauthausen in the fall of 1940. [16]

The fate of both Jewish and non-Jewish children—after 1939 present in increasing numbers in the ghettos, concentration camps, and labor camps —usually fell into one of four patterns: (1) those killed immediately on arrival as, for example, Jewish children sent directly from the ramp to the gas chambers in Birkenau or the Zamosc children, mentioned before, murdered by phenol injections; (2) those killed shortly after birth (not to mention forced abortions), such as 870 infants born in Ravensbrück between 1943 and 1945; (3) those born in ghettos or camps and surviving, such as three-year-old Stefan Georg Zweig, born in 1941 in the Cracow ghetto and deported to Buchenwald in 1944, or Gemma LaGuardia Gluck's infant granddaughter in Ravensbrück; and (4) those children, usually above the age of ten, utilized as prisoners, laborers, and as subjects for medical experiments.

A quick survey of the children interned in Mauthausen between 1938 and 1945 reflects the changing conditions and patterns of internment in the vastly expanded concentration camp system during the war. [17] It is probable that a few Gypsy juveniles were deported from Burgenland and Lower Austria to Mauthausen in 1938–39, arrested as criminals or as so-called asocials (a category that included prostitutes, vagrants, alcoholics, and any person the police thought unfit for civilian society). In the fall of 1940, forty-nine Spanish children aged thirteen to eighteen were deported from the French transit camps to Mauthausen. (Although relatively few Spanish juveniles were sent to Mauthausen, 20,000 republican Spanish children were detained in the southern French camps throughout the war.) [18] During 1944 and 1945, increasing numbers of Polish and Hungarian Jewish children arrived. The last transport to Mauthausen on March 9, 1945, included Gypsy infants and children transferred from Ravensbrück. Most children were assigned to work as stonemasons, in the armament factories, or in construction. Several of the Spanish juveniles were released from Mauthausen and assigned to compulsory labor for local firms. [19] The weaker children were assigned to KP duty peeling potatoes.

The available Mauthausen inmate statistics from the spring of 1943 show 2,400 prisoners below the age of twenty, 12.8 percent of the 18,655-inmate population. (For our concern, the cutoff age of twenty is too high; however, it does give some indications about the number of juveniles present.) By late March 1945, the number of juvenile prisoners in Mauthausen increased to 15,048 or 19.1 percent of the 78,547 Mauthausen inmates. The number of incarcerated children increased 6.2 times, whereas the total number of prisoners in the same period multiplied by a factor of only four. [20] These numbers reflect the increasing use of Polish, Czech, Russian, and Balkan teenagers as slave labor as the war continued. Statistics showing the composition of the juvenile inmates shortly before liberation reveal the following major child prisoner subgroups: 5,809 foreign civilian laborers; 5,055 political prisoners; 3,654 Jews; and 330 Russian POWs. There were also 23 Gypsy children, 20 asocials, 6 Spaniards, and 3 Jehovah's Witnesses. [21] Mauthausen's children are probably representative of the composition of child prisoners in the camps after 1940.

There is probably no need to stress that children were among the most vulnerable of prisoners. Homeless, orphaned, and often present at the death of parents or siblings, they also faced malnutrition, epidemics, physical abuse, medical experimentation, and long hours of work. Unlike the adults, younger children were unprepared with specific strategies of survival; however, their youth permitted them to adapt more easily to camp conditions than the adults. Still, they depended heavily on assistance from supportive adults. Thus, Stefan Georg Zweig, born in 1941 in the Cracow ghetto, was hidden at the age of three by his father and carried in a specially prepared rucksack during transports to the forced-labor camp at Cracow-Prokocim (Julag II) and to Buchenwald. In the latter camp, German Communist prisoners hid and protected the child, and both father and son survived.[22] Other vignettes from memoirs show that women prisoners collectively saved bread and marmalade to provide extra rations as gifts for the incarcerated children in Ravensbrück during Christmas 1944.[23] Extending and stretching the already limited quantities of food was familiar to most adult women, who could draw on previously acquired household management skills that became survival strategies in the camps. Women also taught one another and the children songs, poetry, and even foreign languages. Children also continued to improvise games; a popular one in Ravensbrück in 1944 was called *Appell,* "modeled on the camp's daily roll calls."[24] Rags and straw were used to make puppets; children's plays were performed, and children's choirs performed in Buchenwald, Ravensbrück, and Bergen-Belsen.[25]

Moreover, in Theresienstadt where only 1,000 of the 15,000 Jewish children survived, the Jews assisted the small Lutheran and Catholic communities in helping Christian children celebrate Christmas. (The Lutheran and Catholic communities consisted of converts, *Mischlinge,* and even some Jews arrested with forged identity papers that nominally changed their religious affiliation.) In late 1943, the Jewish Elder Dr. Murmelstein assisted the Lutherans in finding and decorating a Christmas tree with handmade ornaments and candle stubs; he also arranged the performance of Christmas carols by a children's choir, several children's plays, and even a magic act to entertain the children. The adult Lutheran prisoners also held Bible study groups, lectures, and religious services, which were attended by both children and adult inmates.[26]

Although the elimination of Jews was central to Nazi policy, other groups—especially Romani and Sinti—were equally vulnerable. The persecution of German and Austrian Gypsies intensified after 1936, when they were arrested as asocials, and 1938 Gypsy children were expelled from Austrian schools. Surviving photographs of the deportation of a Gypsy caravan on the Simmeringer Hauptstrasse, in Vienna's eleventh ward, during the summer of 1939, show children playing near their parents' wagons as the police arrived. [27] Once the deportation of German Gypsies to the concentration camps of the East commenced in May 1940, Gypsy children were to be deported together with their families. Himmler's so-called Auschwitz Order of December 16, 1942, concerning Gypsies stipulated in Section IV, Item 1:

Families are to be sent *en bloc* to the camps, including all children who are not economically independent. If such children have been placed in special homes, schools, or institutions, they are to be reunited with their clan *[Sippe]* at the earliest opportunity prior to their arrest. The same applies to Gypsy children whose parents are deceased, already in concentration camps, or held elsewhere. [28]

There was one exception to this rule. In November 1938, as part of the increasingly restrictive policies toward Gypsy children in Wuerttemberg as well as in response to changes in state welfare legislation, all pure Gypsy children in St. Josefspflege were not reunited with their parents before the latter were deported in May 1943. This exception probably can be attributed to the fact that these children were the subject of "racial biological research" conducted by Eva Justin. Justin, a former nurse and associate of Dr. Robert Ritter, was completing a dissertation and study for Ritter's *Rassenhygienisches und Bevoelkerungsbiologisches Institut* in the *Reichsgesundheitsamt* in Berlin. Upon completion of her research, the children were deported in January 1944 to Auschwitz BIIe, the Gypsy camp in Birkenau, where most perished. [29]

I hope that these case studies about non-Jewish children open the way for further discussion and research. Nevertheless, it is important to stress that this subject must always be treated in the context of the fate of European Jewish children.

NOTES

1. See Henry Friedlander and Sybil Milton, "Surviving," in *Genocide: Critical Issues of the Holocaust,* ed. Alex Grobman, Daniel Landes, and Sybil Milton (New York and Los Angeles, 1983), pp. 233–35.
2. Office of United States Chief of Council for Prosection of Axis Criminality, *Nazi Conspiracy and Aggression* (Red Series), 8 vols., 2 suppls. (Washington, 1946–48), 7:752–54 (Document L-3). See also Winfried Baumgart, "Zur Ansprache Hitlers vor den Fuehrern der Wehrmacht am 22. August 1939,"

Vierteljahrshefte für Zeitgeschichte 16 (1968): 120–49; ibid., 19 (1971): 294–304; and Kevork B. Bardakjian, *Hitler and the Armenian Genocide* (Cambridge, Mass., 1985), pp. 52–58.

3. *Trials of War Criminals before the Nuremberg Military Tribunals under Control Council Law No. 10* (Green Series), 14 vols. (Washington, 1950–52), 13:147–51 (Documents NO-1880 and NO-1881). See also H[elmut] Kr[ausnick], "Denkschrift Himmlers über die Behandlung der Fremdvuelkischen im Osten, Mai 1940," *Vierteljahrshefte für Zeitgeschichte* 5 (1957):194–98.

4. Washington, National Archives and Records Administration Record Group 238 (hereafter cited as NARA, RG 238), Document NO-3188. I would like to thank Harry E. Rilley of Modern Military Records Reference Branch, NARA, for providing me with photocopies of these documents. The quoted excerpt can also be found with a slightly different translation in Green Series 5:103.

5. NARA, RG 238, Document NO-5875, Situation report from SS Captain Hellmut Mueller, Lublin, to SS Major General Hofmann, Berlin, October 15, 1941 (2½ typed pages).

6. Roman Hrabar, Zofia Tokarz, and Jack E. Wilczur, *The Fate of Polish Children during the Last War* (Warsaw, 1981), p. 51.

7. Zygmunt Klukowski, "How the Eviction of the Poles by the Germans from the Area of Zamosc Was Carried Out," in *German Crimes in Poland*, ed. Main Commission for the Investigation of Nazi Crimes in Poland, 2 vols. in one (n.p., 1946–47; reprinted New York, 1982), 2:67–85; idem, *Verbrechen an polnischen Kindern, 1939–1945: Eine Dokumentation* (Munich, Salzburg, and Warsaw, 1973).

8. Kazimierz Smolen et al., *From the History of the KL Auschwitz* (New York, 1982), p. 199.

9. NARA, RG 238, Document NO-2513, Übersicht über bisherige Anordnungen und Anregungen betr. Bandenkinderunterbringung.

10. Ibid., p. 2.

11. Ibid.

12. Ibid., p. 5.

13. Sybil Milton, "Women and the Holocaust: The Case of German and German-Jewish Women," in *When Biology Became Destiny: Women in Weimar and Nazi Germany*, ed. Renate Bridenthal, Atina Grossman, and Marion Kaplan (New York, 1984), p. 299.

14. New York, Leo Baeck Institute Archives, E. J. Gumbel Papers, chronological press clippings, "Frauen als Geisel," *Sonderdienst der deutschen Informationen: Das Martyrium der Frauen in deutschen Konzentrationslagern*, no. 41 (June 11, 1936), mimeographed.

15. Hauptstaatsarchiv Duesseldorf, RW 18-3, p. 60, circular from Staatspolizeistelle fuer den Regierungsbezirk Koeln, November 11, 1935, concerning "Schutzhaft gegen Bibelforscher."

16. See G. Zoerner, ed., *Frauen-KZ Ravensbrueck* (Berlin, 1977), p. 52; and Hans Marsalek, *Die Geschichte des Konzentrationslagers Mauthausen: Dokumente* (Vienna, 1980), pp. 111–13, 137–39. See also Sybil Milton, "The Community of

Fate: The Interaction of German and Spanish Refugees, 1938–1945" (Paper presented at the Conference for Exile Studies, College Station, Texas, October 1986; conference proceedings now in press).

17. On the camp system, see Henry Friedlander, "The Nazi Concentration Camps," in *Human Responses to the Holocaust,* ed. Michael Ryan (New York and Toronto, 1981), pp. 33–69.

18. Louis Stein, *Beyond Death and Exile: The Spanish Republicans in France, 1939– 1955* (Cambridge, Mass., 1979), does not deal with the Spanish children. For the figure 20,000 children, see Hoover Institution, Stanford, Calif., *Informe del Comité de Coordinación e información de Ayuda à la República Espanola* (Mexico, 1940), unpaginated; see also the records of the American Friends Service Committee, Philadelphia.

19. Marsalek, *Mauthausen,* pp. 137–39.

20. Ibid., p. 138.

21. Ibid.

22. Internationales Lagerkomitee Buchenwald, *Konzentrationslager Buchenwald* (Weimar, n.d.), pp. 42–45. That incident was the basis for Bruno Apitz's 1958 novel *Naked Among the Wolves.*

23. Zoerner, *Ravensbrueck,* pp. 54–55, and Milton, "Women and the Holocaust," pp. 311–12.

24. Gemma Gluck, *My Story* (New York, 1961), pp. 38–39. Gemma LaGuardia Gluck was the sister of the New York mayor Fiorello LaGuardia; she had married a Hungarian Jew and was deported to the *Prominentenbaracke* in Ravensbrück in 1944, along with her daughter and grandchild.

25. See Milton, "Women and the Holocaust," pp. 311–14.

26. Arthur Goldschmidt, *Geschichte der evangelischen Gemeinde Theresienstadt, 1942– 1945* (Tuebingen, 1948), p. 17.

27. Vienna, Dokumentationsarchiv des Österreichischen Widerstandes, files 1127/ 3, 2041/1–3.

28. The entire text of this order is reproduced in Selma Steinmetz, *Oesterreichs Zigeuner im NS-Staat* (Vienna and Frankfurt, 1966), pp. 53–55.

29. Johannes Meister, "Schicksale der Zigeunerkinder aus der St. Josefspflege in Mulfingen," *Württembergisch Franken Jahrbuch* (1984), pp. 197–229; Christoph Knoedler and Hans-Joachim Treumann, "Zigeunerkinder in Mulfingen," in *Alltag im Nationalsozialismus 1933 bis 1939: Jahrbuch zum Schülerwettbewerb Deutsche Geschichte um den Preis des Bundespraesidenten,* ed. Dieter Galinski and Ulla Lachauer (Hamburg, 1982), pp. 246–58.

CHAPTER 16

Non-Jewish Victims in
the Concentration Camps

Konnilyn Feig

The concentration camp system employed organized abuse as the means of solving a variety of real and imagined problems. The Nazis and their collaborators targeted many groups for a range of special abuses as they sought to impose several types of solutions—temporary, partial, haphazard as well as a total, systematized, Final Solution.

The Holocaust, the Final Solution to the Jewish problem, marked all Jews for extinction. Yet the Nazis were determined to solve within the concentration camp system other irritating, threatening, or distasteful problems by targeting other groups for carefully conceived solutions that always included suffering, dehumanization, degradation, and, more often than not, death.

The systematic annihilation of a group of six million people crossing all country boundaries quickly became a demanding, multinational program. It depended on controlled organizational culture and shared behavior molded into a comprehensive structure welded together by the authoritarian power of a state. As an evolutionary experiment, the Final Solution was far more complex than Hitler's other solutions. The Jews were always at risk; they were exterminated everywhere the Nazis came to power. A majority of Jews spent time in ghetto or transient camps. Many of them starved there. Einsatzgruppen shot another large group in eastern Europe. During his last moments on earth, Hitler reaffirmed the unique, singular place the Jews occupied in his life, his wars, and all of his solutions. In his last statement, he wrote not against the Poles or the Gypsies, but against the Jews: "Centuries will pass . . . but our hate will ever be renewed toward the people who are in the final analysis responsible, whom we have to thank for all this: international Jewry; . . . which is actually to blame for this murderous battle."

The solutions imposed by the Nazis relentlessly eliminated Germany's effective and imagined enemies at home and wherever the Nazis moved. Non-Jews were killed everywhere throughout the system. Clearly, important differences existed among the groups, particularly in the rules legislated for them and the proper behavior demanded of them. The means of death differed among the groups the Nazis targeted. Thus, some groups could hope to survive while others lived under a sentence of death. Choice mattered. Some victims were targeted because of what they did; others because of what they were. The Nazis' objective toward the different groups varied from political reeducation to subservience, from behavioral modification to genocide. Efforts to struggle, fight, and be strong could have an impact on the fate of some victim groups but not on all. It mattered if the Nazis wanted to kill one's mind, spirit, soul, and integrity before the victim was murdered.

The final and partial solutions to the Nazis' perceived problems involved much more than mere death. The system was in a constant state of expansion and flux. It seemed always on the move, striving to catch up. It was forced to evolve from a primitive incarceration project to a vast, unprecedented network for the suppression, containment, exploitation, and extermination of millions of people of various nationalities designated as enemies of the state or as members of subhuman, inferior, or irritating groups.

No one knows exactly how many camps existed, but they numbered in the thousands. The sheer enormity, complexity, constant movement, and, at times, chaos of the multinational system precludes a precise determination of the number of victims. We know that at least eighteen million Europeans passed through the system, that at least eleven million died in it, and that at least four million died at Auschwitz/Birkenau alone. We know that the Nazis murdered approximately six million Jews. The Nazis also purposefully and systematically murdered at least another five million non-Jews. More than a million children were murdered, many of them tiny or newborn or unborn infants.

The system included major and official camps and hundreds of subsidiary camps and *Kommandos,* each with its central mother camps, stretched like giant spiderwebs over the whole of Europe. The *modus operandi* changed; the aims conflicted; the categories and purposes of the camps and the characteristics of the impacted groups differed as did the degrees of abuse.

Who were these groups? Picture a cattle car. The Jews emerge first. Most are selected for instant extermination, others to contribute their bodies for labor and medical experimentation before inevitable death, interrupted only by chance or a rare kindness. Out of the second car spill the Gypsy families, an array of bright colors standing in sharp contrast to the gray surroundings, with faces filled with confusion and bewilderment. They move off in a group to the family camp—to recover, they think, from their journey, but in truth to spend their days idly until the proper night when the gas chambers and crematoria are freed to erase the entire conclave.

The doors of the third car open and the homosexuals spill forth, males only, because as Himmler concluded, "lesbians can give birth." The taunting, jeers, and blows of the guards stun the men. They will stay a night and then be rerouted to Sachsenhausen and Buchenwald to be with their kind. The pink triangle they will soon wear is a result of a judgment that they have broken Article 175A, by sexual act, by kissing, by embracing, by fantasy and thought. Some will be given an opportunity to recant by successfully completing sexual activity with a woman in the camp brothel. Most others will find themselves tormented from all sides as they struggle to avoid being assaulted, raped, worked, and beaten to death.

Out of a fourth car step recalcitrant clergy; priests, nuns, congregants of all Christian faiths—there because of some act of affirmation, some deed of decency—whose fate differs: some shall be given favored treatment; others shall rise to martyrdom; others are to be spit upon and worked to death. They are joined in line by the prisoners of conscience—the Jehovah's Witnesses, who reaffirm the supremacy of their Bible over the ideology of the Third Reich, and whose fate varies from death to eventual release.

From car five stumble the Russian POWs, whose brutal treatment in the camps violates every standard of warfare. Out of car six come those the Nazis deemed subhuman—Poles, Slavs, Slovaks, Ukrainians, Lithuanians, Russians. They will contribute their labor to the war effort if they do not die in the process. The next car contains the politicals—primarily Communists and Socialists whose fate will depend on whim, chance, will, and the camp of ultimate destination. They are followed by resistance fighters from every nation, caught in acts against the Nazis, who have lived through torture and avoided the firing squad. Where possible, both groups formed the internal core of camp resistance.

From the eighth car emerge the physically disabled, including hunchbacks and dwarfs who will be killed, their bodies stripped, and their skeletons subjected to careful analysis by Nazi anatomists. Those with skulls of unusual shape will also be killed, their skulls deftly separated from their bodies and studied. Twins will be examined, tested, and operated on by Dr. Mengele in his favorite research project.

The ninth car, slyly termed the *medical center,* disgorges those the euthanasia program missed: older women and men and a coughing, stumbling mass of ill people—sick from the full range of human diseases—as well as a disoriented assortment of mentally ill patients. The crippled with crutches, wheelchairs, missing limbs, and the widest variety of artificial limbs fall off the train. The ramp selectors quickly move the entire group to the gas chamber line for immediate extermination. The Sonderkommando later collects all the crutches, artificial limbs, prostheses, and wheelchairs and stores them in barracks.

Those alighting from the next car are deaf, dumb, or blind. From car eleven step a conglomeration of notables, common criminals, and those people whom an individual Nazi simply did not like. Out of the last car, car twelve, come a stunningly large group of women, the many pregnant women, and children. These women and children are of all nationalities, languages, religions, joined together by their sex or merely because they are mothers of young children or pregnant.

This then is the concentration camp universe. Every one of these humans can anticipate brutal treatment, starvation, torture, overwork, disease —at the very least. The distinctions are blurred as they move down the mud paths to the disinfection rooms and their barracks—where the moments of shared truth await.

The Holocaust is an experience of intended total extermination for all Jews. It is best to leave the Holocaust to them. Hitler had several other deadly solutions in mind for a variety of problems. They may not have been final or total, but once those camp gates clanged shut, all prisoners, whatever distinctions they had among themselves, were united by the obscene systematic abuse they suffered. As a survivor of Flossenburg noted:

You don't die of anything
except death.
Suffering doesn't kill you.
Only death.[1]

The Poles The Polish nation, caught as it was in a vicious vise between Russia and Germany, experienced both the wrath and the disdain of Hitler and the terror of Stalin. The German occupation lasted longer in Poland than in most other countries and was by far the most severe. Hitler intended to clear large areas of Poland for Germany's expanding population. He designated the General Government, which already contained 45 percent of the Polish populations, as the gathering place for Poles and Jews—a reservoir of slave labor, a dumping ground for undesirables, and an extermination reservation with the two huge labor/extermination complexes, Majdanek and Auschwitz. Hitler moved in two million Poles from the incorporated territories.

Hitler harbored a great distaste for the Poles and outlined specific steps he would take in Poland when the war ended. Poles for whom Aryanization was either impossible or undesirable were to be reduced to an animal state. In several regions, Hitler would halt Polish education.

Stutthof near the Baltic coast became the wartime site of one of the strictest and most primitive of the official concentration camps. It was the first camp established on Polish territory and the last in occupied Europe to be liberated. About 120,000 prisoners passed through its gates, citizens of many European countries. Stutthof played a major role in the extermination and incarceration of the Polish people.[2] First came the Polish activists, then the POWs, the postmen, railroad employees, firemen, soldiers, famous professors, journalists, writers, judges, mayors, and 250 priests. When Hitler invaded additional countries, Norwegian policemen, Danish Communists, Lithuanian and Ukrainian officials and intellectuals, and Russian POWs arrived. The most serious feature of Stutthof was labor; most inmates died of work, starvation, and disease, in addition to being beaten, tortured to death. Because the Poles did not starve fast enough, the SS hanged them from trees, drowned them in the mud, and burned them alive in wood furnaces.[3]

In Sachsenhausen, considered an easy camp, the SS punished and harassed the Polish prisoners ceaselessly, as they did in Buchenwald, the "Little Camp." In Buchenwald, considered a moderate camp, most prisoners simply died. Polish and French prisoners lived in tents. Wet, dirty, exhausted, sick, and starving, they fought to remain alive in the impossible conditions. Inmates referred to Buchenwald as the "camp of slow death."[4]

The "Hangman of Buchenwald," Martin Sommer, did not like Poles, and he forced the men to immerse their testicles in ice-cold or boiling water, then painted them with iodine as their skin came off in strips. "He chained seven young Poles to their cots with a diet of saltwater and pickles.

They perished after the entire camp heard their screams and moans for several days."[5]

When the Nazis took over Poland, Himmler's document, *Reflections on the Treatment of Peoples of Alien Races in the East,* directed the SS to select from that conglomeration of inferior people living in the General Government the racially valuable and bring them to Germany for assimilation. The Nazis initiated an extensive program of kidnapping foreign children with good racial and physical characteristics and sending them to Germany to special camps. Himmler's directive was as follows: "The conditions in which these people live . . . are a matter of complete indifference to us. They interest me only to the extent that we need them as slaves for our culture."[6]

In eastern Europe, the Germans hunted for their future little Germans throughout the playgrounds and orphanages, among adopted and illegitimate children, children with Polish guardians, children of mixed marriages and of divorced, deported, or banished parents, children born in camps, and children who happened to be walking down the street. The Germans kidnapped an estimated 200,000 Polish children. "The boys with whom the Nazi indoctrination methods succeeded were to become SS mercenaries. Many smaller girls brought to Germany and selected as slaves were sterilized at the age of four, five, six, or seven; the young boys were castrated. Young girls between eight and twelve were placed in medical centers and given hormone injections to accelerate puberty, and then selected to breed. After bearing three or four children in SS maternity homes, they would be given an injection and simply cease to exist."[7]

One Polish child survivor of the kidnapping system wrote that many children went out of their minds:

Children who wetted their beds were sent to Block 8, which had no doors or windows. The children were given blankets that were as thin an spiders' webs, . . . and during the night they froze. Next morning we had to use picks to cut the stiff bodies away from the plank beds.
. . . We flung them into a mass grave, threw lime over them and covered them with earth. Sometimes they were not quite dead. When they began to suffocate through lack of air, the earth over the grave moved like a cornfield in the wind. . . . On an average day, 120 of the 3,000 or 4,000 children died.[8]

In spite of the approaching end of the war and the advancing Allied armies, the Germans continued to gather Polish children, stuff them into boxcars without food or blankets, and try to ship them to Germany. The cars of Polish children, referred to as death trains, were filled with babies who died en route. Only about 20,000 Polish children were returned to their country after the war.[9]

The Gypsies The Nazis were determined to exterminate the Gypsies, based on the law of 1935: "In Europe generally only Jews and Gypsies are of foreign blood." By a December 1942 decree, the Nazis were to deport all German Gypsies to Auschwitz, regardless of age or sex. On March 29, 1943, the order was given to deport all Dutch Gypsies to Austria. The Nazis then destroyed the European Gypsy communities and deported many to Jewish ghettos and the camps. Gypsy names appear on the death lists throughout the system.[10]

The Nazis sent convoys of Gypsy families from all over central Europe to Birkenau. About 21,000 Gypsies passed through the camp. Birkenau overflowed with Gypsy children. When Himmler visited, he saw the Gypsy children, ravaged by filth and starvation, with grotesquely twisted bodies, their faces without noses, and teeth protruding through skinless cheeks. He took pity and ordered everyone in the Gypsy compound to be gassed.[11]

In Sachsenhausen the Germans performed experiments on Gypsies in an attempt to show they had different blood from Germans.[12] The first transport arrived in 1939 at Ravensbrück—Gypsy children with their mothers. Later Dr. Clauberg sterilized all the Gypsy women and their young daughters between the ages of five and eight. After sterilization, the Gypsy children "used to come out crying, asking their mothers what had been done to them."[13]

Buchenwald had a special section created for Gypsies. In the spring of 1939, a Gypsy tried to escape. After recapturing him,

Commandant Koch had him placed in a wooden box, one side covered by chicken wire. The box was only large enough to permit the prisoner to crouch. He then had large nails driven through the boards, piercing the victim's flesh at the slightest movement. The Gypsy . . . was kept in the roll call area for two days and three nights, without food. His dreadful screams had long since lost any semblance of humanity.[14]

One Gypsy told of the death of her sister and niece:

First the girl was forced to dig a ditch, while her mother, seven months pregnant, was left tied to a tree. With a knife they opened the belly of the mother, took out the baby and threw it in the ditch. Then they threw in the mother and the girl, after raping her. They covered them with earth while they were still alive.[15]

The Nazi Gypsy Solution killed three-quarters of the German and one-half of the Austrian Gypsies. By 1945, the Nazis had murdered at least 220,000 of the estimated 700,000 European Gypsies.[16]

Accused Homosexuals   When Himmler opened his war against homosexuality in 1933, he estimated the number of homosexually inclined men in Germany at one million, or 10 percent of male Germans. He thought it impossible to lock up and reeducate millions; therefore he preached their eradication. No one has a final count of the accused homosexuals killed in the camps, but the Nazis categorized as the worst subhumans Jews, homosexuals, and Gypsies. They were the scum of humanity who had no right to live and who suffered most frequently and severely from tortures, beating, and every medical examination that could be performed on humans—and animals.[17]

The Nazis collected Germany's homosexuals, threw them into jails and camps, and labeled them with pink triangles on their camp uniforms. Many camps had homosexual inmates but Sachsenhausen and Buchenwald housed the largest numbers, in their "queer blocks"—for "back-breaking labor, murder, hunger, and torture."[18]

We know how the SS brutally assaulted and sexually abused the Sachsenhausen homosexuals, calling them "filthy queers."[19] As one survivor recalled: "I was the only available target on whom everyone was free to vent his aggressions." Another survivor described an ordinary death of a young healthy homosexual. The guards beat him to a pulp, calling him a pervert, and then put him in an icy shower. Thoroughly drenched, he was forced to stand outside in the bitter cold night:

When morning came, his breathing had become an audible rattle. Before he died, he was again beaten and kicked. Then he was tied to a post and placed under an arc lamp until he began to sweat, again put under a cold shower and so on. He died toward evening.[20]

When demands for labor by essential industries reached a hysterical level, the Nazis allowed some of the Sachsenhausen homosexuals to be rehabilitated and released as civilian laborers. Rehabilitation took two forms. If a candidate performed "properly" with a prostitute, he might be released as cured. If he failed and agreed to castration, he might be released for heavy labor.[21]

The Recalcitrant Clergy, Christians, and Prisoners of Conscience In 1940, Himmler designated Dachau for the incarceration of all clergy scattered throughout the system. It became a meeting place for the clergy of all nations, of different creeds—a majority of whom were Poles.[22] In 1960 on the day of the dedication of the Monument of Atonement in Dachau, a thousand Catholic young men walked from Munich carrying a heavy cross followed by a hundred priests wearing white robes, priests who as inmates had marched on the camp street in stripped uniforms. Former prisoner Archbishop Adam Kozlowiecki celebrated the pontifical mass, and the congregants joined in a special atonement for the particularly bitter persecution of the Jews and the hatred shown to other races. In the sermon, the bishop grappled with the symbol of Dachau: "Here inhumanity became the law of man. It is fatal to fall into the hands of man."[23]

The Jehovah's Witnesses or the "Bible students, Bible-worms, bible-bees," as they were called, refused to acknowledge the supremacy of the nation over God or to sign a statement repudiating their religion. The abuse experienced by those prisoners of conscience ranged from extremely mild abuse to torture and murder. Martin Gilbert reminds us that the Nazis murdered the Witnesses at Mauthausen along with the Jews and homosexuals. But at Auschwitz, Commandant Hoess blindly wrote of the women as "contented with their lot":

They hoped that, by suffering in captivity for Jehovah's sake, they would be given good positions in His kingdom, which they expected to enter very soon.
. . . I have always regarded Jehovah's Witnesses as poor, misguided creatures, who were nevertheless happy in their way.[24]

The Russian POWs Commandant Hoess wrote about the cruel extermination of the Soviet POWs, of whom only a very few survived. He witnessed the gassing of 900 Russian POWs at Auschwitz. The commandant of Gross-Rosen killed 65,000 Russian inmates in six months by feeding them soup made of grass, water, and quantities of salt followed by quantities of cold water.[25] In Flossenburg, the SS burned the Russian POWs alive, and in Majdanek, they shot them into trenches.

In 1945, in Mauthausen, the SS determined to kill 1,700 new arrivals —predominantly Russians and Poles. They sent them outside nude. That night the temperature dropped below freezing. The prisoners stood in the square for four hours as they were sprayed alternately with hot water.

Icicles formed all over their bodies. One remarkable prisoner, the Russian general Karbychev, walked among them, giving them comfort. He promised to set an example by dying on his feet. "At the next shower of water he leaned against the wall and immediately thick ice formed a coffin around him."[26]

Euthanasia Euthanasia: The Law for the Prevention of Offspring with Hereditary Diseases, 1933, provided that "anyone who is suffering from a hereditary disease can be sterilized by a surgical operation." A German medical economist in 1943 lamented the high cost of caring for deaf-mutes, cripples, mentally ill, or deficient persons. He objected that the state spent far more for the existence of these actually worthless compatriots than for the salary of a healthy man. It was no surprise that the first category of victims were the *Ausschusskinder,* or "garbage children," previously institutionalized or sterilized. By 1940 with the liquidation of children well under way, the Nazis turned to the adults—the insane, feebleminded, epileptic, crippled, old, ill—with all the activity used as a training ground for methods and personnel in the subsequent Hitlerian solutions.[27]

Gross-Rosen became a major Polish camp active in the euthanasia program and in Hitler's subjugation of the Polish people. Many inmates were the undesirables for whom the final solution was euthanasia. Gross-Rosen participated in the project more actively than any other camp. The purpose was to eliminate the "useless eaters," drawn from every German mental institution and hospital for crippled and old, and from the groups of mentally and bodily deficient children, insane Russians and Poles, and those with arteriosclerosis, tuberculosis, and cancer—persons no longer of any value to the state.[28]

The Oddities Clearly to be different in Nazi Germany and wartime Europe was to be placed in extreme peril. Particularly dangerous was tattooed skin. A Czech doctor, Franz Blaha, testified before the Nuremberg Tribunal that in Dachau he had flayed the skin off bodies, after which it was chemically treated and placed in the sun to dry. He then used it for a variety of leather merchandise.[29] Tattooed skin was big business in Sachenhausen, and the pathology department kept its eyes open for richly tattooed prisoners. The Mauthausen doctors also operated a thriving skin business. They skinned bodies of prisoners with interesting tattoos and sent the skin to processing for book covers, gloves, luggage, and lamp shades.[30]

In Buchenwald, "the SS immediately cataloged every tattooed prisoner on entering the camp, and when his order came up, the doctors called him to the dispensary and killed him by injection." The doctors sent some skin to the tattoo collection at a special museum in Berlin. They also found that the skin made excellent lamp shades, several of which were expressly fitted for Frau Koch, wife of the commandant. Decorators pleaded for tattooed skins for their customers.[31]

The Sachsenhausen pathology department supplied universities and anatomical institutes with skulls, skeletons, and organs, and murdered patients who aroused their strange medical interests. In Natzweiler, professors from Strasbourg selected from the prisoners who died there, whom had been pickled in pits, those with the most unusual heads; they placed the bodies in trucks and took them to the Strasbourg medical school.[32]

The Buchenwald researchers collected and prepared human skins, heads, and skulls for the SS. The medical chief of Department D of the WVHA, Dr. Loeling, wrote several times to the pathological section director in Buchenwald: "I need immediately ten entire skeletons, twelve skulls, or individual parts of the body, or we need some interesting bullet wounds." Hunchbacks or other persons whose physiognomy was of medical interest "excited the anatomical and macabre avarice of half-crazed doctors who were not averse to killing to obtain the skeletons to incorporate into the collections of the SS doctors or the display in the SS Medical Academy at Graz." A clerk in the pathology department testified that one day the camp physician pointed at a passing inmate and told the clerk that he wanted that skull on his desk the next day. "The next day he [the inmate] was on my autopsy table and the skull was taken apart, and it was turned over."[33] One former inmate, who worked in medical experimentation areas, told me it was like being confined to a zoo—surrounded by skulls, bones, and bottles of organs.

The SS spent much time on the selection platforms hunting for the twins and dwarfs of Europe. In Dr. Mengele's secret lab in Auschwitz, he murdered twins, dwarfs, and hunchbacks to provide the Berlin Institute of Anthropology with human organs and to discover the secrets of multiple birth.

Women of All Races In general the Nazis declared all Aryan men superior to all women, but Aryan women could bear the vital next generation of Aryan men. The non-Aryan could not. The Nazis therefore developed a program aimed at destroying non-Aryans and eliminating and suppressing ethnic groups and national characteristics. They implemented their program by kidnapping children, by forcing women to have abortions, by taking away the infants of eastern workers, by severely punishing them for sexual intercourse with Germans, by preventing mixed marriages, by hampering reproduction of enemy nationals.

The Nazis' motto was, "Aryan women out of the factories, non-Aryan women in." While the Aryan woman left the factory for the home, the non-Aryan woman left her home for the labor squads and the factories if she was fortunate, for the camps and the gas chambers if not. Aryan babies and children were cherished; non-Aryan babies were destroyed at birth or aborted during pregnancy. In many instances the non-Aryan's pregnancy was considered such an audacity that the SS killed two birds with one stone by throwing the pregnant woman into the gas chamber. Non-Aryan children suffered and died or were experimented on, or worked and died.

In the camps, Commandant Hoess wrote:

Everything was much more difficult, harsher and more depressing for the women, since general living conditions in the women's camp were incomparably worse. . . . The sanitary and hygienic conditions were notably inferior. . . . The general congestion was far greater than in the men's camp.

[In Birkenau,] from every point of view, and at all times, the worst conditions prevailed in the women's camp. This was so even at the very beginning, when it still formed part of the base camp. . . . the survival of a Jewess in Birkenau was twice as improbable as the survival of non-Jewish prisoners—improbable as that was too.[34]

Ravensbrück, the only major camp for women, contained a great mixtures of cultures, including Polish and French women, almost all female Jehovah's Witnesses, resisters, politicals, Jews, and, of course, always the children. One hundred thirty thousand women and children passed through, 90,000 to their death.

A Polish woman who had escaped the Ravensbrück gas chamber told what happened to her countrywomen:

During the winter, the SS on one day nailed shut the windows of their block's washroom, crammed in as many women as possible, and locked the doors. After a few days they decided to see how the experiment had worked—by setting up a motion-picture camera to film the emerging survivors. These prisoners had torn away the chimney bricks to try to get air and had ripped off all their clothing; several had died or were unconscious, others had evidently gone mad.[35]

After filming the scene, the SS sent all the women to the crematorium.

Medical experiments on women were especially frequent, gruesome, and interventionist. In Auschwitz a hospital orderly wrote of his assignment one day to a corpse removal squad:

On the left lay about seven exceptionally beautiful dead women. The breasts of the dead women had been cut off, as had been the flesh from many parts of their bodies —the sides, for example. The yard sloped steeply and the drains were clogged with blood. We waded in blood over our ankles. [36]

The Rabbit Guinea Pigs—a strange group drawn together as the female subjects of Ravensbrück's experimental operations—were subject to one of the most horrifying crimes in the concentration camp system. The experiments used primarily young, healthy Polish women like rabbits in a laboratory, infecting them with various diseases and performing on them the most disfiguring, disgusting, and bizarre of all surgical operations in the long history of the Third Reich's experimental medical program. The sadistic experiments included infectious operations on limbs; regeneration testing on bones (breaking, removal, grafting), on muscles (removal, grafting), on nerves; amputation of limbs and bone transplantation; and sterilization with surgery, X-rays, chemotherapy into the uterus. [37] The Nazis sought to develop an inexpensive, unobtrusive and rapid method of sterilization that could be used to wipe out Russians, Poles, Jews, and other people. At Auschwitz, Dr. Clauberg sterilized several thousand Jewish and Gypsy women by injecting inflammatory liquid into the uterus.

The operations on a special group of feebleminded or mentally ill women in Ravensbrück concerned the removal of certain limbs. The doctors amputated the lower extremities with a disarticulation in the hip joint. They performed the same operation on the upper extremities, with the elimination of the shoulder. To see if bones could be transplanted to German soldiers, they sent the amputated limbs, wrapped in operating sheets, to the military hospital. [38]

What was it like to be pregnant in Birkenau, or to bear a child? What happened to women who brought children with them? For Aryan women, the treatment was sometimes different than for non-Aryans, but for both it was inhuman. A midwife in the Aryan hospital recalled that about three thousand children were born with her help. "All newborn babies until 1943 were drowned in a small barrel. After each delivery, loud gurgles and the splashing of water could be heard in the next room. Later the new mother would see her baby's body thrown outside and torn apart by rats."[39] Of the three thousand babies born in the midwife's section, only thirty survived after 1943.

The Children of All Nations Historians estimate the number of murdered young people below the age of eighteen at one million. The concentration camp system of organized abuse evidenced its greatest antipathy toward the group called children. The SS separated thousands of children from their parents and sent them to Buchenwald. Most were Jewish and Polish children or the children of executed partisans. Only nine hundred survived. In the fall of 1944 the SS suddenly herded together all the Jewish and Gypsy youngsters and shipped the "screaming, sobbing children" to the Auschwitz gas chambers. When a convoy of Polish parents and their children arrived at Gusen, a team of *Kapos* killed many of the children in a mass axing orgy. The screams carried through the camp.

The SS took special care of the large group of inmate children in the Auschwitz/Birkenau complex: special brutality, cruelty, and experimentation, beyond even the ability of the hardened prisoners, so used to death, to watch and tolerate. When the gas chambers were full of adults, the SS dug pits and threw many children into them alive. A guard would grab a child's arms and legs, and hurl the baby through the air. They also laughed as they threw live children into the pond next to the crematorium. Witnesses testified at the Nuremberg trials that several thousand children were burned alive in Birkenau in 1944. When an SS man felt pity toward children, "he took the child and beat the head against a stone first before putting it on the pile of firewood, so that the child lost consciousness."[40]

When the Gypsy children died of starvation, they were thrown in heaps. One witness testified, "I saw a mountain of children's corpses. And scurrying among them the rats." Other witnesses remembered seeing SS men killing children by bending them over their knees like sticks of wood and breaking their spines. Often, when the Sonderkommando pulled the dead from the chambers, the hearts of some children were still beating. The conditions for children led one woman to make this pledge: "Together we will endure death. Even life."[41]

The Nazis usually did not allow children to be born at Birkenau. Pregnant Jewish women went to the gas chambers; any children were killed. In 1943 Aryan children born in the camp could remain alive with the unofficial consent of the SS. After they were entered in the camp register, their camp numbers had to be tattooed on the behinds or thighs because their little arms were too tiny. Most died within a week. The Soviets found only 156 children when they evacuated Birkenau.

Many children lived in Ravensbrück. They came in transports with their mothers or by themselves. Undernourished and with threadbare clothes, they were miserable creatures, little ragged skeletons. Eight hundred sixty children were born in Ravensbrück between 1943 and 1945. Without nourishment, diapers, or water, most babies died within a few days of birth by "natural" means. Also, the midwives drowned or smothered them.[42]

In Auschwitz, Polish prisoner Maria Zarebinska-Broniewska came in touch with the tragedy of children of all nationalities. Initially, as a mother who left her daughter behind, she believed like other inmates that children would survive the selections and the murders. But it was not to be. On one occasion, for example,

the children were given some milk soup with sugar as their supper, and a few hours later they started to pick them up for the crematorium. All crematoria were in use, but it became clear that the number of ovens was not sufficient. Therefore they ordered large pits to be dug, and there they burned the children in large piles. I saw hundreds of children, who climbed out of the trains and went to their deaths. Now that I am writing this, I am myself surprised, that as a mother, who loves not only her child, but all children of this world, I did not go crazy."[43]

Obscenity and Abuse as Public Policy Although the Nazis designed the camps, psychologically and technically, to destroy the inmates' basic humanity, it has always been clear that the camps were to be centers for dying. Except for the killing centers, the two major tasks of the camps' prisoners were to work and to die. Often they managed the dying alone; but the SS carefully planned the work in cooperation with Germany's major industrial firms. For the non-Jewish prisoners, however, the situation was far more complex. The goals for them varied from time to time, because the Nazis could not seem to arrive at a consensus. Yet the exploitation of prisoner labor to advance the war effort was a major and primary short-term goal for all non-Jewish inmates, simply working them to death and replenishing the labor supply from the always available pool. For a small number of prisoners, the task was to have a "change of heart" and a "fright" before being released back to polite society. At the very least, no one in the hierarchy ever objected to the "accidental" death of any prisoner, not even of notables.

Hitler attacked the old, the sick, the mentally ill, the deaf, the dumb, the blind, and the crippled. He sought to kill all Jews and most Gypsies. He classified as subhumans, persecuted, and murdered Poles, Russians, Slavs, and Soviet prisoners of war. He also attacked those he presumed were odd, including the physically unusual or unacceptable, twins, hunchbacks, those with unusual tattoos, skulls, or skeletons. He similarly targeted the politicals including Socialists and Communists, and he attacked prisoners of conscience and recalcitrant Christians including the Jehovah's Witnesses, Eastern Orthodox, Lutherans, Catholics, priests and ministers, male homosexuals, resistance fighters, women, and children.

In Elie Wiesel's *The Oath*, an old wanderer, Azriel, implores: "There is no beautiful death. Nor is there a just death. Every death is absurd. Useless. And ugly. . . . All you get in return is a corpse. And corpses stink."[44]

NOTES

1. Isabella Leitner, *Fragments of Isabella* (New York, 1978), preface.
2. Tadeusz Matusiak, *Stutthof* (Gdansk, 1974), pp. 8–9; and Richard Lukas, *The Forgotten Holocaust: The Poles under German Occupation, 1939–1944* (Lexington, Ky., 1986).
3. *German Crimes in Poland, I and II* (Warsaw, 1947), 2:119 (hereafter cited as GCP); and Matusiak, *Stutthof*, p. 16.
4. David Rousset, "The Days of Our Death," *Politics*, July–August 1957, pp. 151–52; and Annadora Miethe, ed., *Buchenwald* (DDR, 1974).
5. Eugene Kogan, *The Theory and Practice of Hell* (New York, 1950), pp. 209–10.
6. Marc Hillel, *Of Pure Blood* (New York, 1976), p. 150.
7. Ibid., p. 165.
8. Ibid., p. 174.
9. *Trials of Major War Criminals before the International Military Tribunal*, 42 vols. (Nuremberg, 1947–49), 5:367–68 (hereafter cited as TWC).
10. Phillip Friedman, "Nazi Extermination of the Gypsies," *Jewish Frontier*, vol. 1, no. 12; J. Schectman, "The Gypsy Problem," *Midstream* (November 1966), pp. 56–57; Miriam Novitch, "Half a Million Gypsies, Victims of the Nazi Terror," *UNESCO Courier* (October 1984), p. 24; and Miriam Novitch, *L'extermination des Tziganes* (Paris, 1969).
11. Rudolf Hoess, *Commandant of Auschwitz* (London, 1953), pp. 137–38.
12. TWC 1:13, 47, 631–32; Josef Bogusz, *Auschwitz: An Anthology on Inhuman Medicine* (Warsaw, 1970–74), vol. 1, pt. 1, p. 191.
13. "Experimental Operations in the Ravensbrueck Concentration Camp," GCP

2:133–50; Bogusz, *Auschwitz*, vol. 1, pt. 2; Eduard Ullmann, *Ravensbrueck* (DDR, 1964); and Stefan Kanfer, *The Eighth Sin* (New York, 1968), p. 282.

14. Kogan, *Theory and Practice of Hell*, p. 199.
15. Donald Kendrick, *The Destiny of Europe's Gypsies* (New York, 1972), p. 113.
16. Martin Gilbert, *Atlas of the Holocaust* (New York, 1982).
17. Heinz Heger, *The Men with the Pink Triangle* (New York, 1980), p. 143; Wolfgang Harthauser, "Der Massenmord an Homosexuellen im Dritten Reich," in Wilhart Schlegal, ed., *Das Grosser Tabu* (Munich, 1976); and R. Lautmann, "Pink Triangle: The Persecution of Male Homosexuality in Concentration Camps" (my review of the manuscript for *Journal of Homosexuality*, 1981).
18. Heger, ibid., p. 39.
19. Ibid., p. 35.
20. James Steakley, *The Homosexual Emancipation Movement in Germany* (New York, 1975), pp. 114, 116.
21. Richard Plant, "The Men with the Pink Triangles," *Christopher Street* (February 1977), no. 10; and Franz Seidler, *Prostitution, Homosexuality, Selbstverstummelung: Probleme der deutschen Sanitatsfuhrung, 1939–1945* (Vowinckel, 1977).
22. Paul Berben, *Dachau, 1933–1945* (London, 1975), p. 145.
23. Johann Neuhausler, *V.'hat Was It Like in the Concentration Camp at Dachau?* (Munich, 1960), p. 70.
24. Rudolf Hoess, in Jadwiga Bezwinska, ed., *KL Auschwitz, Seen by the SS* (Fertig, 1984), p. 79; Michael Kater, "Die Ernsten Bibelforscher im Dritten Reich," in *Vierteljahrshefte fuer Zeitgeschichte* (17, Jhrg., 1. Heft, 1969), pp. 181–218; Barbara Distel and Ruth Jakusch, eds., *Concentration Camp Dachau* (Munich, 1978), p. 62; and Christine E. King, *The Nazi State and the New Religions* (New York, 1983).
25. Paul Trepman, *Among Men and Beasts* (New York, 1978), pp. 168–69.
26. Evelyn LeChene, *Mauthausen* (London, 1975), pp. 119–20.
27. Robert Conot, *Judgment at Nuremberg* (New York, 1983), p. 205.
28. International Tracing Services: *Catalogue of Camps and Prisoners in Germany and German-Occupied Territories* (Arolsen, West Germany, 1945, 1950, 1951), 2:210 (hereafter cited as *ITS*); TWC 5:444, 464, 859–61, 794–801.
29. Conot, *Judgment at Nuremberg*, p. 288.
30. LeChene, *Mauthausen*, p. 88.
31. TWC 5:1088–89; and Miethe, *Buchenwald*.
32. TWC 1:318–24, 12–15, 54–55, 88–89; and John Sehn, "Some Legal Aspects of the So-called Experiments," *Auschwitz*, vol. 1, pt. 1, pp. 64–65.
33. Miethe, *Buchenwald*, p. 18; TWC 5:1088.
34. Rudolf Hoess, *KL Auschwitz*, pp. 75–76, 79; and Ella Lingens-Reiner, *Prisoner of Fear* (London, 1948), p. 118.
35. Olga Lengyel, *Five Chimneys* (Chicago, 1947), pp. 24–25.
36. Martin Gilbert, *Atlas;* and Bernd Nauman, *Auschwitz* (New York, 1966), p. 371.
37. Wanda Poltawska, " 'Guinea Pigs' in the Ravensbrueck Camp," *Auschwitz*, B. I., pt. 2, p. 140; Poltawska, "Experimental Operations," in *GCP*, vol. 1.

38. Ibid.
39. Stanislawa Leszczynska, "Report of a Midwife from Auschwitz," *Auschwitz*, vol. 2, pt. 2, pp. 181–92, 186.
40. Judith Newman, *In the Hell of Auschwitz* (New York, 1963), p. 52; and *TWC* 5:663–64.
41. Nauman, *Auschwitz*, pp. 103, 133; Kazimerz Smjolen, *Auschwitz* (Oswiecim, 1961), pp. 69–70.
42. Gemma Gluck, *My Story* (New York, 1961), pp. 38–39; Wanda Kiedrzynska, *Ravensbrück* (Ravensbrück Archives, 1961).
43. Roman Hraber et al., *Kriegschicksale Polnischer Kinder* (Warsaw, 1981), pp. 9–10.
44. Elie Wiesel, *The Oath* (New York, 1972), p. 20.

CHAPTER 17

Between Cross and Swastika:
The Position of German Catholicism

John S. Conway

In 1963 a young German author, Rolf Hochhuth, published his polemical play, *The Deputy*, which was highly critical of Roman Catholicism and in particular of Pope Pius XII for his alleged capitulation to Nazi terrorism and aggression.[1] Two years later, in 1965, the American scholar Guenter Lewy wrote his equally critical account of the relationship between the Catholic church and Nazi Germany, which remains the only comprehensive account in English so far.[2] In reply to these criticisms, Catholic scholars in Germany and abroad have published a whole series of documentary volumes. These include the eleven volumes of the *Actes et Documents du Saint Siege*,[3] which describe in detail the diplomatic policies of the Vatican, and the six large volumes of the *Akten deutscher Bischofe*,[4] recording the activities of the German Catholic episcopate. In addition, we now have a whole series of Nazi records from the local regions, which demonstrate in great detail how the policies of the Third Reich affected the daily lives of Catholics. All these sources provide the raw material on which a more scholarly assessment can be made about the response of the Catholic church to Nazi persecution.

The fact remains that much of the scholarly investigation has been defensive in tone. From 1945 onward, it was the policy of the German Catholic church to depict itself as the victim of Nazi aggression, as the unwilling subordinate to Nazi machinations, or as the faithful remnant who refused to worship at the shrine of Germanic racism. The leading German Catholic historians have followed this line by stressing the extent of the church's opposition, by minimizing the extent of its collaboration and compromises, and in particular giving an interpretation of events that justifies the safeguarding of the church's autonomy, even at the expense of

wider social and humanitarian rights, in the face of the Nazis' unprecedented and highly unwelcome onslaught.[5] It was left to a few younger
scholars, or to Protestants such as the late Klaus Scholder, to provide a
more critical account of Catholic attitudes, particularly on the crucial issue
of the making of the Reich Concordat of 1933[6] and its consequences. The
controversy raised by these issues still continues, but I would suggest that
the debate would be more fruitful if the Catholic historians could be
induced to take a broader view of denominational loyalty and to act more
according to the motto of Pope Leo XIII, "Let nothing untrue be said, and
nothing true be unsaid."

From a wider perspective, the Nazi campaign against the churches needs
to be put into the context of the politics of persecution. By concentrating so
closely on the plight of the German Catholics as victims of Nazi harassment
and intolerance, Catholic historians have in my view insufficiently recognized the dynamic force of the Nazi desire to remodel society along totalitarian and racial lines. This gigantic piece of political engineering sought not
only to redraw the map of Europe but to change entirely the nature of its
racial composition by the elimination of all unwanted elements that stood in
the way. The Jews were of course the prime target of this revolution. But
increasingly so were the Christian churches. Not enough stress has been
placed on the significant connections between the persecution of both
groups, connections that became increasingly apparent in the thinking of
the Nazi leaders, particularly of Hitler and his closest associate in his final
years, Martin Bormann. By the end of the Nazi era, the intimate association between Nazi anti-Semitism and Nazi anti-Christianity was expressed
clearly in the frequent pejorative references to both Judaism and Christianity in Hitler's *Table Talk*. The total domination of the *Volksgemeinschaft*
demanded by the Nazi leadership finally left no room either for the Jewish
community or for the concepts of Christianity, which as Bormann noted,
"in their essential points have been taken over from Jewry."[7] In 1941 Hitler
himself made the connection unequivocally:

The heaviest blow that ever struck humanity was the coming of Christianity.
Bolshevism is Christianity's illegitimate child. Both are inventions of the Jew.[8]

To eliminate the total Judaeo-Christian heritage was to be the prime duty
of the new "scientific" Weltanschauung based on the Nazi doctrines of
racial purity and German power. It was part of the Führer's determination
to rid Germany of all "Jewish" filth and priestly twaddle."

The war will be over one day. I shall then consider that my life's final task will be to solve the religious problem. Only then will the life of the German native be guaranteed once and for all.[9]

For various reasons, historians of Nazi Germany have not stressed this ideologically motivated link between the anti-Semitic and anti-Christian aspects of Nazi totalitarianism. General historians of the Nazi era have usually seen the attacks on the churches solely in terms of power politics, as an attempt to curb the churches' institutional life, or to sever any unwanted international connections (e.g., with the Vatican). By concentrating on the fate of their own members, church historians have rarely given sufficient weight to the parallels with the Nazi campaigns against the other victims, and have thus obscured the crucial point, on which the historians of both the "intentionalist" and the "functionalist" schools agree, of the "cumulative radicalization" in the Nazis' plans for a final settlement against all their enemies.

In part, the failure to stress this connection arose because of the obvious difference in tactics. At the beginning of the Nazi rise to power, Hitler had widely divergent strategies for dealing with Jews and Christians. To gain control of Germany, the Nazis needed the support of churchmen who composed—at least nominally—95 percent of the population. The Jews, on the other hand, were a tiny minority and already the object of widespread anti-Semitic feeling. A shrewd awareness of the number of adherents to Christianity obliged Hitler to curb the anticlerical ambitions of his more radical supporters for dealing with the churches, even while their antipathies were given free rein against the Jews.

Second, Hitler's antipathy to the churches was never announced as a public policy. Despite the unceasing persecution against individual priests, or against different aspects of church life from the beginning of 1933, many Catholics continued to believe that allegiance to nazism and to the Church were entirely compatible. Although Hitler was violently critical of the churches in private—as can be seen from the vitriolic outbursts dating from 1932–33, recorded by Rauschning in his book *Hitler Speaks*—he was careful not to reveal his intentions in public. Not until June 1941 were his feelings made plain, in the highly important memorandum issued by Bormann to the Gauleiters, which opened with the incisive pronouncement: "National Socialism and Christianity are irreconcilable."[10] This was followed a few months later by the equally clear policy statement to a conference of Gestapo officials: "Our final goal is the complete elimination of the whole of Christianity."[11] Only the exigencies of the war caused this plan to be postponed.

The third factor precluding the recognition of the similarities of the persecution process arose out of the compliant attitude of German Catholicism, in particular the continued readiness of its leaders to maintain the claim that the position of the church had been guaranteed by the provisions of the 1933 concordat. Despite the ever-growing evidence that the Nazi regime had no intention of honoring its terms, the German bishops strove to retain their belief that the government could be recalled to legally secured and morally defensible positions. A policy of accommodation rather than outright resistance even to the Gestapo's most flagrant breaches of the concordat was consistently followed by the presiding bishop, Cardinal Bertram of Breslau. At no time, as Gordon Zahn pointed out many years ago, were German Catholics taught to recognize the demonic nature of the Nazi regime.[12] The Bishops continued to stress their absolute national loyalty and had decided views about the impossibility of promoting any form of political resistance.

Since 1945 Catholic historians have repeatedly asserted that the authoritarian and conservative stance of their leadership was best suited to preserve the traditional Catholic way of life, which the Nazis were attempting to penetrate and destroy. To be sure, Catholic communities, particularly in the rural areas, retained a strong attachment to their church, and resistance was staunchest where the Nazis sought to sweep away the ancient customs of popular piety. The readiness of Catholics to come to the defense of their own institutions and their own followers was attested to in their protests not only against the so-called euthanasia program, but also in the vigorous opposition to the iconoclastic attempts to remove crucifixes from Catholic schools. These cases aroused the Catholic population because they immediately and visibly challenged the entrenched feelings of the parishioners on their home ground and in their own family lives. These protests reinforced the image of the Catholic church as a closed community on the defensive against a hostile world and government. As a result, the conclusion has been drawn that the Catholic church, by raising the drawbridge and retreating into the fortress of its own community life, successfully resisted the onslaughts of Nazi totalitarianism, and indeed survived better than any comparable group in German society.[13]

Such assertions ignore the fact that the Nazi campaign against German churches was restrained during the war, not so much by Catholic intransigence, but by Hitler's decision to postpone any final settlement until victory was achieved. For this reason the full weight of Nazi repression was not launched against the German Catholic church, in contrast to the situation in Poland. No German Catholic bishop, not even the outspoken bishop of Munster, Count Galen, was imprisoned or tortured. But it is clear that major figures in the Nazi party were unhappy with the Führer's decision. Heydrich encouraged the Gestapo to take repressive measures that went far beyond any that could be justified by wartime necessity. Bormann's initiative in confiscating monasteries in early 1941 was designed as a warning to the church not to expect that its effusive expressions of wartime loyalty would be rewarded later on. The action of Gauleiter Wagner of Bavaria in April 1941 ordering the removal of crucifixes from all schools was evidence of the Nazi desire to capitalize on the euphoria created by Germany's military victories. Now was the time to promote anti-Catholic feelings. And the recently published final volume of Goebbels' diary for the war years shows unequivocally that the Nazi determination to gain total ideological mastery of the German people remained unchanged.[14]

It would be highly instructive if researchers began to use the extensive source materials now available dealing with German popular opinion to analyze for the whole country the reactions to Nazi policies on the church question, along the lines developed for Bavaria by Ian Kershaw,[15] or as thoroughly as Kulka and Rodrique have examined these sources for the Jewish question.[16] Such a study would provide a more discriminating assessment of the success of the Nazi ideological penetration through the cumulative effects of its propaganda campaigns and repressive police measures. Contrary to the apologetic and often self-congratulatory tone of postwar Catholic historians, I believe the picture would reveal that, had the Nazi onslaught been resumed as a central focus of government policy, the outcome for the Catholic church would have been very different. Hitler's continuing ideologically motivated obsession was to obliterate the discredited creeds of Christianity that had misled Germans for too long. If victory still eluded him, this was because his policies of exorcism and persecution had not been radical enough. The Catholic church leaders' readiness to support the authoritarian, nationalist, and anti-Semitic goals of the Nazi regime demonstrated how unprepared they were, institutionally or theologically, to mobilize their following in any campaign beyond the defense of the immediate interests of their own community. Just as the extermination of the Jews had shown how the regime could overthrow all moral barriers to political extremism to implement its paranoid plans, so there can be little doubt that the often-proclaimed determination to root out Christianity altogether would have ended in the persecution of outspoken and committed Catholics by the same methods that had so effectively been used to deal with the Jews.

It would be comforting, but in my view unrealistic, to believe that the Catholic church could have mounted a successful opposition to this process. Whereas in the occupied countries both nationalist and ecclesiastical interests combined to support anti-Nazi resistance, the situation in Germany was far more ambivalent. The pervasive impact of the Nazi ideological indoctrination and intimidation campaigns had already precluded active collective popular resistance, except in the narrowest possible areas. It is therefore difficult to resist Kershaw's incisive conclusion:

So far in history no other advanced society has experienced a collapse of moral consciousness and individual civil morality approximating to the steepness of the decline in Germany after 1933.[17]

The Nazi regime was not overthrown from within. Only the victory of its external enemies saved its intended victims, including the Catholic church, from the full force of Nazi tyranny.

It is instructive to contrast the Catholic and Protestant assessments of the lessons of the church struggle. Catholic historians regard the Nazi era as an unfortunate episode and praise the staunchness of the Catholic milieu in resisting Nazi pretensions. On this basis they welcome the restoration in West Germany of the Catholic church's 1933 position and privileges, including the guarantees provided in the Reich Concordat. After 1945, when these Catholics were seeking to erect barriers against the equally dangerous menace of communism, the defensive strategy of their leaders in the Nazi period seemed particularly appropriate for the determination of future policy.

The Protestant commentators have taken a wider view. Beginning with the famous Stuttgart Declaration of Guilt of October 1945, and much influenced by the thinking of their leading theologian, Dietrich Bonhoeffer, who was executed by the Nazis shortly before the end of the regime, the Protestant churches have sought to learn a very different lesson from their church struggle. In such bodies as the World Council of Churches, the role of the Church is now seen as calling for a direct and prophetic condemnation of the misuse of state power, and for an explicit commitment to the victims of oppression. As the voice of the voiceless, and in solidarity with the poor and suffering masses, the Church must seek to oppose the inhumanity and bureaucratized violence of established powers, and hence to support the cause of freedom and liberation. The failure to follow this course during the Nazi regime is thus seen by Protestants as a fateful legacy.

With the advantage of hindsight, we can now see that the triumph of national socialism raised fundamental questions about the exercise of power and the moral basis of modern society in a totalitarian state. As I have pointed out elsewhere, the failure of the churches to take a stand against the ideology and nihilism of the Nazis was a product of both historical and theological conditioning. On the one hand, there is the undeniable fact of the readiness of the Catholic church to give enthusiastic endorsements to so many parts of the Nazi program. On the other hand, the churches continued to be the source of an alternative system of values to the incessantly propagated Nazi racial ideology. Even if weakly and ineffectually defended by the institutional church, this inheritance provided the basis for the witness of the courageous if small minority of Catholic opponents, such as Bernhard Lichtenberg, Alfred Delp, and Max Joseph Metzger, who died for their beliefs. It remains, however, and open question whether the adherence of the Catholic milieu to their traditional ways in the face of the force of Nazi *Gleichschaltung* should be described as *Widerstand*.[18]

Since 1945 the wider significance of the Nazi period for church-state relations has become clear. The twelve years of Hitler's rule demonstrated both rapidly and ominously the ongoing collapse of every credible religious or moral restraint on the state, the extraordinarily powerful force of propaganda, the growth of dehumanizing ideologies of various kinds, and the erosion of religious traditions. At a time of unprecedented and menacing challenge, the experience of German Catholicism during the Nazi era provides an instructive case study, not only of institutional supineness and human fallibility, but also, on occasion, of personal heroism and authentic religious obedience.

NOTES

1. Rolf Hochhuth, *Der Stellvertreter* (Hamburg, 1963); English ed., *The Representative* (London, 1963); American ed., *The Deputy* (New York, 1964); see also E. Bentley, ed., *The Storm over the Deputy* (New York, 1964).
2. Guenter Lewy, *The Catholic Church and Nazi Germany* (New York, 1965).

3. *Actes et documents du Saint Siege relatifs a la seconde guerre mondiale*, 11 vols. (Vatican City, 1967–81).

4. *Akten deutscher Bischofe über die Lage der Kirche 1933–1945*, 6 vols. (Mainz, 1968–85).

5. Johann Neuhausler, *Kreuz und Hakenkreuz. Der Kampf des Nationalsozialismus gegen die katholische Kirche und der kirchliche Widerstand* (Munich, 1946); Dieter Albrecht, ed., *Katholische Kirche im Dritten Reich. Eine Aufsatzsammlung zum Verhaltnis von Papsttum, Episkopat und deutschen Katholiken zum Nationalsozialismus 1933–1945* (Mainz, 1976); Klaus Gotto und Konrad Repgen, eds., *Kirche, Katholiken und Nationalsozialismus*, (Mainz, 1980).

6. Klaus Scholder, *Die Kirchen und das Dritte Reich*, vol. 1 (Berlin, 1977); Hans Muller, *Katholische Kirche und Nationalsozialismus* (Munich, 1963); E. W. Bockenforde, "Der deutsche Katholizismus im Jahre 1933," in *Hochland* 53 (1960–61); but see also Ludwig Volk, *Das Reichskonkordat vom 20 Juli 1933. Von den Ansatzen in der Weimarer Republik bis zur Ratifizierung am 10 September 1933* ser. B, vol. 5 (Mainz, 1972); K. Repgen, "Ueber die Entstehung der Reichskonkordats-Offerte im Fruhjahr 1933 und die Bedeutung des Reichskonkordat," in *Vierteljahrshefte fuer Zeitgeschichte* 26 (1978).

7. International Military Tribunal, Trials of the Major War Criminals, Document 075-D, quoted in John S. Conway, *The Nazi Persecution of the Churches 1933–1945* (London, 1968), p. 363.

8. *Hitler's Secret Conversations 1941–1944* with an introduction by H. R. Trevor Roper (New York, 1953), p. 37.

9. Ibid., p. 158; numerous and very similar examples of Hitler's views are quoted in the recently published volumes of Goebbels' diaries, 1932–41. See Hans G. Hockerts, "Die Goebbels-Tagebucher 1932–1941. Eine neue Hauptquelle zur Erforschung der nationalsozialistischen Kirchenpolitik," in D. Albrecht *et al.*, eds., *Politik und Konfession. Festschrift fuer Konrad Repgen* (Berlin, 1983), p. 359–92.

10. Conway, *Nazi Persecution*, p. 363.

11. Unpublished notes of Gestapo conference of September 1941, compiled by SS-Obersturmführer Heinrich, and cited in J. S. Conway, *Die Nationalsozialistische Kirchenpolitik* (Munich, 1969), p. 299.

12. Gordon Zahn, *German Catholics and Hitler's Wars* (New York, 1962), p. 73.

13. Heinz Hurten, "Selbstbehauptung und Widerstand der katholischen Kirche," in Jurgen Schmadeke and Peter Steinbach, eds., *Der Widerstand gegen den Nationalsozialismus. Die deutsche Gesellschaft und der Widerstand gegen Hitler* (Berlin, 1985), p. 248.

14. See note 9.

15. Ian Kershaw, *Popular Opinion and Political Dissent in the Third Reich: Bavaria 1933–1945* (Oxford, 1983), chaps. 4, 5, and 8.

16. Otto Dov Kulka and Aron Rodrique, "The German Population and the Jews in the Third Reich: Recent Publications and Trends in Research on German Society and the 'Jewish Question,' " in *Yad Vashem Studies*, vol. 16 (Jerusalem, 1984); O. D. Kulka, " 'Public Opinion' in National Socialist Germany and the

'Jewish Question,' " in *Zion: Quarterly for Research in Jewish History* 40 (1975):186–290 (Hebrew with English summary, documentation in German).

17. I. Kershaw, "German Popular Opinion and the 'Jewish Question,' 1939–1943: Some Further Reflections," in Arnold Paucker, ed., *Die Juden im Nationalsozialistischen Deutschland/The Jews in Nazi Germany 1933–1943* (Tuebingen, 1986), p. 385.

18. See the discussion in *Der Widerstand gegen den Nationalsozialismus* (note 13), p. 227–326.

CHAPTER 18

Jehovah's Witnesses under Nazism

Christine King

The Jehovah's Witness movement was founded in America in the 1870s and came to Germany in the 1890s. Witnesses to Jehovah believe that the world is in its last age and under the sway of Satan. They are members of Jehovah's kingdom and witnesses to Jehovah in the midst of evil. They await the end of the world and the establishment of Christ's rule on earth in the millennium. While honest and law-abiding, as far as their faith allows, Jehovah's Witnesses see themselves as citizens of another state and members of another army. Thus they cannot vote in, or fight for, an "earthly" state. They will "render unto Caesar" but cannot take dual citizenship.

Although Jehovah's Witnesses will not enlist or fight in an "earthly" army, they do not see themselves as pacifists. They are soldiers of Jehovah in the spiritual war between good and evil and expect to see the battle of Armageddon, which will herald the millennium, when Jehovah's forces will defeat those of Satan. The Witnesses' part in this war will be a spiritual one; yet the battle will be physical and real, heralded by a world war on earth.

In times of peace under liberal regimes, Jehovah's Witnesses present few real problems to the state. Their numbers are small and their identification as heretics by the mainstream churches as well as the persistence of their door-to-door preaching means they have few friends. While they may be marginalized or ridiculed, they rarely suffer harassment or persecution on any large scale.

The nature of national socialism, however, was such that it put under an intense spotlight every issue of social and political life. To a regime inclined to control the hearts and minds of all its citizens, the Jehovah's

Witnesses presented a serious challenge. Not only did they stand outside the new German society, but they were publicly perceived as being outside the mainstream. Because of their distribution of "unsuitable" literature and their door-to-door preaching, they were marginalized in Nazi society.

A regime more confident of its roots and its future might ignore such a threat, but the Nazis reacted with extremity and violence. Thus the Witnesses, unlike any other religious group, were isolated and harangued from 1933 onward.[1] Suspicion and harassment turned into bitter persecution as the Witnesses refused to surrender, and the two sides were thrown into a pitched battle with dramatic results for each.

The reasons for the suddenness and violence of this conflict are complex and often contradictory, and go a long way toward revealing the muddled nature of Nazi policy-making and implementation. As a result of early party investigations, the Witnesses were believed to have American connections and internationalist aspirations.[2] Neither characteristic need spell inevitable disaster for the group. Other religious groups who suffered little or no persecution, such as the Mormons, for example, had both these characteristics; nor were American connections necessarily unacceptable before 1941.

The Witnesses were identified as communist. In their refusal to undertake certain civic duties, they were clearly suspect. The Nazis read a political message into the Witnesses' graphic descriptions of the chaos, anarchy, and revolution that would precede the coming of the millennium. To add to their other "crimes," the Witnesses were identified as Zionist. Their supposed Zionism was seen to spring from their prophecies about the return of the Jews to the Holy Land at the imminent end of the present world.[3]

When their alleged and equally groundless freemasonic sympathies and connections were added to the list, the charge completed the catalog and ensured disaster for the Witnesses. Although it is possible that some zealous local officials believed what they were instructed to find in the Witness movement, it is highly unlikely that the policymakers were that naive. It is clear that in the highest circles the Witnesses were recognized as harmless, albeit fanatical. Indeed, they were held up by more than one Nazi as a model of devotion and obedience that the SS might do well to follow. Himmler even had plans to settle the Witnesses in the East as a pacifist buffer state, once the war was won.[4]

There were other reasons for the choice of the Witnesses as the first strike against religious freedom. The closure could be swift, easy, and public—a cheap victory to appease the major churches by the extermination of a heresy and to offer a threat for the future, should church leadership not conform to party wishes. It could also offer a sop to those in the party, like Martin Bormann, who wished to see draconian measures taken against all Christians. An easily identifiable target would also allow the brutality of the SA some "legitimate" crusade.

The primary reason the Nazis identified the Witnesses as enemies was because they recognized in them a rival ideology. The reasons for the initial attack remained, but as the struggle to suppress the movement took more and more police time and failed visibly, the struggle turned into a crusade. Invincible national socialism, already quasi-religious in its claims and practices, would move closer to its millennial goal by crushing this deviant nuisance. Each prophesied a millennium; in building theirs, the Nazis could tolerate no false gods.

The Nazi state had only one weapon and that was force. In the face of this force, the Witnesses had three clear choices. They could collaborate, as did some other religious groups, by making concessions and offering moral legitimation to the regime and financial support to the party. They could compromise by offering the minimum but appearing to bow the knee as had other groups. Finally, they could resist and take the consequences.

The Witnesses unhesitatingly took the third path. They resisted national socialism with a fury the Nazis did not understand and could not have anticipated. The Nazis had created their own Leviathan and had catapulted this harmless group into an eschatological battle, in which torture and martyrdom merely reinforced the Witnesses and gave them strength.

The Witnesses were a small group, some twenty thousand[5] out of a total German population of sixty-five million, with twenty million Catholics and forty million Protestants.[6] Battle lines were drawn early in 1933 and remained in force until 1945. After 1937 the fight spilled over into the concentration camps, where approximately one-quarter of the membership lost their lives.

Outside of the camps, Witnesses lost children, jobs, pensions, and all civil rights. They were brought before special courts for refusing to enlist, undertake air-raid watch, give the Hitler greeting, or stop meeting and proselytizing. In prison, as in the camps, they were subject to extreme and well-documented ridicule and torture.

Throughout all their trials, individuals kept their faith and the movement survived. When one local leader was arrested, another took his or her place. Witnesses not only continued to meet, but also to preach and distribute literature. Posters and tracts were even delivered to the party headquarters. Everywhere it was evident that the Gestapo was failing to crush the Witnesses.

In the camps, the purple triangles survived with the help of a strong network and their own powerful interpretation of history. Once a Witness was admitted to a camp, he or she was met and protected by coreligionists who were able to give practical and moral support and help the inmate overcome the disorientation and depression associated with camp imprisonment. Unlike many other inmates, the Witnesses had a family structure into which they could fit, the comfort of a shared faith, a set of values, and the hope of divine justification. If the most difficult thing to cope with was the loss of these surroundings, the Witnesses had strengths on all counts. While this was no real protection against the physical horrors, it did provide some psychological and emotional protection. Unlike many others, the Witnesses not only knew, but also understood why they were in the camps. Moreover, inside or out, they lived in Jehovah's world, and thus the separation from family and friends was not as drastic as it was for the others.

Also unlike most other prisoners, the Witnesses stayed in the camps by choice. Freedom could be bought by a signature on a simple document denouncing the Jehovah's Witness movement, yet very few signed.[7] Witnesses met, prayed, and converted others. They performed secret baptisms and distributed copies of the *Watchtower*, often smuggled into the camp by local Witnesses. In spite of the torture and murder of many of their number, their faith was unbroken. In punishment cells they sang hymns, and on roll call they preached to the commandant.[8] The SS isolated them, then tried to break them by putting them into specially tough blocks, but all to no avail. In the camps, as in society, the Witnesses not only were not broken but refused to keep quiet about the fact. As Michael Kater suggests, the Witnesses' beliefs immunized them against the SS.[9]

In their battle against Jehovah's Witnesses, the Nazis had taken on an enemy they did not understand. Their normal arsenal of weapons strengthened instead of weakened the resolve of the Witnesses. Ridicule was met by dignity and was seen as a fulfillment of prophecy, a further proof that the Witness was correct in his or her faith. The authorities were puzzled.

The public face of the struggle was an embarrassment to Nazi authorities. Complaints were being received from court officials about the blatant misuse of the law in relation to the Witnesses,[10] and members of the public were refusing to hand over either Witness literature or Witnesses themselves.

Essentially conservative and nonpolitical people, the Witnesses began to identify in very wide terms the evil of the regime. Thus, despite being viewed as hostile to the Jews whom they labeled as the "killers of Christ," the Witnesses, in their worldwide literature, identified the evils the Nazis were promulgating, not just against Witnesses, but also against other Germans, Jews, women, and children.

An ideological battle ensued between two "total" organizations, one very large, one very small, both with all-encompassing eschatological worldviews. Once the battle lines were drawn, neither side could or would surrender. The moral victors were the Witnesses, who emerged with one-quarter of their number dead and many others emotionally and physically battered, but with a belief system intact. To the end, Witnesses would not lie, steal, or kill, even against their enemies. They had served as servants to the SS (who else among the prisoners could be trusted to shave his SS master with a cutthroat razor?).[11] Yet the Witnesses retained the respect of most of their fellow inmates.

At the liberation, the Witnesses were active, moving among the confused and depressed with the message, "There is purpose to all of this; there is a God. Contact. . . ."[12] They continued to make converts.

NOTES

1. C. E. King, *The Nazi State and the New Religions* (New York, 1982).
2. P. Braeunlich, *Die Ernsten Bibelforscher Als Opfer Bolschewittischer Religionspotter* (Leipzig, 1926).
3. F. Schleget, *Die Wahrheit über die ernsten Bibelforscher, Freiburg im Breisgau,* 1928.
4. G. Ritter, "Wunschtraume Heinrich Himmlers 21 July 1944," in *Geschichte in Wissenschafte nd Unterricht,* no. 3, 1954, pp. 162–68.
5. M. Kater, "*Die Ernsten Bibelforscher im dritten Reich,* in *Vierteljahrshefte fuer Zeitgeschichte,* vol. 17 (Munich, 1969), p. 181.
6. *Statistisches Jahrbuch fuer das Deutsche Reich, 1933* (Berlin, 1933).
7. M. Buber, *Under Two Dictators* (London, 1950), p. 130.
8. Ibid., p. 231.

9. M. Kater, op. cit.
10. Bavarian State Archives 42296, July 15, 1940.
11. Evelyn LeChene, *Mauthausen* (London, 1971), p. 130.
12. Author's interview with Dorota Wind, October 19, 1978. Dorota Wind, who was Jewish, survived the camps and became a Jehovah's Witness.

CHAPTER 19

Pacifists during the
Third Reich

Gordon C. Zahn

As a conceptual convenience, it might be well to introduce a threefold breakdown of Nazi victims instead of the usual (and easily justified) tendency to speak only of Jews and "others." The first category were those who became victims because of *what they were* in terms of genetic (or, to a lesser extent, cultural) origins. Here, of course, we have the victims of the Final Solution, the Jews who, by Nazi definition, represented the "antirace" whose only purpose in existing was to defile and destroy the contributions of the Aryan "master" race. Some other groups—most notably perhaps, the Gypsies—shared the designation as human refuse suitable only for extermination. Close to these were the "lesser races"—ethnic, cultural, or national in identity—who, though not altogether worthy of existence, could be "put to use." Thus, we have the record of Slavs and other non-Aryans who were admitted into the Nazi forces or assigned as guards or even more responsible roles denied Jews and Gypsies as a matter of course.

The second category consists of those who became victims because of *what they did.* It is well to distinguish those who engaged in "ordinary" crimes and violations of generally accepted moral values (the homosexual victims, for example) from others whose crimes were political—whether it be a matter of defeatist thought and speech, listening to foreign broadcasts, or ranging all the way up to treason and attempted assassination. Some of these victims were pacifist or, at least, peace oriented in their motivation, but not all.

My third category consists of those who became victims because of what they *refused to do.* Included here are men who refused military service altogether and members of the armed forces who refused to comply with orders they considered immoral. This category is of particular interest to me in the light of my past research and personal commitment.

As is the case with most sets of categories, this breakdown leaves the impression of easy classification that cannot, in fact, be achieved. Who, for example, were those priests who suffered and perished in Dachau? Were they there for what they were (i.e., Poles to a great extent but also a suspect vocational group)? Were they there for what they did (keep alive a religious and cultural heritage that represented a threat to Nazi ideology and dominance)? Or were they there for what they refused to do (in most cases, affirm full support for the totalitarian state)? Most likely, we can agree, all three.

Nevertheless, there is a point in making these distinctions. Without in the least justifying the Nazi actions, we must recognize that much of what the Third Reich set out to punish would be considered subject to punishment in most, if not all, other countries—including our own. The moral and political opposition to any war-making authority is almost by definition open to charges of "giving aid and comfort to the enemy" in time of war. If it is true that these charges were too broadly defined in Hitler's Germany and that punishment was too automatic and too extreme, this does not absolve others of their similar violations of justice.

The Japanese relocation program is obviously relevant here, though it did not come anywhere close to the excesses of Nazi practices. Though our nation recognized conscientious objection to service in the armed forces, it did so as a privilege attendant with quite undemocratic restrictions and overtones. The United States is still reluctant to recognize conscientious objection as a basic human right. Some of our allies in the struggle for freedom (including, of course, *religious* freedom) were not willing to go even that far.

It is in this context, then, that I approach the question of pacifism and conscientious objection in Nazi Germany. Prior to Hitler's accession to power in 1933, there was a strong German peace movement or, if that implies too organized a force, a peace sentiment that found expression in a variety of activities and organizations. Some were rooted in religious, and even denominational, commitment. Besides the traditional "peace church" representation, one could find peace sentiments reflected in organizations devoted to internationalism and schemes for the abolition of war; in the ecumenical experiments seeking to reunify the Christian churches; in the emergence of a clearly dominant peace emphasis on the part of newly emergent religious communities or new movements and concentrations within the older, and more established, churches. Finally, there was an upsurge of interest in the German sections of organizations such as the Fellowship of Reconciliation and the War Resisters League.

Needless to say, none of these organizations lasted very long once the Nazis came to power. Consider, for instance, the *Friedensbund deutscher Katholiken* (whose founders included Father Max Metzger). In 1956 as recipient of a Fulbright Senior Fellowship, I went to Germany to study the FDK and the extent, if any, to which its members may have opposed the German war effort. Before the war, my preliminary study had told me, the movement had claimed a membership in the tens of thousands (including the Kolping Society as a "corporate member") and more than one thousand local groups. As things turned out, however, there was little research for me to do: the Friedensbund had the dubious distinction of being the first religion-related organization to be disbanded by government order, and its leader, the Dominican priest Franziskus Stratmann, retired into voluntary exile in Holland for the duration.

So, too, with Eberhard Arnold's fledgling Bruderhof community. Correctly reading the signs of the time, he arranged for draft-age men to leave the country and, in due time, the entire community followed suit. This was the general experience of the "organized" peace movement. We may take it for granted that some leaders and officials of such movements found their way into concentration camps or prison. Others would pay for their past activity with their lives. Still others would become victims under my third category, either as conscientious objectors in their own right or for encouraging and supporting those who took that stand.

Such actions fell under the special military law against *Zersetzung der Wehrkraft*, or what we would call "undermining" or "subverting" the armed forces, and were punishable by death. To refuse or encourage others to refuse to serve in the German forces (or those of Germany's allies); to encourage or assist a soldier or someone subject to conscription to evade such service, or to be absent without leave or otherwise weaken the morale of members of the armed forces; to counsel or resort to self-mutilation or similar devices to escape service—any and all of these were capital crimes.

Anyone who would seek to research the extent of such crimes and the toll taken in punishment will discover an almost complete lack of records or other available data. The few known cases have been discovered by chance or only slowly brought to public attention by families or surviving friends of the victims. Why slowly? To understand the reason, shocking though we may find it, it is necessary to understand German culture and the military traditions of the past. For many, such a death was—and, it is probably safe to say, for many still is—a matter of shame.

Consider the case of Michael Lerpscher, who was probably the first Catholic to refuse the military oath of unconditional obedience to Adolf Hitler by name. Lerpscher was beheaded on September 5, 1940. Because of the shame and scandal, Lerpscher's father burned all of his son's belongings in the family stove. Brother Michael (one of Metzger's followers, incidentally) may have been the first, but he was not to be the last to lose his head. Nor were all those beheaded Catholic.

In 1956 I happened upon a reference to an Austrian peasant named Franz Jaegerstaetter in a volume summarizing the so-called resistance of the Catholic church in Austria. (The reference, incidentally, presented him as "a typical example of a singularly unique type.") He, too, had been beheaded in Berlin (August 9, 1943), but in his case the refusal to take part in the war was absolute. All other cases of such refusals that came to my notice either focused on the oath or incorporated the willingness to serve as a medic or in some other noncombat role. A year or so later, I went to Jaegerstaetter's tiny village on the Austrian/Bavarian border to interview those who had known him, and in 1964 I published my book, *In Solitary Witness: The Life and Death of Franz Jaegerstaetter.*[1]

I introduce this bit of oral history with a purpose. In my previous research I had found but one book specifically devoted to a "peace" victim of the Nazis—a book written about a Pallotine priest who, like Lerpscher, refused to take the oath. The author, a former prison chaplain, had known the priest, Father Franz Reinisch, in his last days. A brief appendix about Jaegerstaetter—an untutored farmer, a married man, and father of three little daughters—struck me as providing the subject worthy of deeper study. Since my book appeared, the situation has changed. The latest listing I have seen includes no less than twenty additional studies, most of them brief narratives without analysis. One recent book (Hartmann and Hartmann, *Kriegsdienstverweigerung im Dritten Reich*) summarizes thirty such cases—twelve Jehovah's Witnesses; five Catholics; four Seventh Day Adventists; one each of Baptist, Quaker, Fellowship of Reconciliation, and Social Democrat affiliation. The remaining five cases gave no indication of affiliation.

It is gratifying that more attention is now being paid to these martyrs of conscience—but it is still nowhere near enough. As far as Jaegerstaetter is concerned, he has now been officially recognized as a hero in Austria and is increasingly mentioned as a possible candidate for canonization. His widow, however, is still subjected at times to unpleasantness in the village, and for a time at least, she was ruled ineligible for the reparations funds provided by the government after the war to families of victims of Nazi persecution. The refusal to fight for Hitler's version of *Volk* and *Vaterland* is still not seen as entirely praiseworthy even today.

Let us not be too smug about those simple peasants of St. Radegund, however. In 1984 the *New York Times* reported on the adverse reception given in Salt Lake City to a play about a young German Mormon who was beheaded for speaking out against Hitler. An earlier version of the play had been suppressed seven years before, and there was a question as to how its successor would be received. The *Times* cited the Brigham Young professor who compiled the historical record of the case as saying that in the Nazi era the church authorities *in Utah* counseled German members to support the Third Reich under the traditional teachings of required obedience to "the law of the land."

It is not only the horror of what was done by Nazi Germany that should concern us but, even more, *the horror of the awareness that it was done by human beings like us.* Similar horrors are still taking place and are likely to continue. The basic problem is not measurable in quantitative terms; it involves the very quality of human nature itself.

That, I submit, is why this third category—victims who perished because they refused to do evil—is so important. A soldier named Otto Shimek, court-martialed and executed because he would not obey the order to shoot Polish civilian hostages, gives us hope that someday, somewhere, there will be a serviceperson who will refuse to turn the key or press the button that would destroy millions of human lives. A slight hope, perhaps; but a hope nonetheless.

In response to the prison chaplain's request, Franz Jaegerstaetter prepared a statement explaining why, despite the pleas of friends and family and against the advice of priest and even his bishop, he persisted in his refusal to serve. The opening lines put this third category of victims in its most meaningful perspective:

These few words are being set down here as they come from my mind and my heart. And if I must write them with my hands in chains, I find that much better than if my will were in chains. Neither prison nor chains nor sentence of death can rob a man of the Faith and his free will.[2]

It is remarkable how often those same simple truths—call them pieties if you will—are expressed in the farewell letters written by the pacifist and peace-oriented victims of the Third Reich. Perhaps they have much to tell us about ourselves, much more than we realize. Things we may need to know before too long.

Two eminent reviewers of my book seemed to think so. To Theodore Roszak, the account of Jaegerstaetter's solitary witness "provided us with a measure of our own corruption."[3] Studs Terkel struck a somewhat more hopeful note in the conclusion to his review:

"The question recurs: Was Franz Jaegerstaetter crazy or a saint? Perhaps he was neither. No matter what his impulse in bearing solitary witness, perhaps he was just a man fulfilling man's moral potential. Mr Zahn's fascinating case history is more than about Jaegerstaetter. It's about us."[4]

NOTES

1. Gordon C. Zahn, *In Solitary Witness: The Life and Death of Franz Jaegerstaetter* (New York, 1964).
2. Ibid., p. 233.
3. *The Nation*, vol. 200 (April 19, 1965), p. 426.
4. *Chicago Sun Times*, January 24, 1965.

CHAPTER 20

Gay Prisoners in Concentration Camps as Compared with Jehovah's Witnesses and Political Prisoners

Ruediger Lautmann

Historians in Germany argue about how universal the historical character of national socialism was. One conservative faction would like to view the communist system as responsible for fascism. Because Marxism was victorious in Russia, the Fascist parties were able to win in Italy and Germany. This speculation claims that the destruction of social class distinctions by the Bolsheviks prepared the way for racial murders of the Nazis. The extermination of the Jews is presented as a distorted copy of a previous model, rather than as a unique occurrence.

Other social scientists have protested against viewing Nazi crimes in such a relativistic way. They see an aura of normality being created and fear that the basic antifascist consensus in the Federal republic might end. They are also apprehensive about the analogy to current politics and warn against a restoration by means of history.

The dispute concerns the question: Is the Holocaust continuous with the rest of European history, or does it represent a unique event, a break in the continuum of history? Such exciting and dangerous speculation belongs to a sort of metaphysical thinking that has a long tradition in German historiography. As a sociologist, I would like to take a more modest starting point: Is what the Nazis did to their internal enemies unique or totally surprising?

Investigating concentration camps from a sociological perspective, one does not confront a phenomenon that is singular and interesting, while at the same time ordinary and banal. No special attention is given to the "actors of history." Investigation into the structure and procedures of the concentration camps inevitably leads to comparison with other institutions and some form of differentiation. A morsel of normality is discovered in the atrocities, without in the least belittling them.

Regarding Nazi atrocities in this way has its price; it represses emotion. It focuses on details, rather than on the Holocaust as a whole. Understanding the preconditions of a terror means studying its construction, development, and operation in detail. In this essay, I would like to consider the aims of the terror and concentrate on the non-Jewish categories of prisoners, using homosexuals as an example.

Extermination or Reeducation? The concentration camp was one weapon in the campaign to bring state and society into conformity with fascism. If physical extermination formed the most frightful instrument of that policy, it was not the only one. A range of attempts were made to isolate people and to use fear to inhibit "undesirable" behavior. Whatever the reasons for imprisonment, all incarcerations were the result of Nazi ideology and posed a danger to the prisoner's life. The categories of prisoners differed from one another in how they were selected and treated. Those groups whom the Nazis deemed inimical but not racially undesirable were not completely rounded up, but taken only in random samples. They also fared differently within the camps.

Homosexuals, political prisoners, and Jehovah's Witnesses are among the groups who were sent to the concentration camps for reeducation. They were supposed to renounce their particular orientation. The very fact of their incarceration restrained their ideological comrades outside the camps from becoming active in the struggle against nazism.

Democratic freedom makes pluralism possible. In democracies, deviations from the norm concern not only criminality but also sexuality, ethnicity, religion, and attitudes toward work. The Nazi system was concerned with deviations in all these areas. It classified political, sexual, religious, and working-attitude deviations in separate categories. In all probability, the Hitlerian state required these definitions of the enemy and was, in its own terms, correct in its choice of these groups. Within a society, minority and separationist groups represent a seedbed of possible revolt.

Homosexuality has always and everywhere existed. Hitler considered homosexuality as a predisposition that could not be changed. It was assumed that a homosexual orientation could not be eliminated, that only its manifestations could be blocked. Thus, the pink triangle worn by the homosexual in the concentration camp represented the Nazis' intention to reeducate him. Severe measures were in fact intended only as behavioristic conditioning: a way to cause unlearning through aversion.

No credence was placed in a simple change of opinion by homosexuals, such as was granted to Jehovah's Witnesses, who were not taken entirely seriously, or even to political prisoners. Two categories were seen among homosexuals: the constitutionally hard-boiled homosexual and the occasional offender. Since in neither case was the Aryan status of the homosexual in doubt, all could remain alive. If necessary, homosexuals were to be castrated, but they were permitted to continue to work. As a matter of policy, extermination was therefore restrained. In practice there were other contrary impulses on the part of the SS, and those who wore the pink triangle met an unusually harsh fate. The social controls directed at homosexuals within the camp represented a continuation and an intensification of social controls imposed by society at large.

Continuity of Social Control   At the beginning of this essay, I mentioned the questionable attempt of some historians to deny the uniqueness of the Third Reich, to historicise it and to externalize responsibility. This approach has nothing to do with the connection I would like to establish here between society as a whole and society inside the camps. This continuity remains within the German context and does not seek its origins outside the frontiers of the Reich.

The concentration camp was an extreme instance of social control. It mixed ordinary and singular characteristics of social regulation. For example, it was and is "normal" to categorize and stigmatize people; it is "singular" to ascribe total uselessness to a certain group. It is "normal" to organize the life of an inmate; it is "singular" to view the life of a prisoner as being of almost no value. It is "normal" to devalue homosexual activities and to impose certain disadvantages on those who engage in them; it is "singular" to impose this devaluation by physical force and without constitutional procedures. It is "normal" (up to the present day) to stigmatize homosexuals; it is "singular" to attempt to eliminate homosexual life-styles and to destroy the subculture completely by organizing police raids.

The closer a prisoner's category was to the heart of Nazi ideology, the more dangerous his circumstances in the camp. Furthermore, the more repressively a group was controlled in society, the harder the fate of its members within the camp. Increasing the number of those sentenced, and imposing stricter rules in the military and party organizations, was followed by an increased death rate in the camp. The more marginal the social position of a group, the more marginal their position was within the camp.

The prisoners with the pink triangle had certainly shown "precamp" qualities of survival, but they did not get a chance to apply these qualities in the camp. Because their subculture and organizations outside had been wantonly destroyed, no group solidarity developed inside the camp. Since outside the concentration camp homosexuals were regarded as effete, they were given no tasks of self-administration inside the camps. Since every contact outside was regarded as suspicious, homosexuals did not even dare to speak to one another inside (as numerous survivors have reported in interviews). Since homosexuals were generally regarded as worthless, their fellow prisoners had a lower regard for them. Thus, few accounts of the pink triangles exist, and those that do exist have a spiteful flavor.

Differences between Prisoner Categories   To regard the prisoners according to their categories means distinguishing between major and minor sufferings. Is that permissible? We could even ask: Is social science still possible after Auschwitz? Nevertheless, various developments have virtually given a positive answer to these questions. After 1945 differences in the fate of different groups of prisoners have been recognized by differences in compensation. Research, too, has given varying degrees of attention to the different groups of victims. The color of the assigned triangle (i.e., the prisoner category) was the basis for a collective fate.

In my empirical research, I have sifted all extant documents to examine the names and data on all concentration camp prisoners registered as being homosexual.[1] I found the data for about 1,500 homosexuals (This is a complete survey of the quite incomplete documents). I chose as control groups Jehovah's Witnesses (about 750) and political prisoners (200). Each category of prisoner seemed to possess a characteristic social profile. If we look at the distribution according to age upon committal to a camp, the Jehovah's Witnesses predominate in the somewhat older age group (from 35), and the homosexuals in the second somewhat younger one (20–35).

Committal figures have regular curves, which are quite different for the three groups. For homosexuals the year 1942 marks the peak (with a quarter of all committals), and for Jehovah's Witnesses the years 1937 and 1938 (half of all committals) are the peaks. The committal figures for the politicals remain at the same level, with a slight rise toward the year 1944.

The death rate for homosexual prisoners (60 percent) was one and a half times as high as for political prisoners (41 percent) and Jehovah's Witnesses (35 percent). Some background variables, such as professional status, mar-

TABLE 20. I
Death Rate According to Category and Professional Status

	Lower Classes (%)	Lower Middle (%)	Middle and Above (%)	All (%)
Homosexuals	54.6	52.6	50.1	53.0
	(328)	(114)	(219)	(661)
Jehovah's	34.5	36.6	34.6	34.7
Witnesses	(374)	(52)	(81)	(507)
Politicals	40.2	38.9	42.9	40.5
	(122)	(18)	(28)	(168)

Note: Figures in parentheses are based on social groups of a prisoner category, insofar as its fate is known (dead, liberated, or released).

ital status, and number of children, have been considered. Thus far, the individual variables tested do not cancel the connection between the victim group and the risk of death.

Reading the many reports and asking the prisoners' committees (which still exist today) about the prisoners with the pink triangles, one repeatedly learns that they were there, but nobody can tell you anything about them. Quantitative analysis offers a sad explanation for the extraordinary lack of visibility: the individual pink-triangle prisoner was likely to live for only a short time in the camp and then to disappear from the scene. After four months, one in four had left; after a year, one in two. It was otherwise for the Jehovah Witnesses and politicals: after a year four out of five and two out of three, respectively, were still in the camp. This thinning out is due to deaths: three out of four deaths among the homosexuals occurred within the first year after their committal.

In comparison with the red and violet triangles, the pink triangle seems to signify a category of less value. The destinies of Jews and homosexuals within the camp approximate each other. In the concentration camp, both groups found themselves at the bottom of the current hierarchy below the non-Jewish racially defined groups of prisoners.

The collective devaluation of the wearers of certain triangles supports the idea of a connection between internal camp treatment of the marginal groups and the sociostructural control they were subjected to in society at large. With regard to the homosexuals, there were many reports of how the SS deliberately treated them brutally and how the other prisoners looked

TABLE 20.2

Survival Rate According to Category and Marital Status

	Married (%)	Single, Divorced, Widowed (%)
Homosexuals	51.4	47.7
	(74)	(451)
Jehovah's Witnesses	66.2	66.3
	(361)	(146)
Politicals	65.4	52.4
	(81)	(84)

Note: Figures in parentheses are based on social groups of a prisoner category, insofar as its fate is known (dead, liberated, or released).

TABLE 20.3

Survival Rate According to Category and Number of Children

	With Children (%)	Childless (%)
Homosexuals	56.6	49.2
	(69)	(366)
Jehovah's Witnesses	62.9	59.8
	(240)	(179)
Politicals	60.3	56.9
	(78)	(72)

Note: Figures in parentheses are based on social groups of a prisoner category, insofar as its fate is known (dead, liberated, or released).

down upon them. This contrasts with reports stating that Jehovah's Witnesses were admired outside the camp or that politicals were full of respect for one another's activities.

Analytical scientific literature also draws the connection between the prestige of a triangle and the treatment of the victim category concerned. Insofar as the pink triangle appears at all in the historical literature, the tendency is in the direction of antihomosexual prejudice. There is a tendency of the literature to associate the pink triangle with the criminal green. The few surviving pink-triangle wearers were treated similarly by state and society after 1945, when cautious attempts toward compensation were finally and definitely rejected. Interviews with such survivors revealed that for many years they never told anyone they had been in a concentration camp. The extreme devaluation was accepted as a self-evaluation. Gay interest groups arose again only in the 1950s, and the movement as a whole took until the 1970s to return to the position it had held in 1932. Noticeably often, ex-wearers of the pink triangle report that they subsequently got married.

NOTES

1. See my book *Seminar: Gesellschaft und Homosexualitaet* (Frankfurt am Main, 1977), chap. 8, especially pp. 325–65. For some descriptive results, see my article "The Pink Triangle: The Homosexual Males in Concentration Camps in Nazi Germany," *Journal of Homosexuality* 6 (1981):141–60. This is reprinted in Salvatore J. Licata and Robert P. Peterson, eds., *Historical Perspectives on Homosexuality* (New York, 1981).

CHAPTER 21

The Fate of Gypsies in Czechoslovakia under Nazi Domination

Jiří Lípa

The Gypsies are an ethnic group scattered today almost all over the world but residing mainly in Europe. They have no country. They speak their own language but they do not write it. They are unique in that they have no historical memory of their past. Only an analysis of their language shows that they originated in northern India.

The Gypsies are not a uniform group. Two major differences among them originated after their arrival in Europe.

The first of these divisions was created by the impact of the language and culture of the areas where they lived for several centuries. The Gypsies did not travel just anywhere. Each group had an area within which it moved because they knew its language, its geography, and even the people on whom they depended for their livelihood. In central Europe the Gypsies were cruelly persecuted from the sixteenth to the middle of the eighteenth century. Let us cite Bohemia as an example. The Gypsies never became stationary in Bohemia. Some traveling Gypsies lived by their wits. One of the constant complaints against them was that they satisfied their needs at the expense of the people around them by disregarding private property. In reality, the Gypsies paid for their conflicts with the law by spending portions of their lives in jails, but they were caught up in the centuries-old vicious circle and could not see any way out. The Nazis declared the Gypsies to be "asocials" and decided to exterminate them "preventively." This policy extended to entire families, including children. And as we will see, the Nazis extended this description to Gypsies who had been settled for several generations.

The second major division among the Gypsies centered around the fact that some of them had settled down. In countries that were hospitable to

Gypsies in the past, such as Slovakia, the majority of Gypsies had become stationary. When we talk about hospitality of a country toward Gypsies, however, we have to understand that Gypsies were only tolerated there, more or less as beggars. After several generations, the stationary way of life led to a loss of certain phenomena of the common traveling Gypsy tradition.

The process of gradual assimilation of all Gypsies to their respective European environments was in progress at different paces in different ways throughout Europe. In spite of the fact that sedentary Gypsies spoke the Gypsy language to one another, they had come to be perceived by the surrounding majority population less and less as a different ethnic group and more as a social group with a low social status.

In Czechoslovakia, we find four distinct language and culture groups among the Gypsies:

1. The Slovak-Czech group. The dialects within this group originated under the influence of dialects of the Slovak and Czech languages (which are closely related to each other). The majority of these Gypsies lived in Slovakia, a smaller number of them in Moravia, and the fewest of them in Bohemia. In Slovakia, all the members of this group were stationary. In Moravia, some of them were stationary, others, wandering. Stationary Gypsies settled in the south of Moravia in a continuation of Gypsy settlements from Slovakia. Gypsies in Bohemia continued to wander.

2. The German group. The dialects within this group were influenced by German language dialects. This group called itself *Sinti*. Its members lead a wandering way of life.

3. The Hungarian group. The dialects within this group were influenced by Hungarian dialects. Some Gypsies in Slovakia came under the Hungarian influence; others remained in Slovak ambience. All members of this group were sedentary.

4. The Romanian group. The dialects within this group originated under the influence of dialects of the Romanian language. There were two subgroups of this group living in Czechoslovakia. Both of them led a wandering way of life. One called itself *Vlašika Rrom*. The other group called itself by the name of its traditional trade, *Kettlesmiths*.

Some European countries made special legislation regulating the way of life of the wandering Gypsies; Czechoslovakia was among them. It issued a special law about wandering Gypsies on July 19, 1927, requiring them to be registered. Each wandering Gypsy above the age of 14 obtained a special Gypsy identification, which included his fingerprints. Younger children were registered in the identification of the person with whom they lived. Each family of wandering Gypsies also had to have a special license for wandering that listed members of the family and animals that accompanied them. They also had a registration book into which the mayor of each village had to write permission specifying how many days they were allowed to stay, usually for one week.

Most stationary Gypsies in a way fared worse than wandering Gypsies. Wandering Gypsies were always able to procure food for themselves, but stationary Gypsies were bound to the non-Gypsy community, of which they were generally unwelcome members. Society needed only part of the unskilled labor of those who lived in every Gypsy settlement, or ghetto.

In general, both groups of Gypsies, the wandering and the stationary, presented a serious social problem.

On March 15, 1939, Hitler dissolved the Czechoslovak republic. The Czech-speaking part of it, Bohemia and Moravia, was incorporated into Germany as the Protectorate of Bohemia and Moravia. The eastern, Slovak-speaking part, Slovakia, was granted a more independent status by becoming the Slovak republic, a satellite of Germany. Bohemia and Moravia were under direct control of Hitler's authorities, whereas Slovakia had somewhat more say in her own fate. Germany put pressure on both the protectorate and on Slovakia to persecute their Gypsies. Slovakia was more lenient, whereas the Gypsies from Bohemia and Moravia were sent to the death camps.

Slovakia, 1939–1945 The first measure taken against Gypsies in independent Slovakia was issued on June 23, 1939, by the Central Regional Authority *(krajinský úrad)* in Bratislava. Wandering Gypsies were all obliged to return to their respective legal domicile. They were also prohibited from dealing in horses, and licenses for this trade were to be taken away from them.

On September 25, 1939, a law regulating the citizenship; of Slovakia was issued. According to it, no Jews qualified for citizenship. As far as Gypsies were concerned, some of them qualified for Slovak citizenship others did not, even though Gypsies from both groups were born in Slovakia. Only if it were clear beyond any doubt that such persons (i.e., Gypsies) lived an orderly way of life; had a steady place of residence and employment; and were honorable citizens as reflected in their education, their moral and political trustworthiness, and their activity in their community, could they be included in the Slovak national community. If they did not fulfill the aforementioned conditions, or if they fulfilled them only partially—if they worked only occasionally, if they spoke the Gypsy language among themselves, if their moral and political trustworthiness was doubtful, etc.—they could not be considered members of the Slovak national community.[1] In other words, wandering Gypsies did not qualify for citizenship. This document realistically acknowledged that some Gypsies had been integrated into the Slovak population, and regarded such integration as a commendable phenomenon. The law was not racially motivated; it was meant to be favorable to stationary Gypsies. If its requirements for stationary Gypsies had been strictly applied, however, very few stationary Gypsies would have qualified to be Slovak citizens.

The military draft law, published on January 18, 1940, stated that Gypsies and Jews would not be allowed to perform their military duty as members of the army. Instead, they were to serve in special labor units (pp. 73–74).

On June 18, 1940, the Interior Ministry issued an official definition of a Gypsy, based on this opinion: "Only that member of the Gypsy race is to be regarded as a Gypsy who belongs to it on the side of both parents, and lives in the wandering way of life; or, if he lives in a stationary way, he avoids work" (p. 70). The criterion for being a Gypsy was neither ethnic background nor race but rather the way of life.

On April 2, 1941, the Interior Ministry announced the establishment of so-called labor centers (pracovné strediská) for Jews who had been expelled from their regular jobs, and of so-called labor units (pracovné útvary) for asocial men, including Gypsies. The labor units for asocial men were intended as seasonal institutions and at least six of them started operating in May 1941 (pp. 83, 85–86). In the ensuing years some of the camps were reopened, and new ones were established. In the labor units in Hanušovce nad Topľou, Bystré nad Topľou, Ptičie, and Nižný Hrabovec, Gypsies constituted more than half of the inmates (p. 93). In the camps in Dubnica nad Váhom, Gypsies never constituted less than 45 percent of the inmates (p. 111). Conditions in the labor units were bad. Inmates suffered increasingly from inadequate clothing and shoes, cold, infestation with lice and bedbugs, hunger, and disease, especially trachoma and typhus.

A report on an inspection tour in the labor units for asocial men undertaken September 22–24, 1942, explains how the inmates mutilated themselves in order to be released:

They swallowed cement, one ate rosin and died, they would put their feet on the rails and let wagons full of dirt run over them, they would have the fingers on their right hand crushed, would rub onion over their eyes and cut off their toes with a sharpened pickaxe. In one case an inmate put his finger into quicklime, poured water on it and literally boiled the finger in it; cases are on record that some inmates deliberately infected themselves with gonorrhea or trachoma. (p. 102)

The problems in the camp in Bystré nad Topľou were criticized by a deputy of the Slovak parliament in a letter addressed to the central agency of labor (ústredný úrad práce) and dated April 11, 1943: "The camps were established in order to re-educate the asocial elements, not in order to torture people and bring them into an even worse moral degradation" (p. 107). When the labor unit for asocial men in Ústie nad Oravou was dissolved on December 31, 1944, its non-Gypsy inmates were released. Its Gypsy inmates were transferred into the detention camp for Gypsies in Dubnica nad Váhom (p. 129).

On April 20, 1941, the Interior Ministry announced the regulation of certain aspects of the life of the Gypsies: wandering licenses were rescinded and their owners were to return within eight days to their domiciles or to communities in which they had lived for a long time. In them, they would be under police surveillance and would be allowed to leave only with special permission. They were to sell their wagons and horses within two weeks (pp. 74–75).

In communities where Gypsy huts were built along public roads, the Gypsies had to demolish the huts and rebuild them a few kilometers from the non-Gypsy community in a place that the authorities assigned to them. A representative of the Gypsies was responsible to the mayor of the non-Gypsy community for keeping the regulations. The stationary Gypsies were also prohibited from keeping dogs.

All Gypsies were cautioned against avoiding regular work lest they be sent to labor camps. On July 17, 1941, the central labor agency of the Pohronská regional authority (župa) ordered the establishment of a labor unit in Krupina, combined with a camp for the families of the inmates. Sixty families of wandering Gypsies were to be placed there by force and, in the words of an official report, "taught to get accustomed to live in one place and to intensive, productive self-supporting work." (p. 84). The Gypsy men were to be made to work in quarries in Krupina, Dobrá Niva, and Sása but the construction of this camp was never completed.

On July 21, 1943, the Interior Ministry issued a decree that emphasized the removal of Gypsy dwellings away from busy roads, as had been ordered in 1941. Gypsies had to be prohibited by all means from wandering about and from living by illegal means. The ministry declared that soon a concentration camp for Gypsies would be established; therefore lists of those Gypsies who should be placed in it had to be prepared and submitted to the ministry.

On September 29, 1944, by order of the German military command, the Trenčín regional authority (župný úrad) ordered that Gypsy men from all its districts be placed in the camp of the labor unit in Dubnica nad Váhom. The process had to be stopped on October 10, however, because the camp was full. In a decree of November 2, 1944, the Defense Ministry transformed the camp in Dubnica nad Váhom into a detention camp to hold all Gypsies regardless of their sex and age. All non-Gypsy asocial inmates were released, but Gypsy inmates remained. As of December 23, 1944, there were 729 inmates of both sexes in the camp, of whom about 250 were children.

On December 14, 1944, an epidemic of typhus broke out in the camp. The regimental physician of the German military command in Trenčín inspected the camp and reported that it was "in einem unvorstellbar verwahrlosten und schmutzigen Zustand" (i.e., the conditions were unimaginably desolate and filthy) (p. 136). The next known information about the fate of the camp is that on February 34, 1945, two military trucks came into the camp, and armed German soldiers came out of them ostensibly to take the sick Gypsies to the hospital in Trenčín. The twenty-six people who got on the trucks were taken into a valley where a pit was ready. The Gypsies were forced into the pit and shot. The detention camp in Dubnica nad Váhom was dissolved on April 8, 1945, shortly before the Soviet Army arrived.

The Protectorate of Bohemia and Moravia, 1939–1945 On March 2 and April 28, 1939, decrees were published in the name of the central government according to which all persons older than eighteen years who avoided work and could not prove that they were making a living in a regular way, were to be placed in correctional labor camps. On January 31, 1940, wandering Gypsies were ordered to settle down under penalty of "preventive" imprisonment. On August 10, 1940, two correctional labor camps were opened, one for each of the two regions: one was in Lety (near Písek), in Bohemia; the other in Hodonín (near Kunštát), in Moravia. Their inmates worked on constructing two sections of the express highway that was to connect Plzeň and Moravská Ostrava. Between September 1, 1940, and December 1, 1941, 290 Gypsies were sent to the camp of hard labor in

Lety, comprising some 13.60 percent of its inmates, and 442 Gypsies were sent to Hodonín, or 19.26 percent of the total inmate population (p. 31).

On November 30, 1939, the Interior Ministry published a decree (výnos) ordering that by January 31, 1940, at the latest, all Gypsies were to settle down. Those who would not comply with the order were to be sent to corrective labor camps. Wandering Gypsies who did not have a right of domicile were to settle down in the locality they happened to be in on the night of January 31, 1940 (p. 27).

I remember hearing as a boy in Bohemia some time after Hitler occupied Poland that persons employed by certain employers had to sign a statement that read, "I declare that I am not a Jew nor a Pole nor a Gypsy."

On March 9, 1942, a decree of the central government (vládní nařízení) was published about prevention of criminality through preventive imprisonment of criminals and the so-called asocial elements. This term applied, among others, to Gypsies and to "individuals leading a Gypsy-like way of life." The imprisonment was to take place in one of the six places in the protectorate (in camps Lety or Hodonín, or in the penitentiaries in Ruzyně, Pardubice, Brno, or Olšovec), or in Auschwitz (p. 33).

About 1956, a former member of the protectorate police showed me a sheet of paper torn from a lined school copybook, with a statement on it, written with an unskilled hand in Czech, that said, "I agree to being sterilized." I do not remember the name, but it was one of the typical names of Gypsies from Bohemia. The former policeman told me that in issuing this statement, this Gypsy avoided being sent to a concentration camp. I was surprised by the informal look of the statement, but the policeman assured me it was authentic. What happened to the signer, I do not know. Later I heard from a family of carnival people from western Bohemia about a Gypsy from that area who had been sterilized.

As of August 1, 1942, the correctional labor camps in Lety and in Hodonín were changed to concentration camps for Gypsy families by a decree of the Interior Ministry. The stated purpose was to exclude from society Gypsies, Gypsy half-breeds (Zigeunermischlinge), and persons leading a wandering way of life in Gypsy fashion, and to educate them for work, order, and discipline. All men who were not engaged in regular and useful work were to be placed in these concentration camps together with their wives and children.

In connection with the liquidation of the Lety concentration camp, some of the inmates were set free, but the majority were transferred to the concentration camp in Hodonín or to penitentiaries in Ruzyně and Pardubice.

Those individual inmates who attempted to escape from the Gypsy concentration camps in Lety or Hodonín were put into transports that brought the so-called asocial elements from different places in Bohemia and Moravia to the concentration camp at Auschwitz. Besides transports of individuals, several mass transports were sent from Lety to Auschwitz. The first transport, consisting of 78 women and 16 men, took place on December 3, 1942. The oldest woman was Karolína Růžičková, seventy-eight; the youngest woman, Bohumila Hospodářská, twenty-one. The oldest man was Martin Vrba, ninety-three; the youngest was Robert Waitz, twenty-two (p. 53).

On December 7, 1942, the first mass transport left the camp in Hodonín for Auschwitz. It consisted of 46 men and 29 women. The oldest man was Josef Daniel, seventy-four; the oldest women, Anna Paffnerová and Josefa Pupucová, both seventy-eight. The youngest were Jan Matys and Vlasta Matesová, both eighteen years old (p. 58).

On August 21, 1943, the second mass transport from Hodonín left for Auschwitz. It consisted of 767 inmates. Approximately 80 Gypsies were supposed to remain in the camp, but about half of them did not want to be parted from their relatives and volunteered to go with the transport. It is possible to establish the age of half the people included in the transport. Ten children were under one year of age, 32 children were between two and three years old, 53 children were between three and six years old, 208 children were between six and fourteen years old, 38 boys and 40 girls were between fourteen and eighteen years old, 112 men and 185 women were between eighteen and sixty years old, and 12 men and 14 women were over the age of sixty. After this transport, only 57 inmates were left in Hodonín; 31 of these inmates were sick and could not be transported. The remaining 26 (10 men, 6 women, 10 children) were left to work on the liquidation of the camp.

The concentration camp in Hodonín was liquidated on December 1, 1943. The 31 inmates who were ill at the time of the August 21 transport were sent to Auschwitz in the next transport of asocial persons on January 28, 1944. The 26 inmates who worked on the liquidation of the camp were set free; the reasons given were that they had a "predominant amount of Aryan blood" or that they were non-Gypsies (p. 59).

In 1943 several mass transports of stationary Gypsies from southern Moravia were sent to the Gypsy camp at Auschwitz. These transports were in keeping with the December 16, 1942, order of Heinrich Himmler and the instructions for its execution issued by the *Reichssicherheitshauptamt* on January 29, 1943 (p.59). Gypsy possessions were confiscated and publicly auctioned. The proceeds and the savings of the Gypsies were put under the administration of the local Gestapo offices. An announcement dated March 24, 1943, of public auction of the possessions of Tomáš Daniel of Luhačovice listed the following items besides furniture: eight beehives with colonies of bees, a goat, a rabbit, two hundred kilograms of potatoes, one barrel of sauerkraut, an anvil, a wooden handcart without wheels, and various agricultural tools (p. 60). This man was evidently stationary and self-supporting, and the local authorities knew it. But once the murderous machinery was in motion, nothing mattered; people were destroyed.

NOTES

1. Ctibor Nečas, *Nad osudem českých a slovenských Cikánů* (The Fate of the Czech and Slovak Gypsies) (Brno, 1981), p. 70ff. All further references to *Nad osudem českých a slovenských CikánAů* will be indicated in the text by page number. For my review of this book, see the *Newsletter of the Gypsy Lore Society, North American Chapter,* vol. 8, no. 1 (1985), p. 4.

CHAPTER 22

Doubling: The Acts of the Second Self

Robert Jay Lifton

I want to focus on one particular psychological mechanism, doubling, which was used by the perpetrators of Nazi evil and enabled them to do what they did. Doubling is the formation of a second self that can permit an ordinary person to participate in evil. While researching my book *The Nazi Doctors,* I interviewed the daughter of the former chief doctor at Auschwitz, Eduard Wirths, who as is well known, killed himself at the end of the war. She had loved her father and had bounced on his knee as a little girl, and she was horrified to discover that the place where she had bounced on his knee was Auschwitz. At the end of a long interview, during which I felt quite sympathetic toward her as a middle-aged woman trying to come to terms with her background and past, she asked me, "Can a good man do bad things?" My answer was, "Yes, but when he does so, he's no longer a good man."

There is no simple formula for looking at what Hannah Arendt called the banality of evil. Broadly speaking, what I found in my work on the Nazi doctors was that they were very ordinary banal men. However, what they did was not banal; it was extreme—one could almost call it demonic. In the process, they had to change.

Early in my work, I spoke quite frequently to a friend of mine who is an Auschwitz survivor. He had been a child in Auschwitz and remembered the Nazi doctors. He didn't really know much about them when he was there. He just remembered that he was terrified of them, and he said, "Well, tell me, tell me Robert, when they did what they did, were they men or were they demons?" I responded, "You know very well they were men and that's the problem. That's why I'm doing this study." He said, "Yes, I know, but it is demonic that they were not demonic."

It is much more comfortable to think of a demonic group of evildoers, as opposed to the rest of us good folk. Unfortunately, this is not the way we are constituted. These physicians were ordinary—and my point is about the psychological explanation of the capacity of ordinary people to do evil.

Broadly speaking, evil can be viewed in three ways. One can perceive evil solely as a moral question. As such, it is not the concern of psychologists or other professionals who pursue technical tasks; least of all, scientists. Many people adhere to this definition of evil. A further extension of this viewpoint is the second category, which views evil as a visitation from without—a dark force—that in its extreme manifestations cannot be understood in human terms. The third perspective, which is my own, is that evil is a state of wrongdoing profoundly influenced by historical and psychological features.

Evil can be probed and judged by attempting to grasp these psychological and historical forces without eroding moral concerns. In bringing to bear psychological and other intellectual disciplinary perspectives on questions of evil, we do not exonerate the individuals who engage in evil but rather we explore more deeply the capacity of individuals and the way in which they may have involved themselves in evil.

This perspective clearly contradicts certain principles about the Holocaust advocated by a very sympathetic figure, Rolf Hochhuth, an appealing, gifted, and genuine person. I had the privilege of meeting him and talking about these issues. In his play The Deputy, Hochhuth resorted to a Mengele-type figure about which he wrote: "He has the stature of absolute evil, an uncanny visitant from another world, which contrasts with anything that has been learned about human beings."[1] Hochhuth's point sounds like a medieval morality play. I can well understand his feelings but I respectfully disagree. Mengele or other Nazi doctors were human beings responsible for their actions. There were certain psychological and historical components to their behavior. We do not deepen our understanding of evil if we view evil as a kind of visitation alien to the human experience. When I discussed this issue with Hochhuth, he did not disagree. He threw up his arms in despair at trying to grasp what might motivate that kind of man.

Let me say something about doubling. I am sad to report that doubling is an adaptive psychological mechanism. I found that Nazi doctors formed what I came to call an "Auschwitz self." This Auschwitz-self functioned well and enabled them to do selections. In fact, in enabled them to adapt to the vulgar, brutal, and evil environment of Auschwitz, which included heavy drinking, vulgar jokes, a brutalized and brutalizing way of life.

The doctors seemed to undergo a period of anxiety for some three weeks during which they had nightmares and conflicts. Unfortunately, they overcame their conflicts sufficiently to continue working in Auschwitz. In most cases they had the option of leaving, even though it would not have been easy for them to get reassigned. I have not heard of one officer who made a systematic, continuous, successful effort to leave. One or two persons thought of leaving, and one did make some attempts. A major reason why they did not choose to leave was that they would have been sent to the eastern front. They were in a Waffen SS military unit; it was late in the war, and many people, including doctors, were being killed on the eastern front. Reassignment would pose some physical danger to their survival.

There are certain characteristics in the formation of the functional "second self." The individual achieved a sense of equilibrium, which was relatively autonomous from the prior self but linked to it. The second self had a holistic quality; that is, it was adaptive to the whole environment seething with death. It had a life-death dimension, and it warded off death anxiety. Perpetrators as well as victims experienced death anxiety in Auschwitz.

Doubling also had a psychological function of avoidance of guilt. It is always wrong to say that Nazis in general and Nazi doctors in particular had no conscience or did not experience guilt. They were human beings capable of experiencing guilt and of having a conscience, but a transfer of conscience took place. Instead of standing between them and their victims —where conscience should stand—conscience was transferred to a sense of group loyalty, to a commitment to the Nazi enterprise, to the function of Auschwitz, and to related tasks. Of course, there was an unconscious dimension; yet there was also a conscious desire to adapt to Auschwitz, and a conscious impulse toward doubling. Their adaptation resembles what is often called "splitting" in psychoanalytical literature, but splitting implies a piece of the self being sequestered from the rest of the self or from consciousness, whereas doubling implies a holistic self, a portion of self functioning as a whole self.

Without going into detail, some of the important earlier work is less Freud than Otto Rank, who wrote a very important book in the 1920s called *The Double*[2] taken mostly from examples in German romantic literature. Doubling is an adaptation to extremity. As such, one can speak of doubling for life-enhancing purposes, too. Survivors of Auschwitz have told me, "I was a different person in Auschwitz." They had to be. One had to steel one's self in order to survive, and perhaps the admirable achievement of most survivors was to have retained their humanity in the process.

Doubling is a means of keeping the self intact under extreme conditions, thereby avoiding further breakdown of the self, which some Nazi doctors came close to. Doubling, then, is a psychological means by which one calls forth or can call forth the evil potential of the self. The evil potential is neither inherent in the self nor foreign to it. I am not talking about original sin or a death instinct, if you want to put it in psychological-secular terms, but merely saying that evil is potential in all of us. It can be expressed under certain circumstances. We are responsible for it when we do express it. That's why I reject the assumption that we are all Nazis. Perhaps we're all potential Nazis given the evil expression, and we have the human—and moral—alternative of rejecting that potential.

In that sense doubling is one key to grasping human evil, but it does not explain human evil. In an Auschwitz environment, one had to double in order to stay there. Auschwitz was an atrocity-producing, doubling-producing environment. The environment ran on evil. I would say that the doubling was enhanced by powerful currents essential to the Auschwitz environment.

Nazi ideology was crucial to this process. The ideology seems so absurd, so fragmentary, and in many ways contradictory. Yet it had enormous power for various groups of people. Even when held in fragmented form, it helped people into the doubling process.

Another struggle involved in doubling was the attempt to maintain a professional identity. Ironically, Nazi doctors in Auschwitz liked to continue seeing themselves as doctors, but they reduced everything to technique. As one of them said to me, "Ethics was a word we never used in Auschwitz and no wonder, I would add; we only focused on what worked." The Nazi doctors were involved in a kind of absolute, almost diabolical, pragmatism. They had a sense of omnipotence and impotence; omnipotence in the sense of deciding who could live and who could die, and impotence because they saw themselves as a cog in a machine. I must add that they emphasized their impotence to me as a method of trying to exculpate themselves from moral responsibility. Above all, I would stress the strange impulse in human beings toward creation of meaning. The Nazi doctor in Auschwitz went through the motions every day of reporting to work, making jokes with his secretary and backbiting remarks about rivals, as though he were part of an ordinary institution dedicated to life-enhancing purposes. We are meaning-hungry creatures who will create a meaning structure that functions for virtually anything we do, however evil, however destructive.

In closing I would like to raise a couple of questions that suggest a direction for an answer. Are doctors more prone to doubling than other groups? Perhaps so to some extent, in the sense that there is an extreme process involved in becoming a doctor. One of the initiations into the medical priesthood is having the corpse thrust before you the first day of medical school. That is a message. Death is here in your vision, in your experience, and you must numb yourself to it. I think the numbing also includes a kind of doubling, or at least the need to develop a second self, a professional self. Talented and humane doctors balance the need for professional detachment with a continual sense of humanity and feeling, but not every doctor is a humane doctor.

The second question that should be posed: Are Germans more prone to doubling than others? After all, German culture created the idea of the double and Rank wrote about the double from German romantic literature. There is also the Faust legend, of course, expressed by Goethe and others in German tradition. But once you have said all that, then you have to realize that Christopher Marlowe took up the Faust legend long before Goethe did, and you can find literature of the double in America and Britain (for example, Robert Louis Stevenson's *Dr. Jekyll and Mr. Hyde*), as well as in French literature. So doubling is a universal potential with perhaps particularly strong roots in German culture.

Doubling is a mechanism for adapting to one's immediate group including notably, in this example, a group dedicated to evil. Doubling is the enabling form of adaptation; it enables us to do many things. Some important research by Steven Kull has documented the doubling of nuclear strategists in the United States and no doubt in the Soviet Union and elsewhere, in which ordinary men and women project doomsday scenarios and sometimes advocate positions that might involve the killing of hundreds of millions of people within hours or days. What is adaptive on the small scale becomes the very opposite of adaptive for the species if the immediate group has potentially evil, destructive, or genocidal actions in mind. And that is something to which we must give our attention.

I'll close with a statement of my perspective on these matters. One puts them forward, as Franklin Littell said, in the name of life. The line that always haunts me is from Theodore Roethke, the great lyrical American poet: "In a dark time, the eye begins to see."

NOTES

1. Rolf Hochhuth, *The Deputy* (New York, 1964).
2. Otto Rank, *The Double* (Chapel Hill, N.C., 1971).

CHAPTER 23

Sterilization and Euthanasia

Robert Jay Lifton

In Germany in the twenties, many people believed that one would seek to improve the race by encouraging progeny in the healthier people and discouraging or blocking children in those considered less healthy, less valuable. This very dubious point of view had very wide sway at that time. One man played a key role in the Nazis' use of sterilization—Ernst Rüdin, who was not even a German, but a Swiss who became a German citizen. As one of his students told me during my research, Rüdin was a more fanatical geneticist than he was a fanatical Nazi, but he became a Nazi. And like some people who envisioned biological improvement of the human species, he valued the Nazis because they allowed him to carry out his visionary scheme for what he thought might be a way of eliminating mental disease.

Many doctors to whom I spoke had nothing against sterilization, although they sometimes had qualms about the coercive side of it. Nonetheless, they had many reservations about so-called euthanasia. Euthanasia is what the Nazis called their project, but in my previous writings about it, I always put quotations around it no matter how often I used the word. It was not genuine euthanasia. Euthanasia really means helping the dying to die, the idea that a person should be allowed to have a good death or a dignified death. Under the guise or cloak of euthanasia, the Nazis murdered a hundred thousand people, mostly mental patients. They considered these people to be "life unworthy of life."

That phrase did not originate with the Nazis, although they embraced it and, indeed, their entire project could be said to have been built around "life unworthy of life." The phrase originated in a book written in 1920 by Alfred Hoche, a professor of psychiatry at the University of Leipzig, and Karl Binding, a leading German jurist (Karl Binding and Alfred Hoche, *Die Freigabe der Vernichtung lebensunwerten Lebens: Ihr Mass und ihre Form* [Leipzig, 1920]). Their work took the form of a post–World War I document with a plan for helping to regenerate the devastated German nation and race. The idea was that there should be a kind of mercy killing for sufferers of those forms of impairment that drained the society. Hoche advocated killing those people who could never be fully well in the judgment of physicians. The mercy killing was to be done under strict medical control, but it was an example, to say the least, of medical and legal hubris. The Nazis seized upon the volume. It had not been a position of German psychiatry, but it was there as an idea structure.

In late 1939 under cover of the war, the Nazis initiated their program of so-called euthanasia. Children were the first victims. As some of the doctors who were involved said to me later when I interviewed them, "Well, it seemed a little easier with children." In other words, it didn't seem quite as murderous when it was a very young person with some sort of deformity.

There were special wards and special places for these children, who were put to death with sedatives by increasing the dose gradually. One doctor who was involved said to me, "It didn't feel like murder; it's more like a putting to sleep." When the sedative did not take, injections were used. Later on near-sadistic starvation methods were employed, but by and large in all these programs the Nazis tried to avoid sadism. They tried to do things in a very detached way.

The program was extended to include mental patients who were in some way mentally deficient, schizophrenic, manic-depressive, epileptic, or had various other conditions considered incurable or deformed.

The Nazis discovered the use of the gas chambers in connection with direct medical killing of adults, which was done strictly through medical channels with a very pseduoscientific, pseudomedical registration arrangement. Seeming propriety was employed for mass murder. An effort was made to cloak the killings in legality; in this case a medical justification was employed. The Nazis created what I call an "as if" situation; it was "as if" they were conducting a desirable and necessary medical sequence. In actuality, they were murdering thousands and hundred of thousands of human beings.

One could say that they performed the so-called euthanasia program, the direct medical killing of adults, under the cloak of the war, but a more accurate way of looking at it is to say that the war was in the service of the direct medical killing.

In their so-called euthanasia program, the Nazis had to find a way to kill large numbers of adult mental patients efficiently. They tried injections of morphine derivatives. People can be killed that way, but not so easily. Later on they used a carbon monoxide gas chamber, which showed itself to be much more efficient.

As Karl Brandt later testified at the Nuremberg medical trial, Hitler was a very concerned person, and he wanted the killing to be done in the most humane way. Gas was considered more humane than the injections. It was also more efficient from their standpoint, and they used it.

Most of the death camps in the east were set up with carbon monoxide gas chambers. The Nazis experimented in various ways with vans, but once they had the carbon monoxide gas chamber method, it was used in different ways. A gas chamber could be mobile or stationary. The second and, perhaps still more significant advance technologically, was the discovery of cyanide gas as a more efficient killer. The discovery was apparently made in Auschwitz with the help of the manufacturers. German industry made its contribution to the killing process all along the way. And once cyanide gas was discovered to be more effective in Auschwitz, it was used there exclusively. As is well known, the killing in Auschwitz was done with Zyklon B, which is a cyanide derivative.

When the Nazis stopped the official so-called euthanasia program in 1941, they did so because of protests coming from the churches. That had been the result of rumblings from the people. The euthanasia program was conducted in Germany mostly on German non-Jews. The first genocide involved German non-Jewish victims. While euthanasia was officially ended as a project, the killing of children never stopped. It was never visible. The Nazis began a period that has become known as "wild euthanasia," and they simply didn't use the gas method anymore. They used either injections for adults or starvation. Many people were killed after the program had been officially ended.

There was also a very important "in-between" program, called by the code name 14F13, that involved bringing doctors who were central in the so-called euthanasia program into the camps, ostensibly to weed out the mentally ill. These people could then be taken to the killing centers that had been set up. Six such centers were established in Germany for the euthanasia program. Thus, the euthanasia program was extended into the camps. In effect, ordinary concentration camps became death camps by connecting them to the killing centers.

It happens that Auschwitz has a somewhat different history. It wasn't directly created from the euthanasia program. It was more directly related to the project of killing all the Jews, but it was also linked with the so-called euthanasia program because some of the doctors there had been assigned to, and had been active in, the euthanasia program.

One notorious example is Horst Schumann, who was a leading sterilization experimenter in Auschwitz. Schumann had been the head of one of the euthanasia projects and had been very prominent in that program.

Hitler said in *Mein Kampf* that governments and states really mean nothing except insofar as they serve the strengthening of the race. He saw the primary project to be the biological project of strengthening the Aryan race. He had also written in *Mein Kampf* that there were three kinds of races: the Aryan race, which was the only creative race, the only race that created culture; most of the races of the world, which could sustain culture once it had been created by the Aryan race, but could not create it themselves; and the so-called Jewish race, which was culture destroying.

Hitler and the extreme theorists around him literally believed that the Aryan race had become ill, that it had been rendered ill by the Jewish infection. The Jews were a special problem, but other inferior races were also a problem. Therapy took the form of getting rid of the infection. That meant getting rid of the Jews. The object of therapy was not the Jews or the Gypsies or any other group; it was the Aryan race. The way of curing the Aryan race was to get rid of whatever had made it ill.

In that sense one could say that the Nazis saw their project as a biological one. And they tried to create what should be called a *biocracy*. I use that term in my book *The Nazi Doctors* as a parallel to the idea of theocracy. In a theocracy the priests, or the theologians, run the country. That was never true of doctors or biologists under the Nazis. The political leaders ran the Nazi regime, but they did it in the name of biologists or biology, or of physicians. The Nazis sought to take over the evolutionary process.

And if you read Konrad Lorenz, who became a world-famous figure and a Nobel Prize winner (but he was an ardent Nazi theorist at that time), he says very specifically that humankind has been weakened by the civilizing process. Nature, rather than getting rid of the weaker forms as it used to, has allowed them to survive. Therefore, we human beings have to take over where nature no longer prevails. We must assert control over the evolutionary process.[1]

Two examples illustrate the sense of this biological vision or biocracy: One doctor whom I interviewed was an ardent Nazi of long standing, one of the early so-called old fighters among doctors. He had marched and fought in the streets. He said to me, "I joined the Nazi party the day after I heard Rudolf Hess say, 'national socialism is nothing but applied biology.' "

A second example comes from a leading and very admirable non-Jewish inmate physician, who was standing outside the medical block at Auschwitz and talking to a Nazi doctor. They were looking out at the smoking crematoria when she said to him, "How can you reconcile that with your Hippocratic oath?" His answer was, "When you find a diseased appendix, you must remove it." It was a disease of the body of the German race and had to be extirpated.

Once you have a policy of "life unworthy of life," and the radical impulse of the Nazis to combine the politically extreme ideology with a biomedically extreme ideology, the result can be genocide. Life unworthy of life, of course, can include Gypsies, Poles, Russians, homosexuals, pacifists—anybody considered unworthy of life.

One would be, I think, on very shaky ground to claim that only the Germans have been capable of genocide. We have had too many other genocides in the world. The Germans did it in a very special way, and in the Nazi Holocaust there are indeed unique features. However, genocide is not unique to the Germans.

There tends to be in genocide a sense of one's group or nation as having undergone an extreme trauma, a kind of sickness that has been imposed upon it by history. This sense was very extreme in Germany. It really had to do with the whole German emergence and modernization, which was painful, and then World War I, in particular. World War I was meant to be a great solution to the German problem but turned out instead to be a humiliating defeat and a source of enormous demoralization.

There is, then, a seeking of a cure of that trauma or illness. The cure tends to be as radical as the illness is perceived to be. So the cure tends to be all or nothing, totalistic. The Nazi movement offered a form of revitalization. Revitalization is the key. It promised to provide the German people with a way of becoming strong and vital again.

Strangely and sadly with that cure, there tends to be a kind of euphoria or sense of transcendence as one embraces a mass movement. I found that sense of transcendence in talking to Albert Speer in connection with my research. He spoke of his reaction upon hearing Hitler's method, walking about for hours in a daze, feeling himself in a dream through some of the

Nazi experience.[2] In no way does this mitigate his responsibility, or anyone else's for that matter, but that sense of being part of a great mythic force can be extremely important for genocide.

Finally, there is the principle of killing as therapy. You want to be careful, in any culture, when you say that you must kill or harm groups of people to achieve the greater good in some way. And this approach can resemble various premodern forces such as a purification process. As Mary Douglas and other people have written, what used to be in premodern times thought of as purification in modern experience becomes an extreme version of hygiene.[3] Medicalization is employed, as was so evident with the Nazis. They spoke of racial hygiene and had departments and institutes for mental hygiene. They saw their killing process as a form of racial hygiene, a way to be rid of bad genes and bad races.

In addition to the killing process and those themes I've mentioned, agents are required for killing. Any culture can develop a set of professional killers. Sometimes they are people who have a stronger tendency toward sadism. A group can be mobilized to kill with a certain élan and a certain sense of purpose. From my work with the Nazi doctors, I have come to recognize that killing professionals are also required; that is, professionals who will not only help with the technology of killing, but also its rationale, justification, and legitimization. The Nazis mobilized both the medical and legal professions for their purposes. And the professionals, including the doctors, were all too ready and willing to be mobilized.

In addition to the agents of killing, a technology and a bureaucracy for killing were also required. In the case of the Nazis, the technology was the gas chamber, which at Auschwitz could kill as many as twenty thousand people in a twenty-four hour period. While that may have been high technology for the time, it is nothing compared with our present technology of killing. We can kill hundreds of millions of people with nuclear weapons in a matter of days, perhaps hours. A bureaucracy that is in dialogue with the leadership is also required. It isn't just a faceless bureaucracy, but you do need a bureaucratic killing process that routinizes the killing and separates cause and effect in people's minds. The bureaucracy can have very active people in it so that there can be innovation in the killing process as leading bureaucrats try to imagine what's in the leader's mind.

There is still considerable confusion among historians who are authorities on this issue as to whether Hitler ever issued a clear-cut written order or any order at all for the killing of Jews. There probably was an order, but it was not a clear-cut written order. The bureaucratic back-and-forth process was very much a part of the killing process.

Finally, in that process of genocide, you need a genocidal self. In my study of the Nazi doctors, I talk of the process of doubling, the formation of what is functionally a second self even though it's still the same person. What is remarkable and disturbing about that finding is that through this formation of a functional second self, an individual can do evil things, such as participate in killing, that he or she would not ordinarily do. Yet elements of the prior self can remain relatively more humane, as was the case of Nazi doctors who would visit their wives and children outside of Auschwitz. Any situation that creates an environment that promotes doubling in that way can contribute to a genocidal self. Auschwitz was that kind of environment. You almost had to double in order to stay there if you were a perpetrator. Yet the fact that one doubles, or that one can have a psychological interpretation of this process, does not in any way alter the responsibility of the person involved.

NOTES

1. Robert Jay Lifton, *The Nazi Doctors: Medical Killing and the Psychology of Genocide* (New York, 1986), p. 134.
2. Ibid., pp. 474–75.
3. Ibid., p. 482.

Contributors

MICHAEL BERENBAUM, Hymen Goldman Adjunct Professor of Theology at Georgetown University, is also project director of the United States Holocaust Memorial Museum. Among his other books are *The Vision of the Void* and *After Tragedy and Triumph*.

PETER BLACK, research historian with the Office of Special Investigation of the United States Department of Justice, has done extensive research on forced labor in the Nazi concentration camps.

CHRISTOPHER R. BROWNING, professor of history at Pacific Lutheran University in Tacoma, Washington, has written, among other books, *The Final Solution and the German Foreign Office*.

JOHN S. CONWAY, a historian, has written extensively about the churches during the Nazi era. Among his works is *The Nazi Persecution of the Churches*.

KONNILYN FEIG, the author of *Hitler's Death Camps* is dean of the Business and Social Sciences Division at Foothill College.

ISRAEL GUTMAN, professor of modern Jewish history at the Hebrew University in Jerusalem, is also chairman of the Scientific Advisory Committee of Yad Vashem. He is the coauthor of *Unequal Victims: Poles and Jews During World War II*.

EDWARD HOMZE, professor of history at the University of Nebraska, is the author of works about forced and foreign labor during the Nazi era.

TARAS HUNCZAK, professor of history at Rutgers University, specializes in World War II and the Ukraine.

CHRISTINE KING, a historian and theologian who teaches at Lancashire Polytechnic in Preston, England, is a specialist in Jehovah's Witnesses during the Nazi years.

GEORGILY A. KUMANEV is chairman of the World War II sector of the Institute for History of the Soviet Academy of Sciences.

RUEDIGER LAUTMANN teaches at the University of Bremen in West Germany and is an expert on the fate of homosexuals during the Third Reich.

ROBERT JAY LIFTON, distinguished professor of psychiatry and psychology at the City University of New York, John Jay College of Criminal Justice, is the author of *The Nazi Doctors*. This transcript was taken from an oral paper.

JIŘÍ LÍPA, librarian at Seminary of the Immaculate Conception in Huntington, New York, is a Czech-American linguist who has focused on the Gypsies.

RICHARD C. LUKAS, an authority on Eastern Europe, is the author of five books, including *The Forgotten Holocaust*. He teaches history at Wright State University.

SYBIL MILTON, resident historian at the United States Holocaust Memorial Museum, is the author, among other books, of *Art of the Holocaust* and *Women in the Holocaust*. She has also written numerous articles on photographs as historical evidence of the Holocaust.

RICHARD L. RUBENSTEIN, the Robert O. Lawton Distinguished Professor of Religion at Florida State University, is also president of the Washington Institute for Values in Public Policy. Among his many books are *After Auschwitz* and *The Cunning of History*.

MENACHEM SHELAH is a lecturer in contemporary history at the University of Haifa.

CHRISTIAN STREIT, a West German scholar, has published articles about the fate of Soviet POWs in the concentration camps.

BOHDAN VITVITSKY is the author of *The Other Holocaust: The Many Circles of Hell.*

AHARON WEISS, a senior lecturer at the University of Haifa, is also chief editor of *Yad Vashem Studies.*

GORDON C. ZAHN, professor emeritus of sociology at the University of Massachusetts in Boston and director of the Center on Conscience and War, is the author of *German Catholics and Hitler's Wars* and *In Solitary Witness.*

Index

Birkenau (*Continued*)
Gypsies at, 167
Soviet POWs at, 147
treatment of women at, 172, 173–75
Blacks, as undesirables, 81
Blaha, Franz, 170
Bohemia. *See* Protectorate of Bohemia and Moravia
Böhme, Franz, 69, 70
Bok, Wilhelm, 139
Bonhoeffer, Dietrich, 184
Borkin, Joseph, 26
Bormann, Martin, 89, 118, 180, 181–82, 183, 190
Brandt, Karl, 154, 224
Broszat, Martin, 58
Bruderhof community, 196
Buchenwald
children at, 174
conditions at, 54, 165–66
forced-labor program and, 49–50, 54
Gypsies at, 167
homosexuals at, 168
medical experiments at, 171
Spaniards at, 85
Bureaucracy
American Jewish life and, 30–31
killing process and, 26, 99, 223, 227–28
Byelorussian republic, 132–33

Canaris, Wilhelm, 146
Carter, Jimmy, 23–24
Castration of homosexuals, 168
Catholic Church
in Croatia, 77
in Germany, 179–85
Nazi campaign against, 179–81, 182–84
policy of accommodation, 182
possibilities for successful opposition by, 183–84
Children
age groups among, 150–51
in concentration camps, 150–58, 164, 166–67, 174–75
education of, 151, 152, 154
euthanasia and, 170, 223
extermination of, 153, 155, 174–75, 224
in forced-labor program, 156
Germanization of, 152, 153, 166

Gypsy, 155, 157–58, 167–68
housing of, with mothers, 154
kidnapping of, 152, 166–67, 172
patterns in fate of, 155–56
Polish, 150, 151–53, 166–67
presence of, and adult survival, 205
racial examination and categorization of, 153, 154
sterilization of, 167
Ukrainian, 120
Christianity, view of Judaism in, 11–12, 15
Church-state relations, and Nazi period, 184–85
Citizenship, in Slovakia, 209–10
Civilian population, extermination of
means for, 139–40
in Ukraine, 119–20
Clauberg, Dr., 167
Clergy
in concentration camps, 163, 169
Ukrainian, attitudes of, 109, 112
Collection centers (*Sammellager*), 153, 154
Colonialism, and unintended genocide, 3–9
Colored triangles. *See* Prisoner categories, differences between
Commissar Order of June 6, 1941, 145–46
Communist revolution, genocidal measures in, 10
Communists. *See also* Antibolshevism; Union of Soviet Socialist Republics
German military code of honor and, 147–48
Jehovah's Witnesses seen as, 189
as responsible for fascism, 200
Concentration camps. *See also* Forced-labor program; *specific camps; specific victim groups*
change in, during war, 156, 175
differences between prisoner categories in, 203–6
educational purpose of, 51, 59, 201–2
nationality distributions in, 56
number of, 162
punishment of foreign workers and, 43
as social control, 202–3
treatment of non-Jewish victims in, 161–76
Conscientious objection. *See* Pacifists
Criminals, persecution of, 82

Green, Gerald, 91–92
Grey, Edward, 64
Gross-Rosen, 169
Grot-Rowecki, Stefan, 93
Guilt, and doubling, 218
Gypsies
  in Belgium, 82
  in Bohemia and Moravia, 207, 212–15
  children of, 155, 157–58, 167–68
  in concentration camps, 163, 167–68,
    213–14
  in Croatia, 78
  in Czechoslovakia, 207–15
  definition of, 210
  differences among, 207–9
  documentation on, 78
  in France, 82
  versus Jewish victims, 33
  in labor camps, 210–12
  mass extermination of, 214–15
  in Serbia, 70–71
  United States Holocaust Memorial Council and, 35n3
  as victims for what they were, 194

Harassment
  of German Catholics, 180
  of Jehovah's Witnesses, 189, 190
  of Serbs in Croatia, 76–77
Heath, Leslie O., 85
Hess, Rudolf, 226
Heusinger, General, 90
Heydrich, Reinhardt, 40, 46, 47, 146,
  183
High Command of the Armed Forces
  (OKW), 67
Hilberg, Raul, 26, 32, 104–5
Hilfswilligen, 142
Hill, Christopher, 6
Himmler, Heinrich
  children and, 154
  clergy and, 169
  educative function of camps and, 46
  forced-labor program and, 47, 49–51, 53,
    54, 55, 57, 58, 59
  Gypsies and, 158, 167
  homosexuals and, 168
  Jehovah's Witnesses and, 189

Poles and, 89, 91, 151–53, 166
  political resistance and, 125n9
  Slavs and, 130–31, 135
  Soviet POWs and, 147
Historiography. See also Jewish history
  anti-Semitic stereotypes in, 92
  Catholic, and church response, 180
  Catholic versus Protestant views in, 184–
    85
  in Communist Eastern Europe, 101
  exoneration of individuals in, 114
  link between anti-Semitism and anti-
    Christian persecution, 181–82
  Slavs as victimizers and, 104–5
Hitler, Adolf
  Christianity and, 180–81
  genocide of Serbs and, 76
  homosexuals and, 201
  human targets of, 176
  Lebensraum program, 8–9
  Poles and, 89, 151
  Russia and, 128–30
  Slavic allies and, 65–66
  on strengthening of race, 225
  view of Jews, 100, 161
Hoche, Alfred, 222–23
Hochhuth, Rolf, 179, 217
Hodonin (Czeckoslovakia), 212–14
Holocaust. See also Irrationality; Unique-
    ness; Universality
  Carter's definition of, 23–24
  as term, 25–26
  Wiesenthal's definition of, 20–22
Holocaust museum. See United States Holo-
    caust Memorial Museum
Homicide, as crime, 17
Homogeneity, desire for, 16–17
Homosexuals
  categories of, 202
  in concentration camps, 163, 168, 200–
    206
  versus Jewish victims, 33
  persecution of, 82
  as victims for what they did, 194
Höss, Rudolf, 47, 147, 169, 172
Human nature, and evil, 198, 199, 217,
  219
Human skin, 170–71
Huttenbraucker, Dr., 137

Independent State of Croatia, 74
Individual responsibility, 114. *See also* Doubling
Infants
  Aryan versus non-Aryan, 172
  killing of, 173–75
"Instructions for Special Areas for Directive No. 21," 129, 130
Intelligentsia, 127*n*30
International Brigade, 84
International law, and policies of destruction, 146
Ireland, colonization of, 6–7
Irrationality, 15–17
Italian refugees, in France, 83

Jaegerstaetter, Franz, 197–99
Japanese relocation program, 195
Jasenovac, Serb genocide in, 78
Jehovah's Witnesses
  beliefs of, 188, 192
  children of, 155
  in concentration camps, 163, 169, 191, 200–206
  gay prisoners compared with, 200–206
  under Nazism, 188–92
  resistance by, 190–92
Jewish history
  lachrymose theory of, 26–27
  place of Holocaust in, 29–32
Jewish people
  Christian prisoner communities and, 157
  in compared European countries, 106–7
  complexity of Final Solution and, 161
  demonic interpretation of, 12
  Polish record of aid to, 92, 94
  versus Polish victims, 98
  reprieve for, in forced-labor program, 54–55
  self-characterization of, 21
  in Serbia, 70–71
  and Slavs, comparison of perspectives of, 101–7
  Soviet victimization of, 121
  Ukrainian aid to, 109, 111–12, 113, 114
  unanimity on victimization of, 102
  as victims for what they were, 194
Jewish survivors, views of, 1
Journal of Historical Review, 88

Jurichev, Dijonizije, 74
Justin, Eva, 158

Kampuchea, genocide in, 10
Karbychev (Russian general), 170
Kater, Michael, 191
Kaytn forest massacre, 121
Keitel, Wilhelm, 69, 134, 146
Kershaw, Ian, 183, 184
Kidnapping, 152, 166–67, 172
Kiev (USSR), forced labor from, 137–38
Koch, Erich, 104, 117, 138
Koestler, Arthur, 84
Kozara District (Croatia), 78
Kozlowiecki, Adam, 169
Krumey, Hermann, 152
Kubijovych, Volofymyr, 119–20
Kuhnrich, Heinz, 119
Kull, Steven, 220

Labor camps
  for asocial men, 210–12
  Gypsies in, 212–14
  for Jews, 210
Land use, under German occupation, 135–36
Langbein, Hermann, 84
Langer, Lawrence, 26, 32
Lanzmann, Claude, 92
Laqueur, Walter, 92
Law
  harassment of Serbs, 76–77
  regulation of Gypsies, 208–10, 211, 212–13
  against *Zersetzung der Wehrkraft*, 196
Lebensraum program, and colonial genocide, 8–9
Lemelsen, Lieutenant General, 148
Lerpscher, Michael, 197
Lety (Czechoslovakian labor camp), 212–14
Levi, Primo, 32
Levin, Rabbi Itzhak of Lviv, 112, 113
Lewy, Guenter, 179
Lichtenberg, Bernhard, 185
Liebehenschel, Artur, 55
"Life unworthy of life," 222–23, 226
List, Field Marshal Wilhelm, 64–65, 67, 68–69
Littell, Franklin, 220

Living conditions
    of children, 153, 156–57, 166
    forced-labor program and, 40–43, 55, 57–
        58, 59
    under German occupation, 133
    in Serbian transit camps, 77
    in Slovak labor units, 210–11, 212
    for Soviet POWs, 144–45
    for women, 172–73
Loeling, Dr., 171
Lorenz, Konrad, 225
Lorkovitch, Mladen, 77
Loyalty. *See* Disloyalty, community percep-
    tion of
L'universe concentrainaire, 32

Majdanek, Soviet POWs at, 147, 169
Marital status, and survival rate, 205
Martyrdom, 29, 31–32
Mass extermination
    emancipation of European Jews and, 11
    by forced labor, 47–49, 53, 56, 58–59
    of Gypsies, 214–15
    machinery of, 20
    partisan warfare and, 119
    of Serbs, 68–70
Maurer, Gerhard, 49
Mauthausen
    children in, 156
    Jehovah's Witnesses at, 169
    nationality of prisoners in, 56
    satellite camps and, 51
    Soviet POWs at, 169
    Spanish refugees in, 85
    Wiesenthal in, 21
Meaning, creation of, 219–20
Medical experiments. *See also* Nazi doctors
    children and, 156, 158, 172
    Gypsies and, 167
    oddities and, 170–71
    physically disabled and, 163–64
    women and, 173
Mengele, Dr., 171
Mental patients
    euthanasia and, 222, 223, 224
    medical experiments on, 173
    persecution of, 82
Methodology. *See also* Gas chamber
    bureaucracy and, 26, 99, 223, 227–28

concern for humaneness and, 224
    uniqueness of Holocaust and, 32, 200
Metzger, Max Joseph, 185, 196
Michener, James, 91
Middleman minority theory, 12–14
Military defeat, and genocide, 14–15
Misidentification, and Slavic collaboration,
    107
Modernization
    middleman minorities and, 13
    politics of genocide and, 3–18
Moravia. *See* Protectorate of Bohemia and
    Moravia
Morgenthau, Henry, Jr., 34
Mormons, 198
Mortality rate
    for different prisoner categories, 203–4,
        205
    for Soviet versus Anglo-American POWs,
        142
    starvation and, 143–44
Mueller, Franz, 155
Müller, Heinrich, 52
Murmelstein, Dr., 157

National Armed Forces of NSZ, 94
National Socialism
    as applied biology, 225–26
    Jehovah's Witnesses and, 188–89, 190,
        192
    voice in political order and, 11
National Socialist Germany
    as criminal state, 18
    as genocidal state, 6
National sovereignty, and human rights,
    17–18
Natzweiler, medical experiments at, 171
Nazi doctors. *See also* Medical experiments
    doubling by, 216–21, 228
    euthanasia and, 222
    professionalization of killing and, 227
Nazi ideology
    cult of ruthlessness, 66, 67–71
    doubling process and, 219
    sense of transcendence and, 226–27
Nazi occupation. *See* German occupation
Nazi racism
    biological vision in, 225–26
    occupation policies and, 140

gay prisoners compared with, 200–206
persecution of, in West, 82–86
Pol Pot, 10
Popular press, anti-Semitic stereotypes in,
91–92
Population losses
comparison of, by country, 124
among European Gypsies, 168
from Nazi solutions, 162
in Ukraine, 122–24
Pregnant women, 164
Prisoner categories, differences between,
203–6
Prisoners of war. *See* Political prisoners; So
viet prisoners of war
Prostitutes, 82
Protectorate of Bohemia and Moravia, 207,
209, 212–15
Protestant church, 184–85
Proximity principle, 70
Psychological mechanisms. *See* Doubling
Punishment. *See* Penal regulations

Rabbit Guinea Pigs, 173
Racial taxonomy of peoples, 103–4. *See also*
Nazi racism
Rank, Otto, 218–19
Rationality, instrumental versus value, 15.
See also Irrationality
Ravensbrück
children at, 155, 156, 157, 175
forced-labor program and, 50, 52
Gypsies at, 167
medical experiments at, 173
nationality of prisoners at, 57
Spaniards at, 85
women at, 172–73
Reagan, Ronald, 21
Red Army commissars, policy on, 145–46
Redundant populations, and genocide, 4–5,
7, 8–9
Reeducation. *See* Education
Rehabilitation, of homosexuals, 168. *See*
also Education; Homosexuals
Reich Central Office for Security (RSHA),
47
Reich Concordat of 1933, 180, 183
Reinecke, Hermann, 146
Reinisch, Franz, 197

Religiomythic elements in Christian view of
Jews, 11–12, 15
Religion
impact of Holocaust on faith, 29–31
middleman minorities and, 13
Nazi opposition to freedom of, 190
prisoner communities and, 157
uniqueness of Holocaust and, 11–12
Reprisal measures
executions, 73*n*25
forced-labor program and, 137
100:1 ratio, 69, 70
proximity principle and, 70
Serbs and, 67–68, 69–71
against women and children, 154
Resentments
of Jewish survivors, 1
of non-Jewish survivors, 1–2
Resistance
in Belgium, 85–86
concentration camps and, 163
in France, 85–86
among German Catholics, 182
in Poland, 98–99
of Serbs in Croatia, 77–78
in Ukraine, 118–19
Ritter, Robert, 158
Roethke, Theodore, 221
Romani. *See* Gypsies
Romania, 132
Roosevelt, F. D., 34
Rosenberg, Alfred, 119, 136–37
Roszak, Theodore, 199
Rowecki, Stefan, 98–99
RSHA. *See* Reich Central Office for Secu-
rity
Rubenstein, Richard, 26, 28
Rüdin, Ernst, 222
Russia. *See* Union of Soviet Socialist Repub-
lics

Sabille, Jacques, 75
Sachsenhausen
conditions in, 165
homosexuals in, 168
medical experiments at, 171
Sammellager (collection centers), 153, 154
Sanchuk, Alas, 111
Sarraut, Albert, 82